‘This is a rare and wonderful book. In crisp, beautiful prose, Shannyn Palmer attends to the histories preserved in place, story and memory. The result is a profound act of listening, and a dazzling piece of scholarship.’

Billy Griffiths

UNMAKING ANGAS DOWNS

MYTH AND HISTORY ON A CENTRAL AUSTRALIAN PASTORAL STATION

SHANNYN PALMER

MELBOURNE UNIVERSITY PRESS

MELBOURNE UNIVERSITY PRESS
An imprint of Melbourne University Publishing Limited
Level 1, 715 Swanston Street, Carlton, Victoria 3053, Australia
mup-contact@unimelb.edu.au
www.mup.com.au

First published 2022

Cover design by John Canty
Cover photo of Bloodwood Bore on Angas Downs courtesy Shannyn Palmer
Typeset in 11/15pt Sabon by Cannon Typesetting
Printed in Australia by McPherson's Printing Group

NATIONAL LIBRARY OF AUSTRALIA
A catalogue record for this book is available from the National Library of Australia

9780522878387 (paperback)
9780522878394 (ebook)

For Tjuki Tjukanku Pumpjack and Sandra Armstrong.
I am deeply grateful for your wisdom, generosity,
and the learning that you gifted me.

Contents

Author's notes

Acknowledgement

I acknowledge the traditional custodians of the land and seas of Australia. I pay my respects to the Elders, past and present, and acknowledge them as the original knowledge holders and storytellers of this vast continent.

I acknowledge A<u>n</u>angu and their Elders, past and present, as the knowledge holders and custodians of the places that form the foundations of this book. I am deeply grateful for their generosity with this knowledge and for gifting me the opportunity to share in it.

I acknowledge the Arrernte people, on whose lands I lived and worked while I was researching this book.

I also acknowledge the Ngunnawal and Ngambri people, on whose lands I live and work, and where most of this book was written.

Language and translation

The terms 'A<u>n</u>angu', 'Aboriginal' and 'First Nations' are used throughout this book. Where possible I preference specific First Nations groups. Given that this book focuses on the middle decades of the twentieth century and draws heavily on historical sources, the term Aboriginal is used primarily in this historical context. I use the term First Nations to refer to all Aboriginal and Torres Strait Islander peoples collectively.

Unmaking Angas Downs contains Pitjantjatjara/Yankunytjatjara language words. I acknowledge that there are alternative spellings of some names and words. I have used the spelling commonly used by Aṉangu as represented in the *Pitjantjatjara/Yankunytjatjara to English Dictionary*, published by the Institute for Aboriginal Development Press.

The oral history sources are stylistically different to the rest of the text to indicate that they were recorded in a language other than English. These sources have been translated and transcribed from Pitjantjatjara to English, which is an act of interpretation in itself. Most of the oral histories have been translated and transcribed by Linda Rive and Sam Osborne, which provides a consistent approach to translation throughout the book. Translation details for all oral histories are located in the endnotes.

Indigenous Cultural and Intellectual Property (ICIP)

Unmaking Angas Downs contains references to Indigenous Cultural and Intellectual Property. It is reproduced here with permission. All rights to ICIP remain with the relevant Aṉangu owners of the knowledge and cultural expression. Any further use of this information should only be done with consent.

Warning

This book contains references to deceased First Nations people.

I have reproduced terms and names as they appear in settler Australian historical sources without 'correcting' the spelling, or altering or omitting terms that might be considered offensive. These are included to illustrate settler Australian attitudes and mindsets at the time they were produced. First Nations people should exercise care when reading the excerpts of historical sources.

Prologue: Walara

ANGAS DOWNS WAS the name that William 'Bill' Liddle gave to the sheep run he established around 1928–29 at a place called Walara, situated on the edge of the Western Desert, in the Central Australian ranges. A<u>n</u>angu man Tjuki Tjukanku Pumpjack arrived at Walara sometime in the late 1930s. A young boy at the time, he and his family walked out of the Western Desert and embarked upon a journey, which led them to Liddle's Angas Downs station, situated several hundreds of kilometres to the north of their homelands in the Musgrave Ranges.

People with present-day connections to Angas Downs speak a number of different dialects of a shared Western Desert language. Pitjantjatjara, Yankunytjatjara and Ngaanyatjarra are just a few of the names that were given when white settlers arrived and began asking desert people to define who they were in relation to others. A<u>n</u>angu, which is their word for person or people,[1] is the term they use to refer to themselves.

Tjuki and I travelled to Walara together for the first time in August 2012. To reach the place, we drove west from the community of Imanpa along the Lasseter Highway. Named after one of many white men who came, in search of something, to this part of Australia in the nineteenth and twentieth centuries, the 244-kilometre stretch of bitumen reached ahead in a seemingly interminable straight line on the other side of the windscreen. After turning off onto the Luritja Road in the direction of Watarrka (Kings Canyon—see Map 1) and driving along the bitumen for approximately 30 kilometres, we then turned off the highway onto a rough red dirt track. Not far along, Tjuki pointed west towards a hill that rose up out of the mulga scrub, and, motioning with his hand across the country that lay before us, told me that in the Tjukurpa, which is commonly referred to as the Dreaming, Wati Niru (a man called Niru) had chased the Kungkarangkulpa (the Seven Sisters) right through that country. A little way further down the road, the landscape changed, and the red earth turned white because of hundreds of little rocks that mark the presence of a limestone plain. Tjuki told me that this was where the Angas Downs airstrip used to be.

The dirt track we were travelling along was narrow and rough. Water had worn large crevices and dips into the surface, and the absence of any visible tyre tracks made it appear as though very few people, if any, had driven along that road in recent times. As we wound our way deeper and deeper into the desert, it seemed strange to me that a pastoral station would be located in such densely vegetated desert country. The dirt track we were travelling on came to an end, disappearing into an expanse of spinifex or buffel grass, I wasn't sure which. Tjuki gestured with his hand and told me to stop the car.

The place we stood in was bare of trees, except for some sparsely scattered mulga and two large twin gum trees that stood beside one another, commanding the space. The pale yellow tufts of grass shimmered in the heat and light of the afternoon sun. Red rocky ridges dotted with mulga formed a ring around the open grassy area where we stood, creating a natural boundary. I turned to survey the country behind me, and noticed an old water tank, and a dry creek bed the colour of rust and salt. Bits of stone, an old stove, some timber posts and rusted pieces of scattered machinery amid the grass were the only material traces of Angas Downs that remained in the landscape.

As I stood next to him, Tjuki motioned out across the site and said to me, 'That's my Country, we bin grow up here from kids, me and my brother.' He then grabbed his bushy white beard and, running his hands along it, over and over again, told me that this place was his Country because it was where his beard had grown.

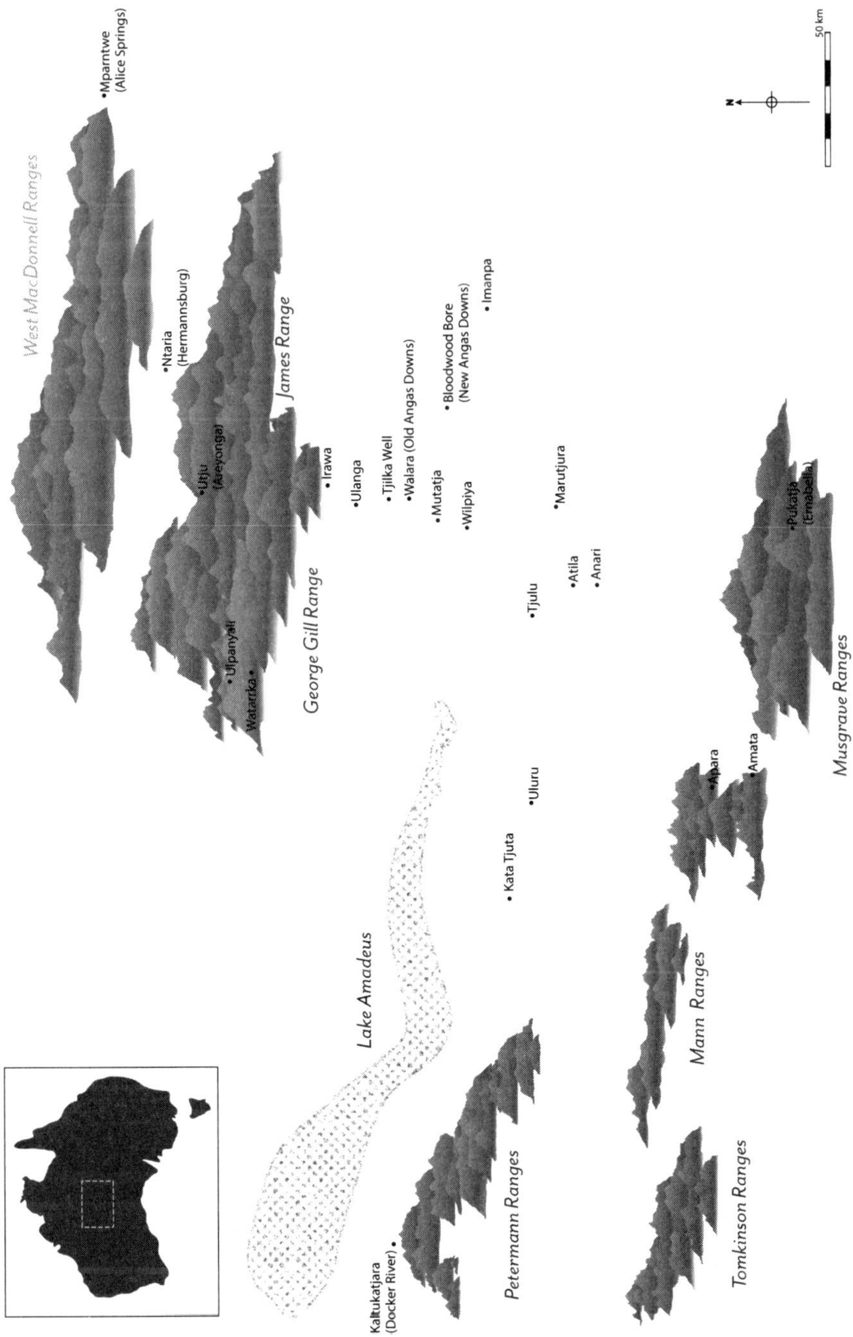

Map 1 is of the southwest region of Central Australia, including various sites on Angas Downs, and places connected to it in the broader regional network of people and places. This area isn't confined within state boundaries, and encompasses part of Western Australia and northern South Australia. *Courtesy Felix Meyer*

Motioning out across the landscape again, Tjuki looked at me and told me to look at the place. He told me that the place was sad. Moving a hand up to his forehead, he proceeded to run it in a downward motion over his face to his chin, closing his eyes as his hand passed over them. With them still closed, he told me that his Country was dying because he was the last one left, and there was no one living on, or 'holding', this place anymore.[2] That day at Walara, I began to see and feel this place was not just the location of an old pastoral station. Rather, as Tjuki described it, the place was alive. It could perceive and feel. It had a past, present and future that he cared for and worried deeply about. As Tjuki described it, the place was a part of him, like the beard on his face, and it was dying because there was no one left to hold it.

Angas Downs was declared an Indigenous Protected Area (IPA) in 2009. Located 300 kilometres southwest of Mparntwe (Alice Springs) and 135 kilometres east from Uluru, it stretches across 320 000 hectares of the Central Australian Ranges. The area is abundant in mulga woodlands, limestone plains, spinifex sand dunes, Desert Oak woodlands, quartzite hills and alluvial plains. It is also home to many species of birds, mammals and reptiles. An IPA information leaflet notes that, as well as being located in an area of rich biodiversity, Angas Downs is of 'great historical and cultural value' and that the Yankunytjatjara and Pitjantjatjara [people] have maintained a continued connection to the property, including its "past life" as a sheep and cattle property'.[3] This place in southern Luritja Country has transformed from desert pastoral property, to reluctantly abandoned settlement, to reclaimed A<u>n</u>angu land in less than a century.[4]

That day at Walara with Tjuki, I wondered how I was to make sense of this place—its history as a pastoral station, and both its ancient and contemporary evocation as Country. What kind of place is Angas Downs? And how can we see it and understand it as a *place*?

A year earlier, I had come across an unusual book, written by an anthropologist, that was set on Angas Downs station. In the black-and-white photographs that captured the station in 1962, it appeared to be situated amid vast plains of dust stripped bare of vegetation. And yet, in 1962 hundreds of A<u>n</u>angu were living there. These people had connections that spanned hundreds of kilometres to the south and west, into the Musgrave and Mann Ranges in South Australia, the Tomkinson and Petermann Ranges in the Northern Territory, and the Warburton Ranges in Western Australia. I wondered what had brought so many of them to this seemingly marginal desert pastoral station.

In 2011 I embarked on a journey into the Central and Western deserts, seeking to understand the history of this place. It began with me assuming it to be a single site of colonial myth making. It ended with an understanding of Angas Downs as a deeply complex place of dynamic interaction and social life—not only lived in, but (un)made by Aṉangu.

INTRODUCTION: ENCOUNTERS IN PLACE

SIXTY YEARS AGO, a British-born anthropologist named Frederick Rose lived at Bloodwood Bore, the site of the second Angas Downs homestead, between July and October 1962. Rose published *The Wind of Change in Central Australia: The Aborigines at Angas Downs, 1962*, several years later, in 1965. Set on a desert cattle station, and concerned with the changes in A<u>n</u>angu social and cultural life brought about by the encounter with a cash economy and commodities, Rose's book was something of an anomaly in the field of anthropology at the time.[1]

For many Australian anthropologists practising throughout the middle decades of the twentieth century, the discipline's primary focus was describing and analysing the 'traditional' life of First Nations people who had experienced minimal contact with white settlers. An imagined dichotomy between 'traditional' and 'non-traditional' peoples was deeply ingrained in the field; those peoples who had been subjected to intense occupation of their lands were assumed to have lost their culture and, therefore, were not seen as a worthy subject of anthropological study. Any anthropological interest in the reaction of First Nations peoples to settler peoples and cultures was investigated under the rubric of 'culture contact', and was largely ignored.[2]

It is not surprising then that *The Wind of Change* has largely been overlooked in the canon of desert ethnography. Fred Rose was only incidentally interested in the traditional or, what he referred to as, the 'cult life' of Aṉangu. A devout Marxist and committed member of the Communist Party, Rose's ethnographic study of change on Angas Downs is filtered through a materialist lens.[3] According to Rose, a process of 'detribalisation', as he called it, was taking place on the station, accelerated by the commodification of material culture and the subsequent encounter with a cash economy that had resulted from the emergence of tourism. As Rose saw it, in 1962 the 'traditional' way of life for Aṉangu on Angas Downs had virtually disappeared.

The strangeness of Rose's ethnography struck me when I first laid eyes on it. As I flicked through the pages, my eyes danced over the text and tables, and came to dwell on the black-and-white photographs scattered throughout that captured people and everyday life on the station. Unlike other ethnographies of the time, people in *The Wind of Change* were photographed wearing settler clothing, collecting rations, receiving haircuts, playing card games and trading with tourists. I was particularly struck by the last pages of the book—150 black-and-white portraits of the people living on Angas Downs during the four months that Rose carried out his fieldwork. The photographs were both immediate and intimate in their close focus on the faces of the people they captured. Some looked uncomfortable, as though Rose's request to photograph them was perhaps an annoyance, while others were smiling and seemed happy to have their picture taken. The portraits were arranged in grids of three-by-three and carried over sixteen pages. There were no names accompanying the photographs. Rather, each portrait was numbered from 1 to 150. As I turned the pages, it occurred to me that there were several generations represented in those pictures. There were so many faces. I wondered who the people in the portraits were and what drew so many of them to this place?

Half a century after it was first published, I took Rose's *The Wind of Change* on a journey back into the country in which it was produced. In 2012 I relocated from Ngunnawal Ngambri Country in the place now known as Canberra, to Mparntwe in Central Arrernte Country, otherwise known as Alice Springs. Not long after I arrived, I took out a loan and bought a green 80 Series Toyota Landcruiser, which soon assumed the role of beloved and trustworthy travelling companion. Over the following four years, we travelled tens of thousands of kilometres throughout the Central and Western deserts. This act of travelling to the heart of the continent echoed the journeys of countless white settlers who came to this place before me, in search of something. Yes, I was seeking to learn about the history of Angas Downs. But I was also searching for answers about the settler historical imagination and ways of seeing the past.

As a white woman settler who grew up in a regional Victorian town where local memory didn't acknowledge that the town was established on Dja Dja Wurrung Country, and as someone troubled by the silences and white noise that dominated Australian history writing throughout much of the twentieth century, I wanted to explore the implications of different ways of knowing the world for historical research and writing in a colonised settler nation. I also wanted to engage with my own nagging sense of dis-location. We all inherit the consequences of colonialism and, as psychologist Craig San Roque describes it, I have felt 'displaced from my integrity by the very act of displacing others from theirs'—and so, in exploring other ways of knowing the past, I have also wanted to explore what it means to belong on stolen land.[4]

When I began this project, I was acutely aware of the ways in which research and colonialism were deeply entangled in what Edward Said referred to as the West's 'will to power'. Here in Australia, as elsewhere, white settler researchers, academics and writers have sought to categorise, describe and speak for the 'Other', in an effort to understand, but also to control, manipulate, even incorporate, First Nations peoples and ways of knowing.[5] As Linda Tuhiwai Smith has highlighted, these practices have been employed to deny First Nations peoples' claim to land and territories, to self-determination, and to the survival of languages and forms of cultural knowledge.[6] Mindful of this, I sought to develop an approach to research that wouldn't own or consume the knowledges I engaged with. Rather, I wanted to explore how engaging with these knowledges might help us to better understand our shared past.

In a move away from seeing history as *collection*, towards seeing history as *process*, I developed a community-engaged research practice that sought to explore ways of collaborating and co-creating knowledge. I was mindful of existing power relations in the settler colonial context and of not taking up too much space as a white settler researcher.[7] Despite my naive assumptions in the beginning, I discovered early in the process that there was no one right way of doing things. Rather, I found myself in a grey area of possibilities and limitations that I had to constantly navigate and negotiate with my collaborators, always aware of my privileged position and the potential for harm in the work.[8] I came to understand that collaborations of this kind are necessarily aspirational and, as artist and language worker Beth Sometimes writes, like the notion of equality itself they are 'elusive, illusory, always in flux [and] dependent upon perspective'.[9] What evolved was an iterative process grounded in an ethics and practice of deep listening, shaped by Aṉangu knowledge and political imperatives.

I couldn't come to know a place like Angas Downs without the stories of the people who lived there. Rose's book was the catalyst for my encounter with Aṉangu in the remote community of Imanpa, a place with strong connections to Angas Downs. Situated 200 kilometres southwest of Mparntwe, 160 kilometres east of Uluru and located a few kilometres off the Lasseter Highway, Imanpa is home to mostly Pitjantjatjara and Yankunytjatjara speakers. *The Wind of Change* is a rare book, and most Aṉangu I met had never seen it before. They had no interest in the ethnography itself. Rather, it was the photographs that they wanted to see. I became known as the 'kungka [young woman] with the book'. When Aṉangu would see my Landcruiser arrive in the community and pull up at the store, I would inevitably hear shouts along the lines of, 'Hey, Kungka, I want to see that book!' Over a four-year period, I travelled from Mparntwe to Imanpa, and beyond, working with Aṉangu and learning how to see and understand this place.

The copy of the *Wind of Change* that I carried with me bears the marks of the process that developed—the front and back covers have fallen away, some pages have come out, and many others are dog-eared, stained and worn thinner by the countless pairs of hands that turned those pages over and over, and over again. These marks are what Elizabeth Edwards calls an 'archaeology of use'—physical traces that are testimony to the active and embodied role that Rose's book played in my encounters with A<u>n</u>angu and Angas Downs station.[10]

As A<u>n</u>angu mobilised Rose's photographs to tell stories, this ethnographic 'artefact' was made into a very different kind of object in their hands. In A<u>n</u>angu telling, Rose's grids of numbered portraits were transformed into a family photo album. Holding the book in their hands, they would move through the portraits, one by one, and tell me who each person was, how they were related to them, and where the person, or their family, was now. Their reading of Rose stretched through time and space, weaving threads of memory that intimately connected the living present with the past world captured in Rose's ethnography.

A<u>n</u>angu stories tracked and traced the various social and cultural practices that intersected at Angas Downs, revealing the ways in which people came to make a place for themselves in the wake of colonialism. Listening to them, I heard histories that are obscured by the single, fixed idea of the pastoral station. What emerged was an understanding of this place as living—made and inhabited by A<u>n</u>angu, even though, at first glance, Angas Downs appears to be the product of white settler intervention.

This book traces a history of colonisation in Central Australia by tracking the rise and demise of a sheep and, later, cattle enterprise over half a century. It also tracks the complex and creative social and cultural practices that A<u>n</u>angu mobilised to make sense of the new places that emerged when white settlers came to the desert. Rather than consider these two facets of the history of Angas Downs as disparate, I look at the ways they combined to make Angas Downs more than merely a pastoral station. In tracing the various cultures of economy, dwelling, and travelling that intersected at this desert locale, I grapple with the question of how people experience dislocation and come to make a place for themselves in the wake of rupture.

Following A<u>n</u>angu stories across the Central and Western deserts, this book exposes the colonial ideologies that have shaped our understanding of the so-called Australian 'outback'. In doing so, *Unmaking Angas Downs* seeks to unmap this long-mythologised place that looms large in the settler Australian imagination, and unmake dominant narratives of white pastoral possession that have overwhelmingly shaped white settler histories and historical understanding of the Northern Territory. Informed as it is by A<u>n</u>angu language and ways of being-in-the-world, this book attends to local knowledge and ways of knowing, to highlight the ways in which A<u>n</u>angu were shaping the world and making place at Angas Downs.

When I first started visiting Imanpa, numerous people told me that if I wanted to learn more about Angas Downs I should seek out Tjuki Pumpjack and Sandra Armstrong, the two recognised as having the longest and deepest association with this place. Both Tjuki's and Sandra's families were some of the earliest arrivals at Angas Downs, and they considered themselves, and are thought of by many, as those with the most knowledge, and therefore the authority, to speak for this place.

I met Tjuki for the first time in June 2012. I had travelled to Imanpa to see Sandra, who I had met previously, by chance, when she grabbed my wrist as I walked past her and asked me to help her retrieve her ATM card from the machine in Yulara. Sandra had no idea who I was at the time, or what my interest in Angas Downs was, but I recognised her immediately. This chance encounter is how our relationship began. On this particular day in June, I had been unable to find her in Imanpa and so went to sit on a bench across from the community store. As I sat there, I noticed Tjuki and his wife Rosie slowly shuffling towards the store. As they approached, I asked them in Pitjantjatjara how they were and then if they had seen Sandra. They hadn't. I explained that I had an old book with lots of photographs from Angas Downs and was hoping to find Sandra to talk to her about the station. Tjuki replied, 'Angie Downs, that my Country.'

Tjuki and Rosie made their way over to where I was sitting on the bench and I handed him Rose's book. He smiled and laughed as he flicked through the pages of photographs, and when he came across the portrait of himself, he turned to me and said, 'That's me when I young fella, no whiskers.' I had heard that Sandra was at Angas Downs, so I asked Tjuki and Rosie if they would like to come for a drive with me to the station to see if she was there. Tjuki stood up without hesitation and looked to me to point out which Landcruiser we would be travelling in. That was the first time I visited Bloodwood Bore, the site of the second Angas Downs homestead, and the only time that I spent on Angas Downs with both Tjuki and Sandra.

The relationship that I developed with each of them evolved quite differently throughout the process. Through listening to the two of them over the following four years, I would come to understand the making and unmaking of Angas Downs.

Tjuki Tjukanku Pumpjack was born around 1926–28. His life history began before white settlers had really begun to penetrate the desert. Over four years we travelled together, recording his stories. It was important to me, and also to his legacy for future generations of his family, that his life history was recorded in his language, Pitjantjatjara. Tjuki, as he liked to be called, was a gifted raconteur, and many of his stories were long and detailed. My grasp of Pitjantjatjara was rudimentary at best when we first started working together, so we collaborated with oral historian and Western Desert language interpreter and translator Linda Rive. She travelled with us, interpreting Tjuki's oral histories in place, and later translating and transcribing into English all the recordings made with him.

Our trips 'out bush' together always gravitated around food. Before leaving, I would prepare a meal in the camp oven, and when we arrived at our destination, we would begin by building a fire. Once we were settled on camping chairs, cups of tea in hand, Tjuki would begin remembering while the food cooked among the coals. Where possible, he chose the locations in which the recordings took place, and who was present. He also decided what stories we would record once we got to a location, and these were inevitably shaped by the place in which we found ourselves. Linda and I were also present, and we too are as much a part of the recordings as Tjuki Pumpjack.

Over the same period, I also worked closely with Sandra Armstrong. She was born in 1942, nearly a generation after Tjuki. When I met with her at Bloodwood Bore on that day in June, Sandra told me that the place where we sat was her Country. She showed me where

A<u>n</u>angu lived on the station; where the old homestead used to be; and the site of the 'chalet' that catered to thousands of tourists who passed through Angas Downs station in the late 1950s and 1960s, on their way to Uluru. As we sat drinking cups of tea, Sandra motioned to the site of the old chalet, and told me that she used to work there, preparing meals for the tourists and cleaning up after them. She also recalled that two men called Captain and Harry Brumby would go from Angas Downs to catch wild camels, and then bring them back to the station to break them in.

When I explained my interest in the station and learning more about her experiences there, she told me that she had recently recorded her oral history with a man called Sam Osborne and that I should see him to 'get that big story'. Sam recorded Sandra's life history over three sessions in 2012–13 as source material for his PhD research investigating A<u>n</u>angu perspectives on education.

After I reached out to Sam to introduce myself, he very kindly invited me to attend the last of these recording sessions at Stuart Lodge in Mparntwe on 5 October 2013. The interviews were recorded in Pitjantjatjara, and translated and transcribed into English by Sam, who is a fluent Pitjantjatjara speaker. While he recorded the interviews for his PhD research, he considered Sandra the owner of the transcripts. When she granted me permission to use them for my research, Sam generously provided me with the transcripts.[11] Over the years that followed, Sandra and I travelled widely together, and much of what I learned from her evolved from many hours spent driving, sitting and talking.

Whereas Tjuki, Linda and I visited various locations on Angas Downs and the surrounding country, Sandra and I travelled further afield in the Central and Western deserts, and as far away as Sydney, as well as spending time together at Bloodwood Bore, Imanpa and Anthelk-Ewlpaye (Charles Creek) town camp in Mpartnwe. The act of travelling is fundamental to this book. Physically travelling to, and experiencing, the landscape was critical in my developing an understanding of this place that is grounded in its physical reality. Visiting ruins, rock art sites, water sources and learning place names informed my developing awareness of Angas Downs as a place steeped in the Tjukurpa, deep time and historical time. Learning while on the move, I also came to understand that mobility is a fundamental fact of desert life, and it was the path, not the place, that was the key to understanding Angas Downs.

Tjuki Pumpjack passed away in 2015. Linda and I spent a lot of time with him in the final months of his life, just sitting with him in the Alice Springs hospital and at his house in Imanpa. He had become thin and frail, and looked a different man from the one we had travelled and talked with all those years. He said often that his time had come. I attended his funeral, having been asked by his granddaughters to give a eulogy and also to read all of the eulogies sent by people who weren't able to attend. I felt profoundly sad at the time, but also deeply grateful that I was able to say goodbye to him in his community, with his family.

Sandra Armstrong passed away in 2020. She was living in the aged care facility in Mutitjulu community at the time. I received word that she was very unwell and then, only a few days later, was told that she had passed away. The COVID-19 pandemic prevented me from travelling to Central Australia, which meant that I was unable to attend her funeral to say goodbye. I still find this very difficult to process.

In 2017 I had travelled out to Imanpa, hoping to see Sandra there, but, as usual, she was on the move. I was living in Canberra at the time, and feared I wouldn't get to see her before I had to leave, and wasn't sure when I would return. Reminiscent of the day we met, I ran into Sandra in Mparntwe, by chance, when she emerged from a taxi as I was walking past. The days that followed at Anthelk-Ewlpaye town camp were the last we spent in each other's company. As always, the conversation centred on Angas Downs.

Both Tjuki and Sandra were on a mission to have their knowledge and their relationship to Angas Downs recorded. They were aware that I wanted to learn more about Angas Downs in order to write a history of this place, but they had their own reasons for choosing to work with me. Despite the different circumstances under which they were recorded, Tjuki's and Sandra's life histories have a certain politics in common. Although their experiences varied, their stories amplify a central statement about their identification with Angas Downs as ngura, or Country. Even though the time period covered in their life histories spans a half a century, they were keenly aware that others might end up hearing their stories. Their oral histories are very much about a present concern that speaks to a fraught politics of place, recognition and sovereignty.

Places accrue people and stories, in multiple layers, over time. Some of these stories come to dominate how we see and interpret a place, while others are obscured from view. While Angas Downs is ostensibly a pastoral station, pastoralism is only a fraction of the story of this place. We can't understand Angas Downs without the stories and the memories of the people who lived there. Listening to them, a very different kind of place emerges from that conjured in the myths and histories of pioneers and pastoralists that have dominated understandings of the past in Australia—particularly in the Northern Territory.

History in Australia, like much of the physical landscape, is contested territory. The past is experienced, remembered and inscribed quite differently by First Nations and settler Australians, and these differences have meant that not everyone has had an equal opportunity to shape the so-called Australian story. Nation-making and popular histories have placed the stories of Federation, the Anzac legend, mateship, the pioneering spirit and the 'opening up' of the great Australian 'outback' as foundational to national identity. Yet, upon closer inspection, these taken-for-granted narratives of Australian beginnings demonstrate the ways in which histories of nations have been imagined and written without including many of the people who live there.

In crude terms, colonisation in Australia can be understood as a confrontation between a Western European culture that structured daily life according to time, and diverse First Nations cultures that oriented themselves in the world according to place.[12] Western time-focused modes of knowledge have dominated historical research and writing in Australia throughout much of the twentieth and into the twenty-first century, which has undermined First Nations ways of knowing the past and being-in-the-world. In seeking to pursue the question of how I could go about researching and writing history that's open to, and shaped by, First Nations perspectives, I've turned to place and its potential to unsettle these taken-for-granted concepts of Western knowledge.[13]

Deborah Bird Rose suggests that in taking a place-centred approach to research and writing, authors destabilise many of the conventional assumptions of Western knowledge. She notes that First Nations peoples have only figured marginally in the settler Australian imagination for long periods of time, and that this is largely because histories of nations and communities can be represented as bounded social groups without having to consider other people who occupy the same time and place. A place-centred project won't let you ignore the people who are there.[14]

How we think about place matters. As Goenpul, Quandamooka scholar Aileen Moreton-Robinson has powerfully demonstrated, settler colonial logic has a tendency to see place as something that is static, and through the lens of white, Western ideas of possession, ownership and property.[15] Similarly, Unangan scholar Eve Tuck and environmental scholar Marcia McKenzie describe the settler colonial relationship to land as one that seeks to remake it into property, and redefine the human relationship to land in terms of ownership—the aim of which is to make place 'ahistorical in order to hack away the narratives that invoke the prior claims and thus reaffirm the myth of terra nullius'.[16] However, as Tuck and McKenzie point out, First Nations Elders, here in Australia and globally, remind us that humans have always enacted more complex and meaningful relationships to land.[17]

Travelling with and learning from Tjuki and Sandra, I came to understand that more than a spatial location, or simple stage for human action, places are complex constructions, made from local cultural material and practices, and the interactions between people, other species and the land.[18] Tjuki Pumpjack evoked Angas Downs as ngura, and cited his family and the growth of his beard as the reasons for relating to this place as his Country. Ngura is the A<u>n</u>angu word for 'camp' and, despite much focus on the Tjukurpa, there is perhaps no finer example of the difficulties of translating the textured and layered meanings of A̲nangu concepts into English. Put simply, ngura can refer both to the place where people live, *and* named and enduring ancestral Country created in the Tjukurpa. The two uses and the dual meanings of the word ngura are bound up with one another through kinship relations. Listening to Tjuki and Sandra, I came to learn that living, sharing, loving, fighting and dying in place were central to the meaning of Country and that, in one sense, walytja, or family, and Country are the same thing.[19]

Place and Country takes a particular form in Tjuki's oral histories especially. Early in my relationship with him, I came to see that his way of remembering the past and narrating his life history was through a series of itineraries—stories spatially anchored to the desert landscape, punctuated by an inventory of places encountered along a lifetime of travelling. It is the journey that organises his stories, and the rhythmic pattern of movement from camp to camp that forms the structural spine of his narratives; this reflects a peripatetic way of being-in-the-world that is articulated in Pitjantjatjara as alternating between ananyi (travelling) and nyinanyi (camping).[20]

This mode of storytelling isn't unique to Tjuki's remembrances. It has been well documented among First Nations people across Australia, and is often articulated in a language of routes, beats, intervals and rhythms.[21] It has also been observed among First Nations cultures elsewhere. Anthropologist Keith Basso observed that all Western Apache narratives he encountered were grounded to points in the land and that the primary spatial anchors 'almost always turned out to be place names'. The Western Apache call this practice 'speaking with names'.[22]

In Australia, this narrative style is commonly associated with the exploits of the Ancestors as they travelled and created the known physical world—human, plant, animal and environment—out of themselves in the Tjukurpa. Like many other white settler Australians growing up in the 1980s, my primary school education led me to believe that the 'Dreamtime', as I knew it then, was a suite of mythical stories explaining how the world was created. This childhood impression of the 'Dreamtime' as little more than folklore was a reflection of an idea deeply embedded in the collective settler Australian psyche that pitted a 'primitive' Aboriginal creation mythology against 'civilised' settler histories of empire, discovery and progress. This way of thinking has been hard at work in Australia, representing First Nations stories and knowledges as inferior to the dominant white settler culture, and insisting on an antagonistic binary between myth and history, and spoken stories and the written word.

Travelling with Tjuki Pumpjack and learning about both past and present places from his perspective, my understanding of the Tjukurpa deepened. Listening to him recount his life, I learned that history, too—the past actions and encounters of human beings—is inscribed in the landscape in a way that echoes the movements of the Ancestors in the Tjukurpa.[23] Over the years, it gradually dawned on me that, more than mythical consciousness, the Tjukurpa represented a mode of orientation to the world, where identity and meaning are embedded in place—or, as Moreton-Robinson describes it, an embodied 'ontological relationship to land'.[24] Listening to and learning from Tjuki, I came to see that his stories were not simply 'oral histories'. Rather, they reflected a culturally specific form of memory that opened up a worldview that has worked to shape my reading of the past and this place in profound ways.

Rather than mine their oral histories for information to be assimilated into my historical analysis, I seek to translate Tjuki's and Sandra's life stories not just from Pitjantjatjara to English but as a particular mode of historical practice that has its own organising principles and conceptual framework.[25] Reading Tjuki's and Sandra's oral histories according to their own narrative logic, and alongside the archival documents, I found that the archives—the cornerstone of the historian's craft—became increasingly 'othered'. I began to see things I would otherwise have missed. Sharing in Tjuki's and Sandra's memories of Angas Downs, I came to understand that it was possible not only to learn something of local language and knowledge but to unlearn something of the white settler colonial mindset that I've inherited.

While the A<u>n</u>angu concept of Country is a central theme in this story, as a white settler Australian I use the concept of place here deliberately. The focus on place in this book highlights the ways in which our orientations to places are both shaped by and determinants of history, colonialism, capitalism and culture. I understand this approach as having the potential not only to reveal local languages and knowledges that have been obscured by settler colonial processes but to unsettle settler colonial claims to knowledge, land and power. I use place here in the hope that it might create space for other settler Australians to radically reimagine their relationships with people, other species, and the stolen land that we seek to belong to, without appropriating or diminishing Country as First Nations ontology.[26]

However, in seeking to respond to the human- and land-based injustices that have resulted from settler colonialism, and been reproduced and sustained in Australian history writing, I understand that there are limitations to this work. As Cobble Cobble woman and pro vice chancellor and professor of law Megan Davis argues, while truth-telling about our shared colonial past is important, it is not *the* pathway to justice for First Nations people in Australia. Following the Uluru Statement in 2017, Davis notes that there has been an enthusiasm among allies for 'truthy jaunts' and 'truthy projects' that are conspicuously 'detached from the political ask'.[27] Heeding Davis' observation, I acknowledge that, while it is critical to produce histories that can create a more truthful understanding of our shared past, this project is subordinate to, but I hope in service of, the greater fight for substantive structural reform and justice—such as a constitutionally enshrined Voice and Treaty—for First Nations peoples.

Angas Downs was a marginal pastoral enterprise, and yet it attracted significant numbers of A<u>n</u>angu around the middle of the twentieth century. These migrations brought people with connections that spanned hundreds of kilometres to the south and west into the Musgrave and Mann Ranges in South Australia, the Tomkinson and Petermann Ranges in the Northern Territory, and the Warburton Ranges in Western Australia. The following chapters traverse a half-century across the Central and Western deserts, and trace the ways in which A<u>n</u>angu relationships to place were reorganised through the act of migration, and the encounter with white settlers, rations, work, tourists and camels.

The book begins with Anangu migrations out of the Western Desert in the late 1920s and early 1930s, and concludes with the demise of the pastoral paradigm. Its structure, while chronological, also seeks to emulate Anangu rhythms of peripatetic movement and modes of historical practice. Time and space combine throughout, to reflect the movement between places and also how places pulse in and out of use over time.

Part 1 begins in the Western Desert, and reinterprets the dominant narrative of 'exodus' that has shaped historical and anthropological understandings of movements in this region when white settlers began to penetrate the desert. These chapters trace some of the journeys to Walara, the site that William Liddle chose to establish the sheep run he called Angas Downs, which is the location of Part 2. Focusing on the environmental knowledge in Tjuki Pumpjack's oral histories and the few letters, diaries and patrol reports that emerged from the period, Walara reveals the ways in which the desert ecology shaped the pastoral enterprise and relations between Anangu and pastoralists, revealing a history of pastoralism quite different from that evoked in the pastoral mythology of the north.

Following World War II, the Liddle family sank a sub-artesian bore, relocated the station, and made the transition from sheep to cattle. Bloodwood Bore was the name of the new site and the location of Part 3. Bloodwood Bore didn't just mark a shift in location; it really was a 'New' Angas Downs, as Anangu sometimes called it. Developments in road making and grading literally paved the way for a greater administrative presence in the region, coinciding with the intensification of the state's assimilation agenda.

However, Welfare Branch patrol officers weren't the only outsiders making inroads into Angas Downs. Roads also opened the way for the first tourists to travel to the long-mythologised 'primitive heart' of the nation. Part 3 reveals a rich and previously unrecognised history of tourism in Central Australia, illuminating the central role that Anangu played in its development. Tracing the story of punu, the carved wooden objects Anangu made to sell to tourists, reveals the ways in which people like Tjuki and Sandra continued to carve a life, and a place, for themselves in the increasingly oppressive postwar assimilation era.

Part 4, 'Itineraries', zooms out, and broadens the perspective on Angas Downs to encompass the wider socioeconomic network in which it was located. A distance of some 250 kilometres separated the mission settlements at Areyonga and Ernabella; yet, travel between these two places was common and is frequently described in Aṉangu oral histories. These two mission settlements, and the stations that lay between them, became the knots that tied threads of travel together in a web that took shape as Aṉangu incorporated new places into existing patterns of movement.

These lines of travel also feature in a series of letters and patrol reports the Northern Territory Welfare Branch produced throughout the 1960s, tracking and monitoring Aṉangu travel between Ernabella and Areyonga. Casting Aṉangu as 'the itinerants', the government documents represent Aṉangu ways of moving through the world as anathema to the prevailing ideology of assimilation. This series of chapters tells the story of a little-known socioeconomic history of the region, revealing the ways in which Aṉangu capitalised on the very few economic opportunities available to them in an economically underdeveloped north *and* how the Welfare Branch tried to stop them from doing so.

Part 5 grapples with the complex transformations of the 1960s and 1970s that resulted in the eventual demise of both Angas Downs and the settler colonial state's assimilation policy agenda. The final chapters are structured around two very different ways of remembering the unmaking of Angas Downs. Sandra Armstrong's memories of the multiple forces of the 'return to Country' and the homelands movement, the start of 'sit-down money' and aspirations for autonomy richly illustrate the complexity of this period. In contrast, Tjuki Pumpjack's story of the station owner's death as the cause of Aṉangu leaving Angas Downs raises the problem of how to explain the 'end' of the station in a way that is both meaningful and truthful. Ruminating on the shifting meanings of Country over half a century of change, Part 5 traces the story of how a cattle station became Country, and the ways in which Tjuki's metaphor of death provides important insights into contemporary politics of place, recognition and sovereignty.

There is much at stake in the stories we tell about places. I don't consider this to be a definitive history of Angas Downs. Focusing on the life histories of two people with a deep connection to it provides scope for a detailed illustration of how people came to make a place for themselves in a period of momentous change. However, there are many more stories from this place that aren't told here. Despite my attempts to engage with some of them, the present-day members of the Liddle family, who are intimately connected to the history of Angas Downs, didn't want to participate in this project.[28] I respect that decision, and acknowledge their memories and stories are integral to that history. Alexis Wright's 2017 book *Tracker* presents another way of seeing and remembering Angas Downs. Told from the perspectives of Tracker Tilmouth, John Liddle, Lawrie Liddle and Tim (Snowy) Lander, Wright's book paints a picture of Angas Downs in the 1960s and 1970s, providing a deeper insight into the Liddle family and their life on the station. These remembrances, like the stories shared in this book, reveal Angas Downs as a place rich in family, language and culture.[29] Both Tjuki Pumpjack and Sandra Armstrong appear briefly in *Tracker* and Tracker Tilmouth makes an appearance in this book, reflecting the entangled nature of people, story and history at Angas Downs.

Both the content and shape of this story have been influenced by the people who I spoke to, and what they chose to remember and share with me, which was undoubtedly influenced by my position as a white woman outsider/settler. Just as there were details about this place that they really wanted me (and you) to know, there are details about this place that we can't know or understand. The following chapters are one story of Angas Downs.

PART 1

EXODUS?

1
WHITEFELLA FOOD

TJUKI PUMPJACK WAS born around 1926–28. He didn't know the exact date. One of the first oral history recordings we made together in 2012 took place on the veranda of his house in the community of Imanpa. In the time that I knew him, he rarely told stories about his life there. We only recorded stories in the community on two occasions, and during those times Tjuki's memory always travelled elsewhere. On this particular day—when we were just getting to know each other—over a period of about two hours, speaking in Pitjantjatjara, he shared his life story with Linda Rive and me. This is where it began:

> My grandmother's country, where she was born, was Ulkiya. She was born there, halfway between there and Yaluriti. I am from Apara. The olden-time name of my place is Apara. That's the proper traditional name of the place. Today, everyone calls that place Amata. But when we were tiny children, we called that area Apara. My grandmother was born at Apara, Ulkiya. My father's mother and my grandmother's mother were born there. They were born there near Amata, near Ulkiya. The old place is called Ulkiya. They lived there and that is where I lived the first few months and years of my life—old enough to be running around on my own two feet, anyway—and I remember seeing my father's father—my

grandfather—there. My father's father is my tjamu. My grandfather. He died where the Amata buildings stand today. He died in that same spot, where the houses are now. The exact spot where he died has a name, which is Apunkintama. My grandfather died when I was a little boy, running around on my own two feet. But I do remember seeing him. When he died, when he fell to his eternal sleep, my father and grandmother and mother did not want to stay around that area anymore. So they decided to walk to Ernabella ... So we went to Ernabella.

Later, houses were built at Amata, but when we were living there, there were no houses or buildings at all. Just the water source. Father was a hunter and he would always be going out hunting kanyala [emu] and bringing the meat back to us. On our journey across to Ernabella we would stop in the afternoons to make camp and sleep the night. One of our camps was a place called Ulayapa. There is water at Ulayapa, and so we stopped there for a while to drink the water. Another camp we stopped at was Kul̲i. At Kul̲i my younger brother was born, Johnny Mulla. He was a tiny little newborn baby, born right there. After that, my father decided that we would go and have a look at this flour that we'd heard about. Flour. Whitefellas had met my father before and told him about it and he used to tell us, 'These whitefellas have got a lot of food stored up, so we are going to go there and get some of it.' So from Kul̲i we changed direction and came around through Fregon way and headed over to Ernabella. The day came when we arrived in Ernabella. We arrived and we sat down there for a while.[1]

As this extract from Tjuki's oral history demonstrates, An̲angu prefer to mark time, and the significant events in their lives, in places. His life story begins in the Musgrave Ranges in South Australia, a place far away from Angas Downs, which is the place he came to think of as his ngura, or Country.

He says that Apara, meaning river red gum in Yankunytjatjara, is where he was born (see Map 1 on page xiii). Apara is nestled among the Musgrave Ranges, located in present-day northern South Australia. A reliable source of water, many explorers and scientists visited it during expeditions into the interior in the early twentieth century. In their writings, naturalist and travel writer HH Finlayson and anthropologist Charles Mountford have rendered this place as Oparrina and Oparinna respectively. However, this is a phonetic impression of how they heard the word Aparanya, the 'nya' being an ending in Pitjantjatjara and Yankunytjatjara that is attached to proper nouns, in order to bind them into a sentence. To elicit the term, Finlayson and Mountford most likely asked Aṉangu at the time, 'Where are we?' or 'What is the name of this place?', to which Aṉangu may have responded, 'Nyangatja ngura Aparanya,' meaning 'This place is Apara.'

Tjuki also tells that where the houses are today in Amata community is where his grandfather died, and that his father and grandmother didn't want to stay in the area after that sad event. For Aṉangu, when someone passes away, it is tradition to leave for an extended period of time the place where the deceased person lived, while they grieve that person. Today, Aṉangu refer to the process as 'sorry business'. It was the death of his grandfather that initiated the journey out of their homeland at Apara.

Much has been assumed and written about Aṉangu migrations in the 1930s out of the Western Desert towards emerging mission settlements and pastoral stations. Referred to overwhelmingly in historical and anthropological writing as the 'exodus' from the Western Desert, it is one of the most significant historical processes to have played out following the arrival of white settlers to the arid interior. The seemingly ubiquitous use of the term exodus to describe Aṉangu mobility at this time suggests a mass one-way movement away from ancestral country towards new settlements. Periods of drought, coinciding with a gradually encroaching white settler society, characterise the cause-and-effect-driven narratives that have converged over time to shape understandings of the migration of desert peoples as a helpless drift, or, as patrol officer TGH Strehlow claimed in 1937, more of a 'flight or rout'.[2]

In seeking to understand the past, historians often pursue questions of 'why' by looking for cause-and-effect relationships that can be explained according to Western logic and chronology. However, Aṉangu oral histories unfold according to their own narrative logic and, as Tjuki Pumpjack's oral history demonstrates, Anangu provide their own interpretations of the journeys they made out of the Western Desert towards pastoral stations and the missions. Anangu oral histories are itineraries—narratives spatially anchored to the desert landscape and punctuated by an inventory of places. Guided by the narrative rhythms of the stories, tracing the places that people went to, and exploring the various motivations for their travels, a more nuanced picture of this so-called exodus begins to emerge.

When Tjuki was really little, his family hardly knew about whitefella food:

> Yes, we were living at Amata. We are the traditional owners of that area and this is where my father lived his whole life, from the early days when everybody was naked. My father was a naked man living in the Amata area, living in the traditional way, before he had ever seen or tasted flour. Later he came to know what flour was because he learned about dingo scalping and how it could be exchanged for flour. After that we started eating flour by kneading it into dough and baking dampers in the hot coals, till they were cooked through, and then we'd pull them out and cut them up with a knife and eat them along with hot tea, dipping the damper into the tea, and eating it like that. After that we walked around the southern area of what is now Amata and walked to Ernabella.[3]

With the expansion of pastoralism came the perceived threat to stock from the dingo. The South Australian Government responded by implementing a bounty on dingo scalps in 1912, with Western Australia and the Northern Territory following suit in the 1920s. The bounty encouraged lone white men, commonly referred to as 'doggers', into the Petermann and Musgrave Ranges, both areas known for plentiful populations of dingo. The incursion of doggers into the desert presented the earliest instances of regular contact between Anangu and white men in the Western Desert; as Tjuki's oral history demonstrates, for many Aṉangu it was also the catalyst for their first encounters with flour, tea and sugar. Aṉangu superior hunting skills, and their sophisticated knowledge of the desert country, meant that they were of great benefit to doggers. Their value as hunters ensured continued contact between them, as Aṉangu sought out the flour, tea and sugar that they could get from doggers in exchange for dingo scalps.

The early 1930s saw increased numbers of white men enter the Southwest and Central Reserves for the purposes of dogging or prospecting. In northwest South Australia, individual doggers often returned to the same base camp year after year, aiming to establish good relations with local Aṉangu. In 1933 anthropologist Norman Tindale noted in his field journal that Aṉangu were travelling and camping in large numbers with individual doggers.[4] After a trip to the Musgrave Ranges in 1935, missionary Charles Duguid made a submission to the South Australian Government to extend the Central Aboriginal Reserve and make it 'inviolate'—which is to say that he wanted to protect Aṉangu within the reserve from harm and violation at the hands of white men. He wanted to rid the reserve of 'undesirables', such as doggers, and ensure that early contact between Aṉangu and white men was with the 'best type of white man', such as himself.[5]

In 1920 the Australian Government gazetted a large tract of desert country in the southwest of the Northern Territory as the Southwest Reserve. By the 1930s the justification for inviolable Aboriginal reserves had begun to shift from earlier ideas of protection and segregation, to assimilation and civilisation. The catalyst for this change was the increasing influence of anthropologist AP Elkin and his advocacy for assimilation. Elkin viewed Aboriginal 'reserves' as training grounds:

> If there were established on each large reserve an institution, practical, educational and religious in nature, which would give the Aborigines a new interest in life, they would not be so readily lured away to white settlements off the Reserve, but rather would themselves be the cause of other natives being attracted to it.[6]

Despite Elkin's increasing influence, in the 1930s there was little consensus among 'white experts' as to the purpose of reserves, and whether they should regulate the transformation of the social and economic lives of Aboriginal people, or segregate them as a means to preserve racial and cultural purity.[7]

In reality, regardless of the debate around their intended purpose, reserves were an administrative imaginary, the borders of which were meaningless to both A<u>n</u>angu, and the white men who roamed as they pleased in country that was, as historian Rani Kerin has described it, both 'unpatrolled and unpatrollable'.[8] While the 'white experts' debated the purpose of the reserves, A<u>n</u>angu and white doggers went about their daily lives, and travelled, hunted, and exchanged scalps for food that was later shared and eaten.

Tjuki explains that his father learned about flour through the exchange of dingo scalps, but he also shares that his father had heard there were whitefellas giving away free food in a place called Ernabella:

> 'Oh, we might go to Ernabella to have a look at this whitefella food.' Whitefellas were giving it out and whitefellas were living in Ernabella. Everybody was thinking about the whitefellas living in Ernabella![9]

Hearing stories of white people giving away food no doubt stirred A<u>n</u>angu curiosity. However, in order to understand the power of food as a driving force in these early encounters, it is necessary to grasp the idea of food as more than material sustenance. For A<u>n</u>angu, it is also a fundamental object of exchange, the sharing of which is an integral part of the social processes that create relationships and connect people to one another as walytja, or kin.

Food and its acquisition is a prominent theme in A<u>n</u>angu oral histories recalling the colonial encounter. Reverend Jim Downing, a Uniting Church minister who worked with Pitjantjatjara people throughout the 1960s and 1970s, noted a recording he made with an A<u>n</u>angu woman called Nganyintja, who told him that her father and uncle walked more than 250 kilometres to Ernabella to 'bring back some of the white man's food'. Nganyintja told Downing that they returned two weeks later with a bag of flour, tea and jam.[10] In an oral history recorded for the Tjanpi Desert Weavers *Kuru Alala* exhibition catalogue, A<u>n</u>angu woman Niningka Lewis, who lives in Ernabella, recalled how her parents came to hear about the white settlers giving away food at the mission:

> Some of them that walked into Ernabella, actually walked huge distances to get there. They walked from many distant places, and my mother and father were amongst those that walked into Ernabella for the first time. They arrived at Ernabella and they stayed for quite a while ... People from all over the country would go to U<u>l</u>panyali to dig out karku [red ochre]. They would get their karku supplies and then carry it all the way back to their country again ... this is when they [Niningka's parents] heard about the white people living at Ernabella. They'd been up getting karku and they heard the news from there. They had heard, 'There are white people living in houses that they've built, and they are giving away free food. They've built this place and have food sent in, and you can go there and get some.' So my parents went there to see for themselves and when they got there they decided to stay.[11]

Niningka's parents heard about the white people at Ernabella and their food while getting karku (red ochre) in U<u>l</u>panyali, situated hundreds of kilometres to the northwest in Watarrka, the place that Ernest Giles called Kings Canyon. When passing through the area in 1932, HH Finlayson recorded seeing this red ochre mine, which he noted was 'of great fame with the blacks', and that the karku was a highly sought-after item 'traded far and wide by the Luritjas'.[12] Niningka says that people travelled from all over the country to U<u>l</u>panyali to get karku, and that her own mother and father travelled there regularly from the Docker River region, several hundreds of kilometres to the south in the Petermann Ranges (see Map 1 on page xiii).

Mobility was a fundamental fact of desert life. The arid environment imposed a particular pattern on the rhythms of movement; these ecological itineraries of travel were punctuated by the soaks, wells and springs that provided the necessary means to move through the country. The unreliability of rainfall and scarcity of resources meant that social isolation in the arid interior was ecologically impossible. People lived day-to-day life in smaller groups of twenty to thirty; yet, collectively they formed a larger regional network that emphasised inclusion and interconnectedness.[13] There is little doubt that word of the white people, and their abundant supplies of food, would have spread rapidly throughout the Musgrave, Mann and Petermann Ranges.

However, Aṉangu were not the only people on the move at the time. Missions and pastoral stations may have been novel, but the places where they were established were not new. The need to believe that the land into which they ventured and the places in which they eventually settled were both unknown and uninhabited gave rise to the perception among white settlers that Aboriginal people were simply drifting in towards pastoral stations and mission settlements. However, the places they chose to establish their settlements were always already known, used and lived in.[14]

Ernabella mission emerged in Aṉangu memories of early migrations as the most significant site in the first sustained encounters between Aṉangu, white settlers and their food. Despite being understood as a 'new' place, and the earliest settlement of its kind in the region, the mission was established somewhere well known to Aṉangu and, as such, complicates white settler narratives of 'exodus' and 'coming in'.

2
THE WHITE EXPERTS

ERNABELLA MISSION WAS established in a place A<u>n</u>angu knew as Pukatja. Winifred Hilliard wrote of the mission's location, on the site of the old Ernabella pastoral station:

> Ernabella, the place which had won so many hearts because of its beauty, was at the end of the mail-run from Oodnadatta. It was thus a regular meeting place for lonely bushmen coming in on mail day each month. The local Aborigines came there to barter their dog scalps, and because it was one of their best permanent waters. It was the obvious centre for this great new venture. All roads led to it.[1]

While Ernabella is known for being the earliest settlement of its kind in the region, it was established at a place that was already significant for A<u>n</u>angu. As Winifred Hilliard observed, '*All roads led to it*', and white settlers were drawn to the area for the same reason A<u>n</u>angu had always been travelling there—water. A<u>n</u>angu were not 'coming in'. Rather, they were returning to Pukatja because it was already there.

Dr Charles Duguid was the driving force behind the establishment of Ernabella in late 1937. He was a medical practitioner, Moderator of the South Australian Assembly of the Presbyterian Church, and self-appointed advocate for the Pitjantjatjara people, and historian Rani Kerin writes that, in light of the relative success of the mission, he is a man who has largely been remembered as a 'visionary'.[2] Proposing the mission as a gesture of the Presbyterian Church to Aboriginal people, at the time Duguid wrote of his motivation for making such a gesture:

> I had seen the Pitjantjatjara people of the Musgrave Ranges were so far uncontaminated by contact with the White man and I was determined that they should be given a chance to survive in their own country. It seemed that the best way to do this would be to establish a Christian mission at the eastern edge of the Ranges ... and that this mission should act as a *buffer* between the Aborigines and the encroaching White man.[3]

The 'buffer' concept was the central and defining characteristic of Ernabella, Duguid claiming in 1938 that:

> First and foremost Ernabella has been called into being to act as a buffer between the white settlers east of it and the Native Reserve west of it.[4]

The notion of missions and reserves as 'buffers' between Aboriginal people and white settlers was not new, and had been used by anthropologists and administrators prior to the establishment of Ernabella. However, the importance of the 'buffer' concept among 'white experts' like Duguid in the mid-1930s was about more than altruistic concern for the future of Aboriginal people. Reputations were riding on it.

A<u>n</u>angu migrations towards the emergent pastoral stations and mission settlements took place amid the increasingly contested domain of Aboriginal politics in Australia. In the mid-1930s professional 'white experts' had begun to intervene in Aboriginal Affairs. Social anthropologists such as AP Elkin, Donald Thomson and WEH Stanner, and medical scientists specialising in physical anthropology, such as Frederic Wood Jones and JB Cleland, and Charles Duguid, all sought to influence the administration of Aboriginal affairs at the time. Throughout the 1930s competing ideas of protection, segregation, preservation and assimilation converged; as historian Geoffrey Gray has noted, blood and culture were conflated, and racist terms such as 'full-blood', 'half-caste', 'traditional' and 'non-traditional' became entangled in administrative and anthropological discourses that sought to categorise Aboriginal people, and influence policy in Aboriginal affairs.[5]

Towards the end of the nineteenth century, most Australian colonies had implemented policies designed to segregate and manage Aboriginal people. The various 'protection' Acts that were introduced rested upon ideas of racial 'caste', which understood race as something that was quantifiable and measured by blood. Racist terms such as 'full-blood' and 'half-caste' in the colonies reflected a wider settler colonial logic that used scientific racism and its technique of blood quantum to govern Aboriginal people. It was assumed that so-called 'full-blood' Aboriginal people would eventually become extinct, while 'half-caste' people would be absorbed into the white settler community and eventually blend into whiteness.

These ideas persisted well into the twentieth century. In the Northern Territory, 'white experts' believed that A_n_angu migrations towards pastoral stations and mission settlements in the 1930s, and the resulting encounter between Aboriginal people and settlers, would inevitably result in the racial and/or cultural decline of A_n_angu. In a 1938 paper called 'The Aborigines', anthropologist WEH Stanner wrote of these migrations in the tropical and arid regions of the north:

> The blacks are ceasing, or have ceased, to make their ancient stone tools. They smoke tobacco. Some of them wear whites' clothes. They are eager for tea and sugar and white flour, and do everything they can ... to obtain manufactured European articles ... They are tending to drift away from their traditional tribal lands to live near white settlements where they can secure more readily the tobacco, tea, sugar, new foods, clothing and manufactured articles they have learned to value and crave. This tribal drift is threatening to dissolve so-called uncivilised tribes into small floating segments, each of which is likely to leave the main tribe and attach itself in parasitic fashion to a cattle station, mission, farm, or settlement. Once this stage has been reached the tribes will never return to the old nomadic life in the bush. Once a tribe is parasitic it is in the half-way house to extinction.[6]

The use of words 'parasitic' and 'parasitism' to describe Aboriginal relationships with white settler society was common in the language of 'white experts' throughout much of the twentieth century. Although it's commonly associated with Elkin, following his coining of the phrase 'intelligent parasitism' in 1951, the term was in use by anthropologists and administrators before then, as Stanner's quote demonstrates.

The use of the word is telling. Parasitism is a biological term, and refers to a species attaching itself to a host and living at the expense of the other species. While the likes of Stanner and Elkin may not have intended the term to be a disparagement, it is deeply offensive and needs to be recognised as such. As Stanner's quote demonstrates, he believed that migrations of Aboriginal people towards white settlements would inevitably result in them attaching themselves 'in parasitic fashion' to these missions and pastoral stations, which would, in turn, lead to their extinction. However, despite Stanner's view on 'parasitism', as historian Heather Goodall has pointed out, it was often the relationship between these 'white experts' and Aboriginal people that was 'parasitic'—men like Duguid and Elkin used it to gain prestige, power and funding, while Aboriginal people received nothing.[7]

Stanner's ideas reflect Gray's observation that anthropological and administrative discourses tended to conflate blood and culture; in his analysis, the 'drift' away from traditional lands and a traditional way of life, in favour of white-settler food, clothes and tools, would somehow result in their elimination as a race of 'so-called uncivilised tribes'. This sentiment is echoed by patrol officer TGH Strehlow, who concluded in 1939 that the government's 'leave 'em alone' policy had done its worst. He lamented that the younger people who had migrated from the Western Desert towards the township of Alice Springs were already 'degenerating into a race of useless wasters'.[8] According to Strehlow, it was urgent that the government act to 'save the Aboriginals from extinction' while there was still time. Stanner's and Strehlow's statements reveal an underlying sentiment that Aboriginal people needed to be saved, not just from extinction but from themselves. These ideas illuminate the anxieties that were emerging, stemming from the assumption that Aboriginal migrations in the 1930s were a result of an abject desire for food and material goods, and would inevitably lead to racial and cultural decline of Aboriginal people, and an increased dependency upon the state.

Like many ideas circulated by administrators, anthropologists and advocates at the time, talk of the 'buffer' concept was not overly concerned with how Aboriginal people approached the missions and stations that were emerging and altering their itineraries. Rather, it reflects the perceived need among 'white experts' to create a barrier between Aboriginal people and white settlers, so as to protect Aboriginal people from racial and cultural 'contamination', as a means to ensure their survival. However, Duguid's idea of Ernabella as a 'buffer' obscures A<u>n</u>angu interpretations of the mission, and their initiative in early encounters with new settlements and stations. As Tjuki's and Niningka's memories attest, word of the mission spread and A<u>n</u>angu began to travel significant distances, largely motivated by the objective of seeking out the white people who had abundant supplies of food. Ernabella was hardly a buffer for A<u>n</u>angu. Rather, it was a new and curious resource, to be explored and then exploited, much like any spring, rockhole or soak in existing patterns of travel.

Despite ideas of inviolability and buffering, by the mid-1930s it was apparent that the establishment of reserves wasn't having the desired effect. In 1939 patrol officer TGH Strehlow, accompanied by Duguid and Lutheran missionary at Hermannsburg Reverend Albrecht, journeyed into the Petermann Ranges to report on conditions within the Southwest Reserve, and also to investigate why so many people were migrating out of it. Strehlow drew the conclusion it was drought conditions that had contributed to the 'alarming depletion' of game and bush foods in the reserve, forcing A<u>n</u>angu to leave their homelands. Strehlow reported that the 'desolation' he encountered had resulted from a series of 'bad seasons' that had created a serious problem. He believed that assuring the food supply in the west would work to 'correct the migration' of desert people to the east, recommending that a ration depot be established to encourage A<u>n</u>angu to stay within the designated borders of the reserve.[9] Duguid, too, reported it was drought that had forced people to migrate in search of food and water, claiming that many had died of starvation. He wrote of the patrol:

> We in the South with a glut of food had left the natives in the Petermanns alone – left them to die of starvation. No one of that 1939 patrol advocates that the natives are best left entirely alone.[10]

The devastation brought by the drought in the desert was a key factor in Duguid's argument that the 'leave-them-alone' policy was not 'practical politics' and that the 'unwisdom of segregation' had been made painfully obvious on his trip to the Petermann Ranges.[11] Strehlow, too, concluded his report by saying that the 'leave 'em alone' policy had done its worst, and it would seem that drought was a critical influence on their respective arguments for increased intervention in A<u>n</u>angu lives, via 'buffer' missions and ration depots.

Drought is, in many ways, a matter of perception and in the arid interior the term's overuse can be misleading. The Bureau of Meteorology states that drought is not simply a matter of low rainfall, and that if it were, 'much of inland Australia would be in almost perpetual drought'.[12] Interesting, then, that much of what has been written about Central Australia and the Western Desert in the past 150 years in journals, reports, newspaper articles, letters and books combines to tell the story of a physical environment in an almost enduring state of 'drought'. Here, in the heart of the continent, rainfall is highly variable, and for prolonged periods, perhaps several years, there might be no rainfall at all. As environmental historian Libby Robin has noted, in the desert average estimates are 'meaningless' and you take the rain when you can get it.[13]

The word desert in the popular imagination conjures images of endless sand dunes, dryness and relative desolation. However, deserts are marked not only by highly variable climatic conditions but vibrant and dynamic places of environmental diversity. The Central Australian Ranges are a large block of desert uplands in the centre of the continent, bordered by the MacDonnell Ranges in the north, and the Mann and Musgrave Ranges in the south. Sweeping west from the edge of the Central Australian Ranges is a group of desert dunefields that form a ring around this continental heart. The Great Sandy Desert, Little Sandy Desert and Gibson Desert are known collectively as the Western Desert.[14] Much of the Central Australian rangelands and the Western Desert are classified as arid, which the United Nations Education, Scientific and Cultural Organization defines as regions characterised by perennial vegetation that is woody succulent, thorny or leafless shrubs, and with an annual rainfall between 80 millimetres to as much as 350 millimetres, and an interannnual rainfall variable of 50 to 100 per cent.[15] The dynamics of deserts such as those of the Australian interior are largely determined by the highly intermittent availability of water. Big rains are rare and yet they structure the characteristics of the arid environment.[16] This variability has been described as a 'pulse-reserve' model, whereby desert ecosystems are largely controlled by infrequent and unpredictable rainfall. Ecologist Walter G Whitford describes 'pulse-reserve' as:

> A rain event triggers a pulse of activity, like the growth of vegetation, a variable portion of which is 'lost' to mortality and/or consumption but some part is put into a reserve such as seeds or reserve energy stores in roots and stems. The magnitude of the 'pulse' varies as a function of the trigger event and season of the year as well as the magnitude and duration of the event.[17]

A familiarity with the fertile soils and reliable rainfall of the British Isles gave Europeans very poor tools, both conceptually and physically, for making sense of, or managing, the Australian environment.[18] Despite attempts to make sense of the Australian interior with vocabularies of British landscapes, the arid rangelands at the heart of the continent confounded the colonists. This unpredictability—and, indeed, indecipherability—of Australia's desert interior led to it being seen as the continent's 'dead heart'.[19] This idea of dryness and desolation came to dominate popular ideas of Australia's deserts from the very earliest European exploration in this region in the latter half of the nineteenth century.

The inability of the British to read the physical world in Central Australia meant that hunger and the risk of perishing from thirst were everyday challenges. Ernest Giles noted that during explorer Charles Sturt's failed attempt to find the fabled inland sea, he seemed to be haunted by the notion that he had got into, and was surrounded by, a 'wilderness the like of which no human being had ever seen or heard of before'.[20] Giles's invocation of extreme wilderness highlighted the perceived difference between 'cultivated' Britain and the 'primitive' Australian interior, which tempered the feverish colonial desire to tame and domesticate the land, due to the very real fear that the country might be too wild and alien for European settlement. It was the lack of water, in particular, and the inability of white men to decipher the patterns that this scarcity imposed on travel, that threatened to thwart British imperial imaginings in Central Australia. Giles lamented during his 1872 expedition that he only wished he could:

> Catch a native, or a dozen, or a thousand; [for] it would be better to die or conquer in a pitched battle for water, than be forever fighting these direful scrubs and getting none.[21]

Following soon after Giles, explorer William Gosse described the interior he encountered in 1873 as the driest country he had ever seen. He wrote that the defining characteristic of the region was there was 'scarcely a water to be depended upon'.[22] It is a telling fact that Gosse recorded the first word from a Central Australian language: kapi, the Pitjantjatjara and Yankunytjatjara word for water.

Drought as a motivating factor for the migration of desert people became a popular assumption among white administrators in the Northern Territory in the early twentieth century. The Chief Protector of Aborigines in Queensland, JW Bleakley, attributed the arrival of a large group of Warlmala people at Wave Hill station in the Northern Territory to the lack of water in the desert brought about by the 1924–29 drought.[23] Stanner, too, wrote of the 'drought-stricken blacks' descending upon Wave Hill, and observed that in 'native Australia' drought conditions occur again and again, and the 'food problem of even the nomadic and uncivilised natives may well be almost as serious as it is for the semi-civilised camps dotted throughout the settled areas'.[24]

In a response to Strehlow's report following his investigation of the Petermann Ranges as part of the McKinnon Inquiry in 1936, the Chief Protector of Aboriginal people in the Northern Territory, Cecil Cook, noted that Strehlow attributed migrations at the time to being motivated by 'the greater facility of life in contact with the white man', and that life within the reserve was becoming very difficult due to 'failure' of waters and shortage of game, and that both factors may have been due to a 'temporary failure of the seasons'.[25] The Commonwealth Meteorologist was unable to provide Cook with rainfall data for the country west of Hermannsburg; however, he assured him that the Hermannsburg data would suffice. Cook's report stated that the 'average' rainfall for the years previous to 1926 was 1200 points, and for the years following:

1926	747 points
1927	478 points
1928	262 points
1929	364 points
1930	1300 points
1931	602 points
1932	873 points
1933	777 points
1934	697 points
1935	583 points

There is no indication of how the 'average' figure of 1200 points for years preceding 1926 was derived, or what this proposed 'average' was based on. Nevertheless, Cook takes it as a benchmark, and observes that in the ten years between 1926 and 1936, the 'average' had only been reached once. He goes on to establish these years as 'rain failures', unable to appreciate the variability of the desert world in which he found himself and see that the so-called 'average' in 1930 was most likely an example of a trigger rain event in the 'pulse-reserve' cycle. The failure at the time was not the rainfall in the years either side of that trigger event but, rather, of the white settler imagination. The dry years were, in fact, the norm in the Australia interior.

Drought looms large in white settler interpretations of A<u>n</u>angu migrations out of the Western Desert. It has come to characterise much of the writing that has contributed to the prevailing historical account of the so-called 'exodus' from the Western Desert, which describes desert Aboriginal people as refugees, forced or pushed out of their homelands in sheer desperation.[26] Strehlow's 1939 report following his second journey to the Petermann Ranges was particularly influential in shaping the idea that a severe drought provoked movement out of the Petermann Ranges towards stations and missions. Strehlow noted that on their journey he and Duguid met only twenty-six people, 'all of whom were forced by lack of food or water to travel in small groups', and that they themselves saw no kangaroo, euro, wallaby or emu during their journey.[27] However, despite the conclusion of drought conditions that Strehlow draws in his report, it also notes that these drought years couldn't have been totally rainless, for 'everywhere was in quite good condition'. Strehlow documents encountering 'fair country' in several parts of the reserve and in the Western Petermann Ranges; he reports seeing 'many fresh tracks of kangaroo and turkeys, also some of emus' and 'many fresh footprints of human beings leading east, north and west'. There were several waters that enabled them to make the trip, one large enough to bathe in. Upon encountering the Docker River, Strehlow wrote:

> Then came the green – oh so beautifully green! – Gums of the Docker River. It burst through a very range here, and its amazingly broad river bed was a mass of lovely gums, full branched, white trunked and full of vitality and beauty.[28]

Despite this, his concluding remarks were that the reserve was desolate and 'virtually empty', providing no other explanation for the migration out of the Petermann Ranges than drought conditions depleting the reserve of game.

In contrast to this story of drought as being a major influence on movements out of the desert, very few A<u>n</u>angu oral histories I've recorded or listened to make any reference to hunger or drought.[29] The very few Anangu oral histories I've heard that mention conditions we've come to think of as 'drought' speak of ailuru or 'hard times'. Anangu observe three seasons: kuli, which describes the hot weather we think of as summertime; piriyakutu, the time of the warm spring winds that blow from the north and west; and nyinnga, the frost season or cold time. Ailuru is the Anangu word for a period of little or no rains, resulting in conditions dry enough to make bush food and game scarce. The reliance on pulses of rainfall to provide the opportunity to procure food around the more ephemeral waters means that in prolonged periods of little to no rainfall, ailuru occurs. In a place of extremes where average rainfall measurements are meaningless, Anangu speak of 'good times' and 'hard times'.

Tjukupati James from Docker River recorded an oral history about her life growing up in the Petermann Ranges, before going to Areyonga mission, and says that there was always abundant food there. She recalls an instance of ailuru when life became very hard due to the lack of water, bush foods and game:

> The country was green and figs, bush onions and desert raisins were everywhere. There were also small ground animals like bandicoots and plenty of water. My mother was always going out to forage for these abundant foods for us. They were great times. But then ailuru came, there was no rain and waterholes dried up. Some small animals survived, and our mother would dig them from the banks of the creek for us to eat. They used to dig for water too, but later even these soaks dried up and life became very hard for us. However, rain eventually came and the creeks flowed and grass appeared and we were able to enjoy desert raisins, bush tomatoes and figs again. Our mothers and all the others were happy. They harvested the seeds of the woolybutt plant and winnowed, ground and kneaded them and cooked us all this wonderful food. It was marvellous: we had been crying with hunger for so long and now we had as much as we could eat.[30]

Tjukupati's family didn't leave Docker River during this time of hardship. Rather, she talks about making the 'mistake' of going to

Areyonga after meeting the pastor while travelling and being taken there for food. Ailuru was a fact of life for Anangu. Efficient land use, detailed knowledge of Country, and fluid and inclusive social relationships were crucial in enabling them to survive 'hard times'. Deborah Bird Rose describes this relationship between people, mobility and place in Victoria River as:

> Not usually a matter of being pushed from place to place as resources become scarce, but rather of being called from place to place as food comes into plenty (and in land claims across the Northern Territory from desert to islands people speak of nomadic travels as joyful engagements with plenty). Victoria River people, like others, have stories of the hardships of drought and flood, and there are sites of refuge as well as stories of people who did not survive, but people speak of these events as exceptions.[31]

In another oral history recorded for Tjanpi Desert Weavers, Nyanu Watson from Kalka reflects Rose's observations of travelling as 'joyful engagements with plenty':

> We would travel around with a mob of donkeys and camels, who would carry our gear. After traveling for the day we would set up camp and everybody would go hunting for meat ... They'd come back at the end of the day with meat, and we'd all be really happy because we knew we'd be having plenty of meat for dinner ... We always had plenty of food, and we got flour from the stations. We were very happy with our way of life and had no need for anything else. We were contented and happy and unaware of anything else in the world. We didn't need anything other than what we had, and we didn't want anything else. It was a great way of life ... We had lovely fresh water to drink, everywhere we went, and our donkeys had a good drink too.[32]

Nyanu also recalls how her grandfather, an Amata man, died young during ailuru. She noted that this particular ailuru happened a long time ago and was fatal for many people. However, this was a one-off event in Nyanu's life story.

Over the four-year period we recorded his life history, Tjuki Pumpjack remembered a single instance of ailuru. In keeping with Rose's observation of 'hard times' as exceptional, Tjuki's memory of the experience was evocative in its description of the weather event as being both out of the ordinary and extreme:

> A very long time ago we walked to Areyonga during a great heat. It was terribly hot. We started out walking from Ulanga [near Walara on Angas Downs]. We started walking from there because the water had run out. We had been living there but the water had run out. One old man left first, carrying a very large piti [digging dish] on his head, to get water, but couldn't find any! So he turned around and came back. We called out to him, 'Old man! Bring the water here to us!' But he called back to us, 'Nothing! I couldn't find any, my son! It is empty!' and he showed us the empty piti. 'Empty!!'. So there we all were, sitting beside the trunk of a tree, while birds fell out of the sky and died all around us. Even the Kanyala [emu] were dying beside Irawa spring [near Ulanga]. Everything was dying from the heatwave, even the birds. Crows died, falling out of the sky dead. We, too, were there, with no water at all. We, too, nearly died. We were this side of Tempe [Tempe Downs station]. This side of Tempe we nearly died. This side of Kings Canyon. We were barely surviving. We hung on. My older brother asked me, 'Are you alright?' I said, 'Yes, I'm alright. Where are we going to find water?' So we decided to leave that night to find some. We walked all night. We came to the rocks [a rockhole hidden up high in a rock face] and my brother picked up a small round pebble and he threw it. 'Hey! It has hit water!' Uru! Uru! Uru! Splash! Without hesitation we leapt into the water, fully clothed, in our trousers and boots, and we drank and drank until we were able to lift ourselves up again. We then got out and lit a fire and slept for the rest of the night. Three of us, my number one kuta [brother], me, and our old man. We were heading for Tempe but we nearly died halfway in that terrible, terrible heat, which killed all the birds. We were so lucky to get away with our lives on that occasion.[33]

While Tjuki's descriptions of birds falling to their death from the sky might sound fantastical, HH Finlayson described a similar experience during his 1932 visit to Central Australia, recording in his diary at the time that he encountered dead or incapacitated birds everywhere, and that the extreme heatwave of 1931–32 prevailed over a very large area, resulting in what he referred to as the 'bird holocaust'.[34] Despite the severity of the conditions described during 'hard times', Tjuki never recounted an instance of A<u>n</u>angu succumbing to these conditions. Rather, it's recalled as an extreme event that caused significant hardship due to lack of food and water. None of the oral histories I've heard or read attribute 'hard times' to being an influence on the journeys that took A<u>n</u>angu out of the Western Desert.

Charles Duguid wrote of his journey into the Petermann Ranges with Strehlow:

> We could not help wondering what would happen to the little families who were so much at the mercy of their surroundings, but there seemed to be very little we could do for them at the time.[35]

Despite Duguid's claims after his trip into the Petermann Ranges that A<u>n</u>angu were dying of starvation, A<u>n</u>angu memories recounting episodes where they are at the mercy of their environment are rare. White settlers' perceptions of difficult and challenging desert lands, and their inevitable misconceptions about the people who lived in them, prevented them from appreciating the sophistication of the desert lifeworld, instead projecting the 'otherness' of their own experience onto people and places they knew little about. White settler environmental sensibilities in the deserts of the interior resulted in the imposition of an idea not suited to Central Australia; yet, drought has persistently shaped historical narratives of one of the most important processes to have taken place in the region.

3

WALYTJA

THE YEAR 1872 is significant in the history of colonialism and cultural encounters in the desert. The Overland Telegraph Line was completed in that year. Three thousand two hundred kilometres of telecommunications cable had been laid along the length of the continent from Port Augusta in the south to Port Darwin in the north, collapsing time and space by linking the Australian colonies with Java in Indonesia and, ultimately, the imperial centre, Great Britain. The twelve repeater stations that punctuated 'The Line' further enabled European exploration of the Australian continent. The year of its completion is also remembered in colonial history as marking the moment of 'first exploration' into the arid interior. That year, Ernest Giles penetrated the country to the west of the Telegraph Line, and, in doing so, ventured into territory where, in his own words, 'for a thousand miles in a straight line, no white man's foot had ever wandered'.[1] Commencing nearly a century after the British first established colonial settlements in the southeast of the continent, the early encounters between Anangu and white settlers set in train movements of people that would come to change significantly the social ecology, and cultural and physical landscapes, of the Western Desert and Central Australia over the next eighty or more years.

Appearing as though mimicking the highly variable arrangement of available resources in the arid interior, the process of colonisation in the desert was sparse and patchy. Established between 1870 and 1885, Henbury, Tempe Downs, Erldunda and Glen Helen were the earliest pastoral stations in the region west of the Overland Telegraph Line. Clustered around the northern edge of the Central Australian Ranges, this early pastoral development didn't greatly increase the number of white settlers living in the region, but it did contribute to an increase in their movements throughout it. Incidents of Aṉangu spearing cattle began on Tempe Downs in the 1870s. It appeared at this time that people began moving in from the deserts beyond the so-called frontier to participate in cattle spearing, and also to seek rations and safety from reprisals at the nearby Hermannsburg mission, which had been established in 1877.[2] However, for nearly half a century after these early stations appeared, pastoral settlement failed to penetrate any deeper into the Central Australian Ranges or the Western Desert, and it would seem that Aṉangu daily life continued relatively undisturbed between the 1870s and 1930s.

The 1930s and 1940s witnessed rapid pastoral expansion in Central Australia. The establishment of Angas Downs, Lyndavale, Curtin Springs and Mount Connor stations in the southwestern corner of the Northern Territory during this period coincided with the establishment of Ernabella mission in 1937 and Areyonga mission in 1943. The rapid expansion in new settlements greatly intensified contact between Aṉangu and white settlers, and began to impact materially upon Aṉangu itineraries of travel.

As Aṉangu walked north and east from the Western Desert, and white settlers moved further to the south and west from Alice Springs and the Overland Telegraph Line, the food that was obtainable at mission settlements and pastoral stations meant that social groupings began to change. The availability of flour, sugar and tea caused Aṉangu to supplement customary bush foods with the new foods that white people had brought. This situation resulted in changes to the 'ecology of survival', which was particularly novel in terms of the larger numbers of people who could be sustained at any one time.[3]

As movements out of the desert intensified, and the periods of time spent exploring and exploiting the new and curious resource bases lengthened, the social ecology of the desert also altered. In the inclusive and interconnected social world of the Western Desert, the departure of kin must have been keenly felt by those who remained. As anthropologist John Carty has observed, as increasing numbers of A<u>n</u>angu travelled to mission settlements and stations, a 'human drought' began to occur in the desert.[4]

Family, as well as food, punctuates the journey narratives of A<u>n</u>angu life histories. Many speak of movements out of homelands as being motivated by the search for kin who had earlier left the desert. A<u>n</u>angu were always travelling, not just to procure food but also to share that food among kin. They also travelled and gathered to share knowledge, conduct ceremonies, and carry out the ritual practices of the Tjukurpa (Dreaming), which were necessary for caring for and maintaining ngura (Country) and walytja (kin). The changing nature of food resources presented new opportunities for social life. Not only could larger numbers of people be sustained in any one place, extended family, who would previously only have been seen intermittently, could now come together for prolonged periods of time.

Tjuki Pumpjack says that while his family were visiting Ernabella, his father decided that he wanted to keep travelling and see his older sister:

> He wanted to see his kangkuru [sister]. He had been asking around, 'What's the name of the place where she is living now? My kangkuru, where is she living now?' The people told him, 'Wilpiya. She's living at Wilpiya, your older sister.' So my father took us to go and search for her. We set off, heading towards Atila. We arrived at Atila, and we asked the people there, 'Does anybody know where my sister is living?'
>
> 'She's living up that way! Up around Wilpiya! There is a big hill at Wilpiya—go there!'
>
> There is indeed a big hill at Wilpiya, and so that is where we headed. At last we arrived in the district, and we could see hundreds of sheep footprints everywhere. We followed them and we finally arrived at the camp. 'There's my auntie! Over there!' And, indeed, there was my auntie, sitting in her camp with her husband, my uncle. That man who had married my auntie was from Docker River.

> He was a Docker River man. They had married at Docker River, and then as a married couple had come to this place.[5]

There at Wilpiya, a place not far from Walara, on Angas Downs station, Tjuki's father found his older sister.

As with many of the white pastoralists in Central Australia, there is a robust mythology around William Liddle and the establishment of Angas Downs station. Born to Scottish parents in Angaston, South Australia, in 1888, Liddle had been in Central Australia, working in various occupations, since 1907. Described by well-known Central Australian tourism proprietor Jim Cotterill as a 'genuine pioneer settler of Central Australia', local lore has it that in 1922, after running cattle at a place called Kings Creek near Watarrka (Kings Canyon), Liddle sold his 500 head of cattle and set out with camels 'to look for greener pastures':[6]

> Whilst going southwards amongst spinifex and sandhills Bill saw hostile natives fighting over a soak, so he went around the natives and found water in a forked desert oak tree. He claimed that this tree saved his life. Going further south Bill found another soak, which he later called Angas Downs. He then travelled south and found another soak later called Wilbia [sic] and then west to another, later called Curtin Springs. He arrived at Ayers Rock in approximately 1922. There was no water in Maggie Springs or any of the rock holes around the base of Ayers Rock so he climbed into a shelf several hundred feet above the ground and found water. Bill then went north to Lake Amadeus and then west to Western Australia. Then he returned by a similar route.[7]

The above story is part of a local legend well known in the region. Similar versions of the story appear in HH Finlayson's diaries, Arthur Groom's book *I Saw a Strange Land* and Bill Harney's book *To Ayers Rock and Beyond*; both Tjuki Pumpjack and Sandra Armstrong told versions of Bill Liddle's founding story as part of their oral histories of Angas Downs station. Legend has it that after purchasing 2000 head of sheep in South Australia, Liddle returned to the second soak he had 'found' on his travels out west and called it Angas Downs, which A<u>n</u>angu knew as Walara. This was sometime around 1928–29, approximately six years after he had first set out from Watarrka.[8] In 1930 the first camel train carrying wool left Walara for Rumbalara railway siding, which lay to the south of Alice Springs.

HH Finlayson stayed with Bill Liddle at Walara during his 1932 visit to Central Australia, at which time he observed that there were approximately six to eight men, ten women and 'many children' who were 'attached to Liddle's show'.[9] While the primary purpose of his expedition was to study indigenous mammals, Finlayson also took many photographs of Aboriginal people during his travels. The collection from his stay at Walara contains twenty-two prints, accompanied by handwritten notes, that include each person's name, approximate age and family information, and are titled 'Petermann Range Natives at Moment Domiciled in Basedow Range'.[10] The information in Finlayson's diary places the A<u>n</u>angu he encountered at Angas Downs as having left the Petermann Ranges around 1920–22, the word 'domiciled' in the title of his collection suggesting that, ten years later, these families were living, somewhat permanently, on the station.

Tjuki's father's older sister, Mimiya, is named 'Mimi' on the back of Finlayson's photograph of her. His own sisters Tjintjiwara, Awutjari and Imbidi are also subjects in Finlayson's photographs. Tjuki says that his auntie and uncle had one son and three daughters, which, according to the A<u>n</u>angu system of relatedness, are his siblings. Finlayson also photographed Tjuki's uncle Tjutjapayi, the Docker River man, and recorded his name as Kurraton. When asked why his auntie went to Angas Downs, Tjuki replied:

> She went there because a Wintalyka man—a Mulga Seed man—from Docker River called her to join him in marriage. That man was originally from Docker River. He called her to join him in marriage. He had already been living there [Angas Downs], and so the two

> of them went straight back there. They went in a straight line from Docker River via Uluru. Wati Wintalyka [Mulga Seed Man].[11]

Tjuki explains that Tjutjapayi had already been living at Angas Downs when he travelled to call Mimiya in marriage. It was customary for men from that area of the Western Desert around the Petermann Ranges to seek marriage partners to the east in the region of the Mann and Musgrave Ranges. After he called Tjuki's auntie in marriage, they then travelled from Docker River back to Angas Downs.

To say that an area in the Petermann Ranges is Wintalyka Country, and that the men connected to it are Wati Wintalyka, is to say that Anangu, and the Mulga Seed of that place, are inextricably intertwined in a mutual relationship that has its beginnings in the Tjukurpa. When the Ancestors 'changed over' after their creative travels, they became the animal or plant relatives of the people with whom they share intimate relationships.[12] Liddle's 'daybook' records Harry Brumby, also a Wintalyka man from the Kikingura area in the Petermann Ranges, as being employed by him in the early years at Walara, around 1939. Anthropologist Fred Rose's fieldwork diaries, produced some two decades later, also reveal strong connections between Angas Downs and Kikingura, which is Mulga Seed Country, in the Petermann Ranges. Exactly what happened during Liddle's journey, or how the Anangu who Finlayson encountered at Walara came to be living at Angas Downs, we don't know. But what does seem likely is that the first group of people Liddle established relations with had strong ritual ties, through those Wati Wintalyka, to the area around Kikingura in the Petermann Ranges.

According to Finlayson, Liddle spoke fluent Pitjantjatjara in 1932, which would indicate that by the time he returned to Walara to establish his sheep run, he already had considerable contact with Anangu. A lone white man wandering with his camels for years over vast distances and through deserts would surely have encountered many Anangu on his travels. He more than likely relied on them to show him the string of water sources that enabled him to make that journey. It is possible that Liddle met with these Wati Wintalyka while they were travelling on ceremonial business somewhere around Watarrka, or perhaps while collecting karku, and established a relationship with them, most likely structured around the provision of food. He may also have met with Wati Wintalyka while in the Petermann Ranges, possibly engaging some of them to hunt dingos on his behalf. TGH Strehlow noted, after visiting Liddle in 1937, that Liddle actively encouraged A<u>n</u>angu to come into the homestead for the purpose of bartering dingo scalps. Furthermore, during a visit to Piltati waterhole in the Petermann Ranges the previous year, he encountered two A<u>n</u>angu males and one woman, who had 'arrived with camels in order to collect dingo scalps for Liddle from the natives living in the Western Petermanns'.[13] Strehlow's observations confirm that the exchange of dingo scalps and food was well established between Liddle and A<u>n</u>angu from the Petermann Ranges by the mid-1930s.

The tracks people traced across vast distances in the desert were anything but 'helpless' or 'passive drift'. Despite ideas circulating at the time that contributed to claims that drought was driving A<u>n</u>angu out of the desert towards mission settlements and pastoral stations, and bolstered arguments for the need to 'buffer' A<u>n</u>angu from the perceived racial and cultural decline that would result from these encounters, A<u>n</u>angu oral histories illuminate the interplay between agency and opportunism. Furthermore, they shed light on the circumstances of a changing world that were imposed on them and were beyond their control. It is not at all surprising that desert people would grasp the opportunity to get good food from faraway places through little effort, doing so, as Tim Rowse has suggested, 'with no sense of disaffiliation from their homelands'.[14] While there is no one story that can explain why A<u>n</u>angu walked out of the Western Desert in large numbers in the 1930s and 1940s, A<u>n</u>angu memories of this period demonstrate that access to new foods and resource bases began to change A<u>n</u>angu itineraries. A<u>n</u>angu engagement with these places was characterised by strategic economic and socioculturally motivated movements between mission settlements, pastoral stations and the bush.

Tjuki Pumpjack says that when he and his family arrived at Walara:

> Happily, we combined our camps and we settled in to live there with them, and that is where I grew up.[15]

At Walara, Tjuki and his family, and the extended network of walytja, began to translate existing relationships of everyday life and exchange into the new context in which they found themselves. Although they couldn't have anticipated the impact at the time, Angas Downs began to reorganise (not replace) Aṉangu relationships to place, thus beginning a process of accommodation and reorientation to the material world that would continue to evolve throughout the twentieth century.

PART 2

WALARA

4
FOUNDING MOMENTS

THE 'OUTBACK' IS a powerful symbol in the Australian national identity. Yet, what and where it is, is not easy to define. Symbols are often slippery like that. Although most Australians live in cities and towns that cling to the continent's coastlines, it is the outback that has been understood as the source of a distinctly Australian character. Taking shape in the myriad legends of the bush that emerged in the late nineteenth century, with the words of radical nationalist writers such as Henry Lawson and Banjo Paterson, these typically Australian traits found their expression most strongly in the itinerant white, male workers of the pastoral industry who historian Russel Ward referred to in his book *The Australian Legend* as the 'nomadic tribesman' of the bush. The strangeness of much of the Australian environment lay at the heart of this idea; scarce rainfall, harsh arid landscapes and great distances were seen to have shaped a distinctive ethos—hard working, rough and ready, swears consistently, gambles often, drinks deeply—that Ward noted was 'overwhelmingly masculine in composition and outlook'.[1]

It is also overwhelmingly colonial in its logic, embedded as it is in the idea of the frontier. Existing 'out back' of the densely populated cities, the vast and varied ecologies of the inland were imagined as marking the edge of civilisation and settlement. As nationhood emerged with the dawning of the twentieth century, settler anxieties about the 'unsettled' and 'empty' north saw the new nation look towards the outback as the continent's final frontier. Alongside Antarctica, New Guinea and the Pacific Islands, it was to be discovered, possessed, known and made productive in the modern Australian nation's re-enactment of European colonisation.

The settler story of the arrival of pastoralists in the Northern Territory is one of pioneer men toiling and triumphing in the outback. Deeply entangled in Ward's notion of an 'Australian legend', stories of pioneering feats in the heart of the continent have been told in the familiar terms of the nomadic tribe of the pastoral industry. The names of the white men who are remembered for 'opening up' Central Australia are circulated in masculine myths of discovery, sacrifice, fortitude and conquest. The stories that surround men such as Bill Liddle, Abe Andrew, Snowy Pearce, Bob Buck, Bryan Bowman and Paddy De Conlay have been passed down by descendants and acquaintances, and reproduced in the widely read writings of travellers such as Hedley Herbert Finlayson, Arthur Groom and Bill Harney.

A 1948 *Walkabout* magazine article called 'People of the Centre: Man and Environment in Central Australia' noted that the 'westward frontier' was maintained by a number of these men:

> Farthest west are the Andrew family of Curtin Springs, north-west of Mt Connor and about 40 miles from Ayers Rock. It was heartening to see this family of three generations standing to the task in a land where house blacks often outnumber the whites ... [and] Angas Downs impressed itself upon us through a great character W.H. (Bill) Liddle ... He is the first white man to have been seen by 500 or 600 blacks, and knows the country right out to the west into the sand ridge desert ... Already his own name appears on official maps in the Liddle Hills, north of the Basedow Range.[2]

Founded in 1934, *Walkabout* magazine became integral to the mid-twentieth-century narration of the nation. Charged with the work of asserting a racially and culturally homogenous Australian identity, *Walkabout* drew heavily upon frontier tropes that represented the inland environment as resistant to settlement, yet rewarding for those men who were tough enough to stay and struggle on with the difficult task of subduing the land.[3] *Walkabout* also had a particular fascination with the imagined timelessness of the desert. Journeys to the centre were often described as an opportunity to travel back in time, and representations relied upon imagery that rendered Aboriginal people as remnants of an earlier period of human history. The assumption that these primitive people and their Stone Age culture would inevitably be eclipsed by civilisation and the modern nation enabled *Walkabout* to represent these pioneering white men as agents of national progress.

Although Aboriginal people were largely displaced in the magazine, *they were there*, and as the above quotation demonstrates, Central Australia was a 'land where house blacks often outnumber[ed] the whites'. Anangu, some of whom would have been the 'house blacks' in the *Walkabout* article, also tell stories of these same 'founding moments' in Central Australia. Tjuki Pumpjack often told the story of how Abe Andrew and 'Old Bill' Liddle travelled together from Alice Springs to 'look for country':

> It was when they started from Alice Springs and were coming out this way. Abe Andrew and old Bill Liddle. Those two old men came out here to see the country and find out what the country was like. They were both looking for a place to set up home, after leaving Alice Springs. Anyway they came out here by way of Watarrka. Andrew saw the land and got excited. 'Hey, this is great country. I might settle down right here.' Abe Andrew was with his old wife, that old white woman. So they established their first place at Irawa waterhole, which is one mile from Ulanga.[4]

It was sometime around 1934, five or six years after Liddle returned to Walara to establish Angas Downs, that Abe Andrew set out from Port Lincoln in South Australia, with his wife Bertha, their daughter Maisie Parker (formerly Arbon), and Maisie's children, Gladys and Ray Arbon.[5] Abe Andrew's son Merv recalls that his father became 'bent' on going to a little well called Ulanga after hearing about it while camped at Port Augusta.[6] Knowledge of the limited water sources in the arid Central Australian environment was crucial and many pastoralists were dependent on local Aboriginal people for this knowledge. While Merv doesn't elaborate on who it was who told his father about Ulanga, Abe's grandson Ray Arbon noted in his recollection of that journey that his grandfather would always go and speak to 'the head man' at Aboriginal camps to find out about game, water and type of country ahead, and that his grandmother always had damper, brownies or soda bread to give to the Aboriginal children.[7]

Tjuki said that the world of A_n_angu started changing when sheep began to walk on the land; this marked the time that he began to 'learn the new way'.[8] However, Tjuki also said that A_n_angu knew the country—they knew where the water was and, because of this, they could go everywhere. But whitefellas, they would just go anywhere![9] Sitting under the canopy of a large desert oak at Ulanga, the place where Abe Andrew and his family decided to settle, Tjuki Pumpjack told me that when A_n_angu see a large body of water, they know there is a wanampi inside it. Popularly understood as the Rainbow Serpent, the wanampi is the most powerful and revered of all the ancestral beings. They came out of the sky and struck the earth, creating the water sources that are their home and sustain life on earth. That warm early October afternoon at Ulanga, I was told that we were in the presence of, but a safe distance from, an old blind wanampi who was known to make a strange grumbling sound if you upset him. Having visited a number of water sources with A_n_angu, I have learned that certain protocols are adhered to, and great care taken, so as not to anger or otherwise upset the wanampi. Upset the wanampi and the water source will dry up. When I suggested to Tjuki that many whitefellas would not believe his story about the wanampi, he said that whitefellas don't understand the wanampi. Nor do they have wanampi of their own. Emphasising that they didn't *know*, he said whitefellas only thought about the location of the water:

> Only like 'em water, white man. He want 'em water. 'Oh, got 'em plenty water here! I might put a station here, somewhere here!' That what he think about, whitefella.[10]

Upon locating Ulanga, and the nearby Irawa waterhole, the Andrew family decided to stay and make a life for themselves on a difficult tract of land jammed between Tempe Downs and Angas Downs stations. They called it Andaloo.

Deserts were difficult for white settlers to travel, which meant that the pastoral settlements in this region were hard to reach. In a letter dated 11 June 1936, some seven years after establishing his sheep run at Walara, Bill Liddle wrote to the Lands Department stating that he:

> [W]ould very much like to have some one visit ... on behalf of the Board so they would know what I am doing here. I have been on this block since June 1929 and have had no one here to see if I am on the right place.[11]

A chief surveyor Shepherd, from the Lands and Survey Branch, noted in a response to Liddle's request that he was located in unsurveyed country and that there was no fixed survey point anywhere near his boundaries. He observed that Liddle's block was an 'isolated one' that was 'entirely surrounded by vacant country',[12] and as a result there was no likelihood of it being surveyed any time soon. There were no roads leading to Angas Downs or Andaloo.

In a 1938 report on one of his patrols of the southwestern station area, TGH Strehlow documented in detail the difficulties he and Constable William McKinnon encountered in trying to reach Andaloo and Angas Downs by vehicle. Rough tracks that provided passage for camel wagons or a tip-dray were not kind to motorcars. When they could find a 'road', Strehlow and McKinnon's vehicle was bogged continuously and received a beating from the steep gutters either side of the narrow tracks. Upon entering sandhill country, Strehlow observed, the road to Andaloo was well marked, but rough and heavy going. When they finally arrived, the camp was deserted, as it had been for months, according to Strehlow.

Rain had washed away the traces of the recent tracks to the new homestead. Remembering that Andrew had a soak to the south, Strehlow decided to follow an old wagon road, never travelled on by car, that led south into heavy sandhill country. However, the sand was heavy and the track kept splitting into countless indeterminate trails. On encountering a huge sandhill that obstructed their passage, Strehlow and McKinnon climbed it, and saw that on the other side the trail split into various sections. At this point, they realised the futility of trying to find Andaloo without a guide:

> It was sunset, and our fruitless trekking in this heavy going was burning up petrol by the gallon. We abandoned the quest, and turned around, glad to leave the eerie silence of the desert oak glades. The car slithered back gratefully over countless unburnt tufts of tall spinifex, and thousands of desert oak needles, beneath which the red sand gleamed mockingly at us – as though the unconquered sandhill desert was frowning upon our poor efforts to conquer it by car.[13]

The next morning, accompanied by Abe Andrew himself, they travelled back to the old camp and again turned into the sandhills to the south, this time leaving the well-marked wagon tracks they had pursued the day before for a faint track that Strehlow had disregarded because of its disused appearance. After travelling for 6½ miles over heavy sandhills, they arrived at a gypsum flat, fringed with desert oaks, where there was a well; a small, new yard; and 'rude bough shed'. Strehlow reported that they spent the day with Andrew, his wife Bertha, and their grandchildren Ray and Gladys, all of whom were 'extremely pleased to have some visitors', given that no one ever strayed out into such 'wilderness'. Bertha Andrew and her daughter Maisie Parker were the only white women in the entire southwest region in the 1930s. Abe and Bertha's other daughter Gladys recalled that when she joined the rest of the family at Andaloo in the early 1940s, her mother hadn't seen another white woman for nine years.[14]

Despite their elevation in the outback imaginary as embodiments of masculine dominance over the desert, these pastoralists can just as easily be characterised as isolated, outnumbered and anxious. Liddle's neighbour and friend Snowy Pearce owned Lyndavale station, which was located at Marutjura waterhole on the edge of Erldunda station. Pearce contacted the police in Alice Springs, and patrol officer Strehlow, on several occasions between 1937 and 1939 to complain about 'bush natives' trespassing on his station. In March 1937 Pearce reported that there were approximately two hundred people from the Petermann Ranges who had turned up at his station, 'travelling through his sheep in all directions', stating matter-of-factly: 'I want them removed off my country'.[15] At around the same time, Bill Liddle wrote to the police in Alice Springs, asking if the group of people who had turned up at his station could be 'shifted from my country'. Like Pearce, Liddle complained that the group of approximately sixty were guilty of wandering through his sheep. He also reported not being able to get any sleep at night, due to 'brawls among them and corroborees'.[16]

Pearce's and Liddle's letters are illuminating. They reveal the perceived difference between the 'myall' or 'wild bush natives' and 'station boys' or 'station blacks', which underpinned white settler pastoralists' ideas about A<u>n</u>angu at the time. Pearce clearly saw a difference between the 'bush natives' trespassing on his country and those over whom he claimed ownership, referring to them as *his* 'natives'. Similarly, Liddle's letter declared that he would not mind if it were *their* country, but objected on the grounds that the 'trespassers' were predominantly from the Mann and Western Petermann Ranges. Inherited from a colonial ideology that created the symbolic opposites of the 'civilising' coloniser and the 'wild' colonised, these distinctions were thoroughly entangled with colonists' claims to country, and often invoked in order to legitimise the contradictions of colonial violence.[17]

In an oral history recorded for the Central Land Council book *Every Hill Got a Story*, Tjuki Pumpjack, in a remembrance of frontier violence, makes a distinction between 'naked' people who 'didn't know' and those who today are 'almost whitefellas':

> Out in the middle there, over on Angas Downs, in the middle, this side of Wilpiya, naked A<u>n</u>angu showed up at an old waterhole.

> You know, they didn't know about trousers, don't know clothes. Those naked Aṉangu they came from the west, came along when there were rations. They started getting rations, clothing, everything. Nowadays they're a bit flash, almost whitefellas. Yes, they sat and ate, naked. They speared a lot of cattle, they didn't understand properly. You know, they were spearing cattle, those naked men, long ago. And McNamara shot them. Pow! Pow! Long ago this side of Areyonga.
>
> Today they say he shot many. It happened a long time ago.[18]

William McNamara established a cattle run in the 1920s at a place called Bowson's Hole, near Tempe Downs, where Bill Liddle built a stone hut for McNamara that Aṉangu refer to as 'Old Station'. It's reported that around the same time as the Coniston Massacre in 1928, he shot somewhere between six and twenty-five people, following the spearing of one of his milking cows.[19] Aṉangu know the incident as the 'Old Station killings'. Tjuki said that this 'happened a long time ago' because 'they didn't understand properly', rendering the violent encounter as a mark of ignorance.

Ideas and imaginings, as well as the fact of violence, are powerful and all frontiers in the colonial encounter have, to varying degrees, relied upon the creation of landscapes of fear in order to take possession of land.[20] The story of McNamara's shooting Aṉangu in retaliation for spearing his cattle was one that was probably passed on as a warning and an important lesson in 'learning the new way'.

This story is one of only three references to violence that appear in the entire body of oral histories recorded with Tjuki Pumpjack. Speaking of the time before he and his family arrived at Walara, he said people used to kill others for nothing back then. However, stories of violent encounters are not characteristic of the oral histories that we recorded together. By the 1930s and 1940s, when station bores and windmills punctuated the marginal pastoral country of the arid southwest, the 'guerrilla warfare' that had characterised the 1880s and 1890s had largely abated. I have found that oral histories from this period of pastoral settlement differ significantly from memories of earlier experiences of violent encounters as a result of the development of the pastoral industry between 1880 and 1930, particularly further north. However, this is not to say that violent encounters didn't take place during this period. Mark McKenna's recent book *Return to Uluru*, in its examination of the death of A<u>n</u>angu man Yokununna at the hands of the white policeman Bill McKinnon at Uluru in 1934, demonstrates that incidences of colonial violence in Central Australia persisted well into the twentieth century.[21]

Isolation necessitated the formation of networks among the stations, and brought white settlers and A<u>n</u>angu into complex relationships with one another. As the letters from Pearce and Liddle demonstrate, some of these relationships were close, while others were distant. Claiming ownership of not just the land but the A<u>n</u>angu who lived with and worked for them was perhaps a way to establish some sense of security and familiarity in an environment that offered little of either. Despite finding good country and water, and claiming it as their land, the arrival of large numbers of desert people moving and looking for food, water and family must have been unsettling. It was a constant reminder that, no matter what they considered their rights to be, they had taken up residency in someone else's country.

5
FOUNDING ENTANGLEMENTS

One of the most memorable oral history recordings I made with Tjuki Pumpjack took place in October 2013, about a year into our relationship. We were at Ulanga, one of the numerous sites that punctuate Tjuki's memories of shepherding. A friend of Tjuki's, a man named Timmy Young, accompanied us and his presence enlivened Tjuki's performance that day. Tjuki relished the status of expert and, as we started recording, he turned to his friend and said to him, '*This is how I talk, Timmy.*' Interpreter Linda Rive noted in the transcript that, on saying this, he changed his tone and adopted what she called his 'high-pitched storytelling voice'.[1]

Timmy interacted with Tjuki constantly throughout: laughing, nodding enthusiastically in agreement, registering shock or surprise, asking questions and requesting more stories. Linda also noted in the transcript the points where Timmy apparently talked too much, prompting Tjuki to raise his voice and draw out his vowels in an effort to reinforce his authority as the storyteller, and drown Timmy out. At one point, Timmy asked Tjuki if he knew about the 'grumpy old wanampi' that lives at Ulanga. Tjuki responded by saying, 'Uwa. Wanti ka nyinara mirama,' which Linda translated as '*Yes. Just leave it and sit there and speak only if you must.*' Timmy didn't seem to mind this at all and proceeded to mimic the deep, grumbling sound that the wanampi makes. Tjuki then added that the wanampi wasn't only old and grumpy, he was also blind. He told us that the wanampi could smell, though, and both Tjuki and Timmy confirmed that he was present at Ulanga that day, listening to us talk and smelling us.

The decaying timber remains of a sheep yard, and an old rusted tank and windmill, are the relics that remain from the time to which Tjuki travelled in his memory that day. Sitting in the shade of the giant desert oak, he told us, '*That old whitefella [Abe Andrew] used to camp right under this tree here, underneath this desert oak*.' I think that it was the combination of Timmy's presence and being in Ulanga that stimulated the most evocative, exquisitely detailed oral histories we recorded during our time together. The transcripts I draw on here can't capture Tjuki's lively and authoritative tone, the co-produced nature of the recording, or the nuance and fine detail of a series of memories that Tjuki skilfully wove together over a period of approximately forty-five minutes. Despite this, they are a rich source for reading how A_n_angu inscribe history in place, and also how this inscriptive practice shows us the ways in which landscape shaped the pastoral enterprise in the desert.

Tjuki Pumpjack's oral history transcripts are lists of points in the landscape that form a network of wells, springs and bores A_n_angu moved between as they shepherded sheep. Characterised by the alternating rhythm of ananyi (travelling) and nyinanyi (sitting down/camping), the names Wilpiya, Irawa, Ulanga and Mutatja appear repeatedly, always followed by a return to Walara (see Map 2 on page 65). These named places that punctuate Tjuki's narratives are evoked as sheep camps. That day at Ulanga, Tjuki Pumpjack took us along on the desert shepherd's journey:

> I came here as a child, when I had no beard. No whiskers. We were living at *Walara*. But *Walara* became very dry. 'Hey! The place has become very dry! No ukiri!' [green grass] So old tjilpi [old man, Elder] Liddle said to us, 'Let's move to where there is green grass. Take the sheep! Take all the sheep!' So we brought all the sheep here [*Ulanga*] from *Walara*. First, we camped at *Tjilka*. Tjilka Well. We camped there, and then we came to *Ulanga*. We arrived at *Ulanga* and we stayed here with all the sheep. It was a really good place

with plenty of green feed .... Anyway, those sheep stayed here for quite a while, all around here, until another time, around two weeks later, when we started to shift them again, this time up to *Irawa*. So off we went with the sheep. A bit later we arrived at *Irawa*. And there we stayed ... We took the sheep up to the waterhole, and kept them there until the grass gave out again.

When the grass was virtually all gone—almost gone—we said, 'Right then! Let's go back again. Let's take the sheep and move back!' So we moved the sheep and started moving them back towards this way again [*Ulanga*]. We camped halfway and stayed around there for two or three weeks. Then we would move them again. And that is how we moved the sheep, stopping and starting. Moving the sheep, keeping them on good feed, moving them again, and stopping again where there was good feed. We moved through the country like that, herding the sheep, until we came to *Tjilka Well*. We got to *Tjilka Well* and camped there for a while ... after a stay there, we moved on and returned to *Walara* ...

But *Walara* became dry again by that time, and we still had a lot of sheep to look after. We still had the sheep. So we had to move them again and this time we took them to *Mutatja*. We took them to *Mutatja* and we stayed there for a very long time with the sheep. Until one day when the mayatja [boss] said to us, 'Take the sheep to *Alice Springs* and sell them. Take them all in one mob and sell them there.' So we took the sheep up along this road here and then along through *Ukaka* and across this side of *Tempe* [*Downs*] and then, heading in a straight line, we went to *Orange Creek*, to *Doctor Stone's*. That's what it was called a long time ago, Doctor Stone's. Nowadays there is a camel farm there. So we took our sheep right through where the camel farm is today. We got them to *Alice Springs* and we sold them there.[2]

Early in my relationship with Tjuki Pumpjack, I came to see that his way of remembering the past and narrating his life history was through a series of itineraries. They were stories spatially anchored to the desert landscape, punctuated by an inventory of places encountered along a lifetime of travelling.

Moving through the country and listening to stories, I came to understand that the 'journey' is central to A<u>n</u>angu storytelling and it's the rhythmic pattern of movement between places that forms the spine of the narrative. This way of speaking is commonly associated with the exploits of the ancestors as they travelled and created the known physical world—human, plant, animal and environment—out of themselves in the Tjukurpa. Yet, history and memory, too, are inscribed in the landscape in this way.

Tjuki didn't recall the past as moments in time but, rather, as events that happened here, or there. I've found this particular way of talking story to be illuminating. As I became more attuned to the way that Tjuki told stories about the past, I began to develop a deeper understanding of the Tjukurpa and its significance for history in Australia.

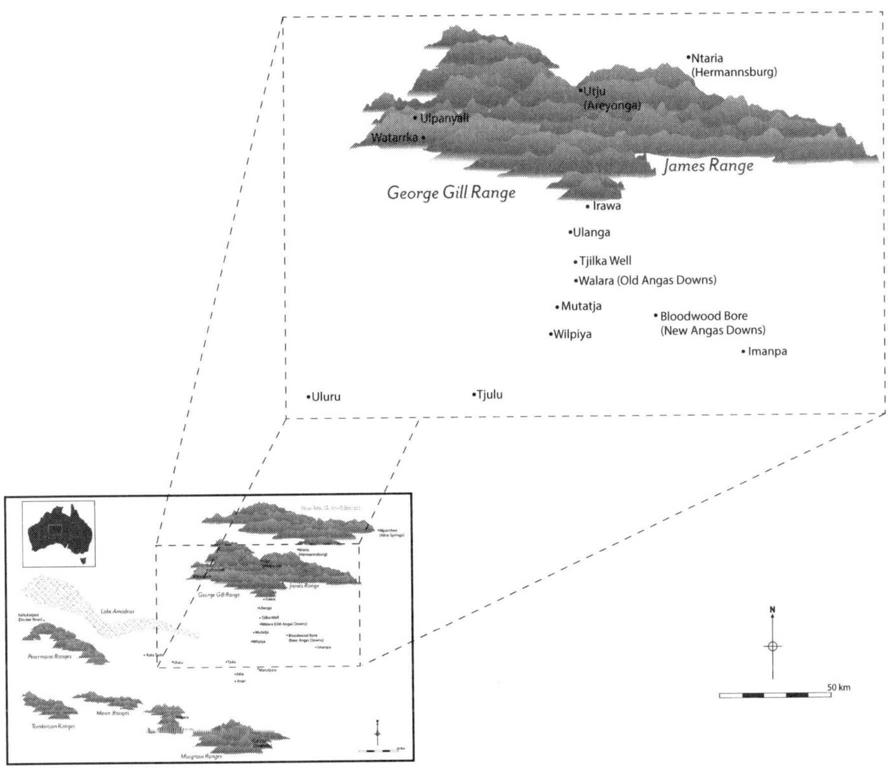

Map 2 is a close-up of the wells, springs, bores and sheep camps that feature in Tjuki Pumpjack's memories of shepherding at Walara. *Courtesy Felix Meyer*

The Dreaming that I encountered in books as a child was a mythology; it was a wonderful suite of stories populated by fantastic beings that had created the world as they travelled over it. Sitting and listening to Tjuki remembering the past, I came to see that the Dreaming was not just mythology, or a set of creation stories, but the basis of his reality—a way of experiencing the world, whereby meaning is embedded in place. I came to see that Tjuki's stories of shepherding Bill Liddle's sheep are structured much the same as stories detailing the creative deeds of the ancestors in the Tjukurpa, spoken as a journey and punctuated by movement from one place to the next.

Tracing these tracks in Tjuki's memory is also to take a journey into the ecology of the desert world. As records of the contours and textures of the environment in which Anangu move, they delineate the location and types of water sources, and reveal how this ecological knowledge shaped pastoral colonialism. The unpredictable 'pulse-reserve' model of rainfall that characterises the arid interior determined these lines and rhythms of travel. Pulses of rain meant that people could move from the relatively reliable water sources of base camp to the more ephemeral waters further afield. The desert imposed itself upon pastoralism in the region in much the same way:

> And so this is how we lived, going backwards and forwards, from big water to another water, one to another. We were always focusing on the need to be around a dependable water source ... And so that's what we would do. We would leave Walara and travel to Tjilka Well, camp there, and then leave Tjilka Well and come here [Ulanga] and camp right here. Then we would go to Irawa waterhole and camp there. Then we would camp at Ukaka waterhole. We would go to Ukaka along the old track, to Tempe. From Tempe we would go to Ila̲ri Spring. That's a big spring the other side of Tempe Down. But it is a dangerous spring, because she's got a big watersnake there, a wanampi lives in the spring. You know? ... That's an ancient place that we've always gone to. But it is too dangerous now. That water snake is a monster. It attacks people ... You'd be going along, near that place, when all of a sudden there would be a great flood

> of water attacking the car! So we would go around that place. That's the route we would take, right up, and go around and then work our way back here again ...
>
> That's what life is like for us living in this country, on all these water sources. We'd be going from Walara to Tjilka Well, then Tjilka Well back to here. After that we'd go to Waterhole. To Irawa ... Yes, we'd camp in one place for a while and then we would be back on the road again. This is when we had that huge flock of sheep. The sheep were the reason we had to keep taking them from place to place. It was one big huge flock we'd be taking, all along those tracks. It wasn't a proper road. There is a very old road going along here somewhere, a very old track, that goes from here, through the sandhills. And so that's how we moved from place to place.[3]

In his evocation of ancestral beings, water sources and shepherding, Tjuki illustrates the entanglement of the ancestral, historical and ecological in an Aṉangu worldview. Water has always been essential to pastoralism, and Anangu knowledge of the whereabouts of water was invaluable to the enterprise.

In the case of Tjuki Pumpjack's oral histories of shepherding at Walara, the environmental knowledge embedded in them is evidence of the ways in which the deserts of the interior shaped and, in some regard, inhibited colonialism and colonial power in this remote location. While much has been written about how First Nations peoples accommodated or incorporated the pastoral industry into their life world, less attention has been given to how pastoralists adapted their enterprises to suit their environment, and the ways in which they were being transformed by the places in which they found themselves. In the arid rangelands, pastoralism met with the ecological limitations of the desert, resulting in a patchwork of smaller, family-owned enterprises that rested upon constant movement amid a network of sites. In adapting to the environment, pastoralists such as Bill Liddle had to learn not just the physical features of the land but a way of *knowing* it and *moving* through it that provided them a place in it that was specific to their mode of land use and occupation.[4]

In February 1932 HH Finlayson described his arrival at Walara:

> Made Liddle's camp about 2 pm – if it could be called that, since the site was marked by a litter of canteens, camel saddles, gins and children; the sole shelter being a more than usually flimsy wurli … The necessity of shepherding and yarding 1200 sheep and some goats every night, and driving them to water every second day, was reducing the country to a sand drift.[5]

The image of Walara evoked in Finlayson's diary differs significantly from the heavily romanticised idea of outback homesteads and cattle drovers forged in the pastoral myths of the north. Constructed in the image of the large, foreign-owned stations that dominated the industry in the far north (such as Victoria River Downs and Wave Hill), such stations covered huge tracts of land, and their employees, black and white, numbered in the hundreds. These large, company-owned enterprises had head station camps that looked like small townships, including amenities such as a kitchen, butcher's shop, blacksmith's shop, saddlery, garage and general store.[6]

Finlayson's description of a sole flimsy wurli, and scattered saddles and humans amid a sand drift, does not resonate with such popular ideas of the outback pastoral industry perpetuated in Baz Lurhmann's film *Australia*. The patchy, highly variable deserts of the southwest produced a kind of nomadic pastoralism like that routinely practised in other semi-arid and arid rangelands around the world, or in the southeast of Australia in the nineteenth and early twentieth centuries before closer settlement.

To Finlayson, the pastoral scene he observed at Walara was more Old Testament in its imagery than reflecting outback mythology. Significant rains fell just after he arrived at Walara and he described the move that followed a few days later:

> Liddle shifted camp to some clay pans 5 miles south of here, which were now full of water. The move was the most amusing affair, and distinctly in the style of the old Biblical patriarchs – the whole camp was pulled up by the roots as it were, tied onto the camels in

> remarkable ways, and then the whole personnel drifted off to the new water – sheep, goats, horses, donkeys, dogs and gins, children, camels and ourselves, all strung out over the landscape.[7]

The claypan that Finlayson wrote of relocating to is Mutatja, one of the many nodes in the pastoral network mapped out in Tjuki's oral histories. It has been assumed that one of the most significant influences white settler pastoralists had on the landscape was the development of a network of stock routes. Tjuki's oral histories challenge this assumption, by showing us the ways in which the environmental imperatives of the desert resulted in pastoralists travelling along well-established pathways, and mimicking A_n_angu itineraries of travel and modes of land use. This observation has been reflected in archaeological fieldwork studying the material traces of past human activities on pastoral stations, revealing that the practice of moving to more remote parts of station leases during good seasons meant pastoral settlement patterns correlated with the archaeological evidence for pre-contact Aboriginal settlement.[8] Despite narratives of hardworking pioneers and hard-won pastoral progress in the outback, pastoralists didn't transform the Central Australian landscape in the way that was hoped. Rather, as Tjuki shows us, the desert environment, and A_n_angu knowledge of how to move through and use it, shaped the kind of pastoralism that developed.

However, it was not just A_n_angu knowledge that served the pastoral enterprise at Walara; the supply of readily available, cheap labour was also critical to any measure of success for pastoralists. While cattle are most prominent in the outback imaginary, it was sheep and goats that formed the basis of the enterprise in Central Australia during the interwar period. Wool was still a highly valuable commodity in the early twentieth century and sheep were far more lucrative than cattle. In a pastoral economy that made almost no use of fences, constant shepherding was required to stop flocks from straying and to protect them from dingoes. Pastoralists came to rely on local people to fulfil the role of shepherds, many of whom would be responsible for flocks at remote camps without supervision. This practice of relying on Aboriginal people for the labour-intensive work of shepherding had been common practice from as early as the 1850s in New South Wales, after the discovery of gold in the colony led to a shortage of European labour.

In Central Australia, entire families would be equipped with rations and sent out for days, or even weeks, at a time—this has been similarly reflected in various times and places in Australia where sheep were the primary focus of pastoral activity and Aboriginal labour was used.[9] In the never-ending cycle of driving sheep to water, the alternating rhythm of travelling and camping was one Tjuki Pumpjack's entire family traced across the landscape together. His memories also emphasise the material dimensions of the entanglement between Bill Liddle and Anangu that was emerging at Walara:

> We used to keep sheep. A lot of sheep. We were shepherds and we kept sheep. We would take the sheep in the morning from the yards, after we had opened the gates to the yards and watered them, out to graze on the feed. We used to take them to where there was green feed. We would stay there and eat our dinner out there. During this time the sheep would stay under the shady trees. We would stay with the sheep all day long, watching them and looking after them. At the day's end we would take them back to the sheep camp at Mutatja. Mutatja sheep camp. We would put them back into their yards in the late afternoon. Yarded up, we would shut the gate and then we wouldn't move from that gate, but we would light a fire near the gate and camp right there. We would camp near the sheep yard gate, caring for those sheep continually. We looked after those sheep twenty-four hours a day. The next morning we would get up again and open up the yard gate and round them up and take them out.
>
> This continued day after day after day. It was a lot of work. It was hard, continual work. Yet we never received any pay for the work. No money. No pay. Even though sheep are funny buggers and difficult, we never received any pay for all the work we did. We still looked after them, though. However, the shepherds always received rations. So we did get rations, trousers and shirts. That's what we got. I think about it now and I realise that we never got any actual pay for the work. So we looked after those sheep for nothing,

> watching over them twenty-four hours a day ... We did a great job caring for them. Yet we were never paid. We cared for those sheep like they were our own children. Yet we were not paid to take care for them, just as parents aren't paid to look after their children.[10]

Anxieties emerged among white society in the first decade of the twentieth century that the rationing relationship was turning Aboriginal people into 'paupers', or 'beggars', by failing to teach them the desired relationship between effort and reward. However, as Tjuki's oral history attests, this fear of 'pauperism' wasn't supported by the reality that on stations, and in towns, Aboriginal people were earning their rations by selling their labour.

Despite Prime Minister Scott Morrison's claim in 2020 that 'there was no slavery' in Australia, it is widely known and documented that First Nations people, in various times and places in Australia's history, were bought and sold as chattel labour, had their movements restricted, and were subjected to forced labour and abuse in the pastoral industry. Like Tjuki, many were paid rations of flour, sugar, tea, tobacco and clothing instead of wages, while many others had their wages withheld and never received them. As the debate that arose following Morrison's comments demonstrates, it's a subject that the settler Australian state is only just beginning to grapple with.[11]

In this context, reading A<u>n</u>angu oral history and memory is complicated. Despite my assumption that their stories would corroborate the idea of the pastoral relationship as exploitative, in reality they reveal a more nuanced perspective on the complexities of early colonial encounters. Senior A<u>n</u>angu man Bruce Breaden, who grew up on Middleton Ponds station, recalled in relation to the time of Abe Andrew and 'old Billy Liddle mob':

> I only ever worked for Bob Buck [at that time] I still never got paid but that was because they were only early settlers and they had no money. So nobody got paid, because nobody had money.[12]

Tjuki Pumpjack also contextualises the receipt of rations and clothes in exchange for his hard work in the 'early days'. He never expressed feelings of ill will about this arrangement. When I asked him specifically if he and A<u>n</u>angu more generally were angry or upset about not being paid for their hard work, he replied:

> No! We just lived anyway! We did not know any different! We just lived anyway. We were really happy about the clothes we got. We really liked the clothes—the cowboy hats. We'd be happy to go to work ... we were happy to start receiving pay when it came in. It was a new idea to us, that had come from white people, and when it happened, we started to learn that new way, the way with money.[13]

Nevertheless, Tjuki did say that, later on, after learning the new way with money, some A<u>n</u>angu did get angry with '*some of those whitefellas who had only ever given us clothing as payment*'. However, he never expressed resentment himself and reiterated that, at the time, A<u>n</u>angu never thought about money, as they didn't know it existed. Despite Tjuki's and Bruce's reluctance to cast the pastoral relationship as exploitative, it is important not to lose sight of the unequal power dynamics that structured these relationships.

While pastoralism was undoubtedly both a capitalist and colonial enterprise, in the 1930s and 1940s in the southwest of the Northern Territory, it is also true that transactions were rarely exacted in cash. In 1933 the employment licensing sections of the 1918 *Aboriginals Ordinance* were amended to enable the Chief Protector to exempt a pastoralist from paying Aboriginal people if he was maintaining their relatives and dependents. While such an amendment may seem overtly exploitative, there was no place to spend money in the bush in the interwar period, and pastoralists themselves were often paid in stock, and lived on fixed rations of flour, sugar and tea they supplemented with their own meat.[14] Merv Andrew worked for Bill Liddle when he first arrived in the Northern Territory in the early 1940s, and recalled he was paid a sheep a week and a horse a month. Andrew also said of the daily diet of rations, beef and damper that 'you didn't enjoy living very much', and that it went on like that for years.[15]

Deprivation and self-denial were not solely a reflection of the absence of cash in the interwar period but, rather, an intrinsic part of the 'asceticism of bush life'.[16] Pastoralism in the arid interior was marginal at best, and was more of a 'tactic' for many prewar pastoralists, who 'were content with a casual lifestyle which accompanied their minimal capital investments and their relative lack of commercial orientation'.[17] What motivated these men to live a life of isolation and obscurity in the outback? What compelled them to live a life of discomfort and privation when the rewards seldom took material form? There is a sense that emerges in the descriptions of deprivation and denial that characterise these men of seeking out and, at the same time, trying to escape, something. Of being both in and out of place.

In a letter to the Chief Protector in 1937, Strehlow described Snowy Pearce:

> He has no car or wireless set, is in relatively poor circumstances, and is a man aged 54 years. He owns a sheep-station, financed by the Government, and still has to repay about 300 pounds on his sheep. He is slowly reducing debt by hard labour and economy. He has no desire of ever returning to the civilised life of townships.[18]

Why precisely these men were avoiding 'civilised life' is hard to know, and what motivated them has been obscured in the mythologies that have been built up around them. The Andrew family, the sole exception to the lone white male running sheep or cattle in the isolated southwest, were staunch socialists. Perhaps it wasn't just a new life that they sought in the desert but also avoidance of the capitalist economy and way of life. In the archival fragments that remain of pastoralists such as Liddle, Pearce and Andrew, there is a sense of these men as the white 'nomad tribesman' of Ward's *Australian Legend*. Perhaps in rejecting 'civilisation', material comforts and wage slavery, they were, in some way, attempting to escape settler society and somehow become 'other'. Ward observed that most of the men he encountered in the Northern Territory in 1930 were there because the remoteness offered them a 'vagabond life free from conventional restraints'.[19] These pastoralists moved beyond just rejecting the 'civilised life of townships', and actively sought to make a place for themselves on the margins by learning how to live in, and move through, the landscape.

Some learned local language, and almost all of them became entangled in local social networks and relationships of exchange. In this sense, as scholar Chris Healy has observed, it's possible to think of these 'white nomads', and their tales of isolation and deprivation, as attempting to escape their own cultural histories.[20]

In Central Australia, these attempts at avoiding 'civilised' life led to lifestyles that undermined bureaucratic attempts to regulate relationships between black and white. This, in turn, often led to criticism on the grounds that pastoralists and local people were too close, too isolated and too mobile. Administrative attitudes at the time regarded open-range pastoralism as not only technologically backward but 'humanly idiosyncratic', with the belief that a resistance to 'the message of industry capitalisation' meant that pastoralists were in danger of being 'assimilated' into the local scene.[21]

Bill Liddle was one of many pastoralists who had a reputation among patrol officers, and other pastoralists, for his relations with local women. Sex and relationships between white men and black women were a significant concern in the government's early surveillance. It has also been the subject of much scholarship since then. Yet in my experience with A<u>n</u>angu remembering this time, the topic of sexual relations and exchange didn't emerge as noteworthy. In fact, it barely rated a mention. People talked about whitefella pastoralists and their A<u>n</u>angu wives, but this wasn't discussed as though it was anything out of the ordinary. Rather, it provided context and connections between people. Tjuki Pumpjack described Bill Liddle as being 'married' to his three 'sisters' and said that he had children with each of them. As he described it, Liddle was his 'brother-in-law' for a while.[22] This information was always relayed matter-of-factly and without any sense that he was speaking about something considered taboo. Yet, Strehlow's reports from the southwestern station area in the late 1930s reveal a preoccupation with attempts at reforming the lifestyles of men like Liddle, as well as the futile attempts to intervene in their affairs, and the impossible task of controlling them.

What developed was a process of entanglement that has been described in similar ways, but given different names, at different places throughout the history of the colonial encounter in Australia.

Bill Liddle had nothing to gain, but something to lose, by disrupting the ties that bound Aṉangu to one another in social life. Thus, pastoral camps such as that at Walara came to fulfil a structural role in the regional economy. The interdependent relationship that developed between Bill Liddle and Aṉangu reflects a regime in which it made sense to conserve the economic, social and cultural dimensions of Aṉangu daily life, in order to maintain a cheap supply of labour. This process of accommodation has been viewed differently depending on perspective; cultural difference obscured exploitation, while at the same time assured a degree of freedom for Aṉangu.

6

FOUND IN TRANSLATION

On the surface, in their English-language interpretation and transcription, Tjuki Pumpjack's oral histories can be read as reinforcing the idea of the colonial relationship on pastoral stations as based in mutually beneficial exchange. Tjuki said that A<u>n</u>angu worked hard shepherding Bill Liddle's sheep and, in exchange for their labour, they received food and clothing. They incorporated the 'new way' into existing social and ecological itineraries and, in doing so, continued to live with one another as kin.

That much of the meaning of his shepherding memories is lost in the English-language transcript says something about the complexities of writing histories of the colonial encounter in Australia. In a place where two different ways of being-in-the-world brought two very different systems of meaning to bear on that shared experience, memory such as that presented here requires translation—not just of language but of the worldview and concepts that shape it and give it meaning. On closer inspection, Tjuki Pumpjack's memories of shepherding take us into a social world where the *giving* and *receiving* of food, material goods and knowledge is how relationships are created, and where the sheep themselves have a part to play in the story.

In Pitjantjatjara, Tjuki repeatedly used the word kanyilpai to describe the work of shepherding at Walara. Kanyini in Pitjantjatjara is a verb that translates as to 'have' or to 'look after'. In the form Tjuki uses it—kanyilpai—it refers to the action he is describing as being 'typical' or 'characteristic' of the situation he is describing. Anthropologist Fred Myers glosses the corresponding Pintupi kanyininpa as 'to have and to hold', and describes it as a concept grounded in the experience of social life as essentially supportive, and one articulated with poetic force:

> The metaphor of 'holding' as the Pintupi invoke it derives from the linguistic expression describing how a small child is held in the arms against the breast.

Myers notes that the model of kanyininpa structures 'society as a series of successive generations, each one "holding" and "looking after" the next'. Authority is thus derived from the responsibility of having to 'look after' and 'hold' those who come after. Or, put another way, authority is derived from nurturance.[1]

Tjuki repeatedly refers to the act of shepherding sheep as kanyilpai and explicitly states that his family 'looked after' those sheep like a parent does their child. In doing so, he invokes a *relationship* that is rooted in kin relations and the responsibility to nurture. His family were 'looking after' those sheep for Bill Liddle, who they referred to as mayatja, meaning 'boss'. In the A<u>n</u>angu lifeworld, a 'boss' is someone who gains authority by 'looking after'. The power to allocate resources elevates the person to a status of one who 'looks after', thus defining them as 'boss'.[2] In the desert, a place where whitefellas have long controlled the distribution of resources, the term 'boss' is regularly extended to white people. Bill Liddle's status as 'boss' didn't derive from his authority as the owner of Angas Downs. Rather, it stemmed from the fact that he 'looked after' A<u>n</u>angu by distributing food and clothing. In living with, and distributing resources among A<u>n</u>angu, Bill Liddle became necessarily entangled in A<u>n</u>angu webs of relatedness.

The relationship that generated the oral histories and knowledge discussed here was not just one that developed between Tjuki Pumpjack and me. Interpreter Linda Rive was there from the very beginning and a constant presence throughout. Without her knowledge, and language skills, telling this story wouldn't be possible.

Over the years, as the relationship between her and Tjuki developed, Linda's knowledge of Tjuki's particular way with language deepened. When I asked for elaboration of her understanding of Tjuki's use of the term kanyini in relation to shepherding Liddle's sheep, Linda said that Tjuki was talking about more than a job. Rather, as she understood it, he was describing something more akin to an 'abiding social contract', bound up with a deep sense of the responsibility to 'look after'.[3] Anthropologist Diane Austin-Broos observed that the concept of 'looking after' produces and reproduces *the social group and the place of which they are a part*:

> The wellsprings of this scheme are kinship and country so that the activities of sitting with, making camp, foraging, hunting and preparing for ceremony describe various practices that reproduce values of social being in place. It is only in the English of market-based sociality that components of this practice also become 'work'.[4]

In this sense, Tjuki's memories of shepherding articulate the ways in which he was translating existing socioeconomic relations, made up of expectations and obligations, into the new context in which he found himself. It was precisely these processes of translation that enabled Anangu to try to make sense of the structures of colonialism they had come into contact with since the 1930s.

However, colonialism was not all that Anangu had to make sense of. Tjuki Pumpjack's oral histories also illuminate a non-human-being-centred view of the world. Sheep are as much a part of his memories as Bill Liddle, rations and travelling, and, as he tells it, his family took responsibility for the sheep and 'looked after' them as if they were their children. For Anangu, every human, animal and plant that exists carries within it what TGH Strehlow called 'an immortal spark of life', which is derived from the original ancestral beings.[5] Totemic is the English word used to try to describe this identification of humans with particular plants, animals and places as living manifestations of the ancestors in the present.

Tjuki Pumpjack was a Wati Papa, or Dingo Man. More than just identifying with the dingo, his life was defined by that animal in a mutual relationship that connected them in the Tjukurpa, the nature of which is impossible for me to describe adequately. His connection to the dingo was an expression of a cosmos where animals perceive and evaluate as humans do, just as they observe and interpret humans, in what Deborah Bird Rose describes as less a chain than a network-of-being, where 'relationships of care' are enacted among all species.[6] It's within this conceptual framework that we must seek to understand Tjuki Pumpjack's memories of 'looking after' and 'holding' Bill Liddle's sheep.

In his imagining of the impact of strange species on the local Wotjobaluk people in mid-nineteenth-century colonial Victoria, historian Robert Kenny wrote that, despite popular assumptions, it was not so much the appearance of European humans that disrupted the worldview of local people but the animals they brought with them. Humans, even though they were white-skinned, were, to some extent, accountable. Sheep and cattle were not. Kenny asks his reader to imagine having lived in a world where the biggest things that moved other than humans—kangaroos and emus—were bipeds similar in size to people. Then into this landscape enter horses, cattle, sheep and camels. When one of the primary perspectival focuses of your life is tracking—reading the world through marks made on the ground—what then to make of the tracks of hard-hoofed quadrupeds and camel wagons?[7]

Tjuki Pumpjack recorded on several occasions the story of his family's arrival at Walara. Each version of the story prefaces the end of the long journey with the sighting of sheep tracks. Hundreds of sheep tracks. They followed them, and eventually arrived at the camp to be reunited with his auntie and uncle. Although Tjuki grew up from a young age with sheep in his world, his mother and father must surely have recalled the encounter somewhat differently. Imagine the stories they must have told. They must have sought to understand these animals within the conceptual framework that shaped their world. Tjuki Pumpjack's father was also a Wati Papa, and his mother's origins were in the ma<u>l</u>u (Kangaroo) Dreaming. The thousands of sheep that made the tracks belonged to Bill Liddle, so surely Tjuki's family assumed that some kind of spiritual connection existed between Liddle and the sheep. Yet, as Kenny explains in his study, the very nature of the relationship between sheep and humans must have been perplexing:

> If you have never known animals domesticated, as are sheep, cattle and horses, what do you see from afar? Humans dedicated to the animals: leading them to feed and water, protecting them from predators, concerned at their every need. You see humans cajoled by animals. You see servants of the sheep. What hold did these animals have over their servants?[8]

The work of shepherding represented an entirely new relationship with animals, and the strangeness of the relationship is reflected in Tjuki's repeated references to sheep as 'funny buggers' and 'difficult'. Just as Kenny described that process as the 'lamb enters the Dreaming', so Tjuki said that his family began 'shepherding sheep and learning the new way'.[9]

As Kenny asked of the Wotjobaluk, I can ask of A<u>n</u>angu how they couldn't have believed that sheep and cattle were whitefella 'totems' to which they were mystically linked.[10] In this light, Tjuki's invoking of kanyini in relation to the sheep takes on a deeper meaning than reciprocating the receiving of rations. His oral histories of shepherding stress that he and his family cared for the sheep continuously, twenty-four hours a day, and yet were not paid for this constant care, *just as parents are not paid to look after their children*. Surely this must have indicated that sheep were of deep symbolic importance to whitefellas and of primary importance in the European Dreaming.[11] Bill Liddle 'looked after' A<u>n</u>angu by distributing food and clothing, and they, in turn, 'looked after' his sheep; as such, the sheep, too, became enmeshed in the enactment of social relations that sought to incorporate strange structures and animals into the A<u>n</u>angu lifeworld at Walara.

In more recent times, Tjuki experienced another kind of rupture in relation to the place of sheep in the world:

> That is how we lived, shepherding the sheep and learning the new way. It was good. But recently, in recent years, I noticed something

> new—sheep living freely without human shepherds watching over them! So all those years, there we were caring for those sheep night and day, and yet they don't need that! Going down towards Port Augusta, I could see the sheep walking around everywhere by themselves! Just roaming freely in the open fields! Nobody looking after them! Nothing! No shepherds![12]

In telling this story, Tjuki sounded truly perplexed by what he'd seen. In its telling, this particular memory was marked by a distinct sense of bewilderment and an air of the almost overwhelming question 'What had all that "looking after" been for?' In a world where relationships of care extend to all species, along came an animal that demanded a level of care and 'looking after' never before experienced. In Rose's description of the network-of-being, she noted that relationships of care were non-hierarchical and that every species is understood to 'have its own right to exist of and for itself'.[13] Surely the work of shepherding disrupted that understanding, in making humans the servants of the sheep. Bill Liddle and his thousands of sheep represented a human–animal relationship of some significance and one in which A<u>n</u>angu became heavily invested. The way Tjuki recalled it, to see sheep without human shepherds was truly shocking. That level of care had served no continuing purpose, so what had all that work been for? Tjuki Pumpjack's epiphany down near Port Augusta illustrates the ways in which he was still trying to make sense, some sixty years later, of the structures of colonialism and the strange animals with which his life had become enmeshed.

Sheep didn't just walk over the land; they instantly began to transform it, and not in the way that had been hoped for. A mere three to four years after establishing his sheep run at Walara, Finlayson's remark that the constant driving of sheep to water had turned the country into a sand drift reveals signs of the significant strain that sheep were placing upon the desert ecology. In 1943 a field officer for the

Northern Territory Lands and Survey Branch, WL Clough, described the situation at Walara as 'precarious':

> With only one water on the whole of his run, sheep running on this area for a number of years has caused the land to be eaten out. He also has 1056 sheep of Stanes' plus this year's lambs boxed with his own and on the count I gave there were 3116 grown sheep and lambs.
>
> However, you will see how impossible it would be for Liddle to carry this number on one water, and on country that I consider second-class country for sheep. I discussed this aspect with Sid Staines of Erldunda who also sees the position as hopeless and has decided to bring his sheep home together with the sheep he purchases from Liddle. This would leave Liddle with approximately 1000 sheep, 25 mixed cattle valued at 75 pounds, 70 light and medium horses at 140 pounds and 10 rams just recently purchased at 70 pounds ...
>
> I recommend that Liddle be allowed to sell sufficient sheep to pay off the mortgage to the Primary Producer's Board and release him of his mortgage to the Crown.[14]

Tjuki Pumpjack associated the end of Walara with the impact of the sheep:

> Eventually all the grass was eaten out. The sheep ate every blade of grass, and so we took the first lot of sheep to Finke. We next took another lot of sheep to Finke as well, and the other men took the rest of the sheep to Alice Springs. So there we were without any sheep.[15]

Tjuki Pumpjack said that after Bill Liddle sold the sheep, he and his family moved from Walara to Mutatja sheep camp, and that they lived there for a 'really long time'. After Mutatja, they went to live in and around all the little camps in the bush. After travelling and camping, possibly for several years, Tjuki and his family moved to Bloodwood Bore, the site of 'New Angas Downs':

> We were living at Bloodwood Bore. The name of that place is Bloodwood Bore, which is on Angas Downs. Some people refer

> to it as Angas Downs, and indeed it was called Angas Downs for a while, but then it got changed properly to Bloodwood Bore. So now it is known as Bloodwood Bore. Anyway, there were a lot of people living there for a long time, and indeed that is where I used to live. Prior to that, I had been living in Walara. I had also lived for a long time at Mutatja. After living at Mutatja for a long while, we left and went to live in the bush for a long time. We wanted to live in the bush for a while. We wanted to be bush people again and move around a lot and make many camps, see a lot of country and be mobile for a while. After that, we moved to Bloodwood Bore.[16]

Time has revealed that the move to Bloodwood Bore represents more than just the relocation of Angas Downs station. Rather, Bloodwood Bore marks the beginning of a new era in the history of the colonial encounter, and a significant transformation in the Aṉangu engagement with whitefellas and the settler capitalist economy.

PART 3

BLOODWOOD BORE

7
RATION TIMES

THE SHEEP HAD turned Walara into a dusty sand drift. It's difficult to pinpoint a precise moment when the station base was relocated to Bloodwood Bore, and, from the records available, it seems that somewhere between three to eight years passed between the sheep finishing the grass at Walara and the new homestead being established at Bloodwood Bore. Liddle's situation was described as 'precarious' and the decision to sell his sheep was made in 1943. Some three years later, Bill Liddle sold the station and 227 head of cattle to his sons Milton and Arthur Liddle, two of the four children he had with his Arrernte wife Mary. A visit to the southern stations that patrol officer Les Penhall undertook in 1949 recorded thirty-three A<u>n</u>angu living at Angas Downs station. However, there's nothing in the report that indicates where the station was at the time.[1] A later inspection report surveying drought relief bores at Angas Downs shows that 'Homestead Bore' was sunk in 1951. In the same report, the well at Walara is called 'Old Station Well'.[2]

Tjuki Pumpjack said that at Walara the sheep became too numerous and ate all the grass, so they had to move and drill a new bore:

> When all the grass died [at Walara] we had to move to New Angas Downs, and drilled a new bore there, near Wilpiya Range. We put a new water bore down in there. We lived at that new bore.[3]

The springs and wells that punctuate Tjuki's memories of shepherding at Walara were fed from the Amadeus Basin, which stores water in the rock's pores, deep down in the earth. Prior to the arrival of white settlers, the water emerged naturally from the basin, through faults or vents, into springs and streams on the earth's surface. Towards the end of the nineteenth century, when white settlers figured out the nature of the basin water supply, the water began to take a shortcut to the surface. The sinking of wells and drilling into the sandstone aquifers transformed the landscape into one pockmarked with bores, windmills and tanks. Niningka Lewis recalled this physical transformation:

> Water would be dug out of soakages and drunk, or drunk from rockholes which had filled from rainfall, which would be drunk until it was all gone, and then we'd move to a new area, to the next soakage, to new water. When that water was gone we'd move off again, and so on. That is how we lived before the windmills came along ... I was just a child when I saw my first ever windmill. It was on a station ... We just stood and stared. But really, we grew up around windmills ... We still had to have them explained to us but it was our mother's generation that would have had a big shock to see such a thing for the first time ... They were the ones who would have just stood there and been blown away by what they saw. They would have wondered what on earth it was.[4]

Niningka said that her parents' and grandparents' generations were 'shocked and amazed' by these new signs and objects that began appearing in their lands.

However, despite the substantial natural pressure and subsequent gushing waters of early bores, by the end of the first decade of the twentieth century, the increasing number of bores gave rise to a decline in the natural pressure, resulting in dwindling water flows.[5] Despite the early enthusiasm for environmental transformation, as historian Michael Cathcart has observed, the 'deserts did not bloom', and fragile desert ecosystems were soon 'trampled into dust' by sheep and cattle.[6]

The degradation brought about by the introduction of sheep, cattle and camels, coupled with the declining water pressure that resulted from increasing numbers of bores, meant that desert springs were particularly vulnerable to failure. In the arid rangelands, expensive pumping technology became necessary in order to extract water from non-flowing, sub-artesian bores.[7] Tjuki's memory reflects the transformation in the relationship to water that was brought about by the drilling of sub-artesian bores:

> Of course we always used to simply drink water for free, from the springs we knew about. There were springs around the place that we knew about, but now they wanted to drill for bore water, for water from bores.[8]

The impact of technology on natural water sources isn't just marked in his experiences and memories—Tjuki's name is also a record of it. A 'pumpjack' is the above ground device that mechanically raises water from underground wells. Tjuki said that Bill Liddle gave his father the name Pumpjack, and it's possible that Tjuki's father, Tjukyntji, earned the name by being the pumpjack operator responsible for pumping water from the well at Walara.

And so it was, in the shade of a mighty bloodwood tree, that the new bore was drilled to a depth of 180 feet. It created a more stable water supply, a more permanent homestead and a new era in the station's history.

Tjuki Pumpjack said that after they drilled the new bore and moved there to live:

> Ration times started up then. A rations station was started by Arthur Liddle and Bessie Liddle. Those two started up the rations. A<u>n</u>angu tjuta [many] began arriving, and many people were around in those days. Many, many people started to come there because of the rations. They were looking for those rations.[9]

Despite having been receiving rations at Walara for some ten years or more, Tjuki Pumpjack associates the move to Bloodwood Bore with the beginning of 'ration times'. Indeed, Bill Liddle had been issuing food to A<u>n</u>angu workers and families from as early as 1928 at Walara.[10] Why then, in Tjuki's memory, is it Bloodwood Bore that's characterised by the issuing of rations?

Tim Rowse's history of rationing, *White Flour, White Power*, clearly demonstrates that food was the primary vehicle for the assimilation project in Central Australia.[11] Following World War II, the policy of assimilation emerged as the dominant paradigm in Aboriginal affairs. According to Rowse, the increased demand for Aboriginal labour during the war, coupled with the democratic sentiments of the anti-fascist struggle, had resulted in the task of governing Aboriginal people becoming 'explicitly normative'. Consequently, policy focus was directed away from the preservation and protection of Aboriginal difference, and instead looked towards educating and training Aboriginal people for Australian citizenship.[12]

In 1953 the Native Affairs Branch was renamed the Welfare Branch. In the same year, the *Aboriginals Ordinance* of 1911 was replaced by the *Welfare Ordinance*, which led to the creation of the Register of Wards. The Director of Welfare became the guardian of all 'wards' and, as such, Aboriginal people were committed to the care of the state. Using the term 'ward' was deliberate. In choosing to refer to 'wards' instead of Aboriginal people, the Northern Territory Administration sought to obscure the overtly racist nature of the policy. According to the administration, a person could be declared a ward simply:

- by reason of his manner of living;
- his inability to manage his own affairs;
- his standard of social habit and behavior; and
- his personal associations … [to be] in need of social care.[13]

A list of so-called 'wards' was published in the *Northern Territory Gazette* in 1957, making public the personal details of thousands of Aboriginal people—the kinds of details that white settler Australians took for granted as being private. The Register of Wards was commonly referred to by the Northern Territory Administration as the 'Stud Book', a dehumanising reference to a book that breeders used to record the pedigree of horses. Documenting some 15 000 Aboriginal people and declaring them 'wards' of the state, it was a mechanism for arbitrarily denying Aboriginal people in the Northern Territory Australian citizenship, on the grounds of a lack of shared humanity.

When Arthur and Milton Liddle began distributing rations to 'wards' on behalf of the government, Bloodwood Bore became a quasi-government settlement. In 1954 the first census reports from Angas Downs began to appear in the Welfare Branch correspondence archive. They occurred regularly from this time onwards, evidence of the administration's attempts to monitor, and *know*, the population at Bloodwood Bore and assert some measure of control over their lives.

In 1956 Milton Liddle sold his share of Angas Downs to his brother Arthur, who then ran it with his wife, a Luritja woman called Bessie Liddle. Tjuki Pumpjack said that Arthur Liddle drilled a new bore and 'started up the rations', and then many A<u>n</u>angu began to arrive. In a 1954 report, patrol officer TC Lovegrove documented that the A<u>n</u>angu who were being given rations received second-hand clothing every month to six weeks; a blanket annually; and weekly rations that consisted of:

- Flour 15 to 20 lbs
- Sugar 2 lbs
- Tea 4 ozs
- Jam or Syrup 1 tin
- Soap 1 cake
- Tobacco plug 2 ozs
- Beef 10 to 12 lbs

Lovegrove added that:

> In addition to the above-mentioned beef, an average of 1 kangaroo per day is shot and supplied to the camp. With the exception of tobacco, children receive half of the above scale of rations. No rice, peas or their alternatives are normally supplied but excess flour, tea and sugar are issued to cover these.[14]

In the early 1950s a population of approximately ten to twelve adults and seven to ten children was recorded as living on the station.[15] In 1959 approximately one hundred Anangu were recorded at Angas Downs,[16] while the largest recorded number at Bloodwood Bore at any one time was 250 people in 1961.[17] Angas Downs was not the only quasi-settlement in Central Australia, and while the distribution of Aboriginal people across pastoral leases was uneven, the numbers across the ten biggest station camps, Angas Downs included, all grew between 1949 and 1965–66.[18]

Tjuki's remembrance of this period as 'ration times' reflects the pervasiveness of rationing as a tool of assimilation policy and affirms the central role that it played in the pastoral relationship at Angas Downs.[19] However, I think that perhaps this way of marking time in Anangu memory also performs a narrative role that represents a particular way of organising historical remembrances. Tjuki marks distinctive phases in the past, or indicates temporal ruptures or shifts in experience, with different 'times'. Temporal markers such as 'early days', 'ration times', 'cattle times' and 'sit-down times' structure his memory in a series of episodes. Rather than describe a single moment or event, these different 'times' represent many events that have assembled in memory over time, and in the case of 'ration times', give particular periods meaning according to pertinent events, or features, like the government's issuing of rations.

Such episodic ways of remembering are not necessarily chronological. 'Times' can and do overlap and, thus, challenge Western knowledge's understandings of linear historical time. Oral historian Alessandro Portelli describes this way of speaking memory as the projection of an image of the past. He observes that while the historian often strives for a linear, chronological sequence, speakers are more interested in 'gathering together bundles of meaning, relationships and themes' across the span of their lives.[20] Tjuki says that after the new bore was drilled, many Anangu began to arrive at Angas Downs 'looking for rations'. Despite having been receiving rations for a decade or more, it is the issuing of them that has come to symbolise this period in his memory. That rations came to represent this period in Tjuki's memory is significant for what it says about the changing relationship between Anangu and the settler state in the postwar period. Rations and 'ration times', in his historical remembrance, can be understood as a reflection of the impact and experience of assimilation policy—in particular, the systematic use of rationing as a technique of colonial governance and a tool for intervening in Anangu lives.

An anthropologist called Frederick Rose lived at Bloodwood Bore for four months, between July and October 1962. He was there to carry out fieldwork and hoped to further pursue questions of kinship, which had emerged from his earlier fieldwork on Groote Eylandt in 1938–41.[21] Rose had limited funds to carry out his research, and so entered into a 'gentlemen's agreement' with Arthur Liddle—for his 'board and lodging' at Bloodwood Bore, he accepted the responsibility of looking after the homestead while the Liddles were away. This duty, sometimes carried out for days at a time, entailed distributing the weekly pension and rations to Anangu. Rose observed that although it may not have been legitimate to compare quantities of rations issued by Bill Liddle with those issued by Arthur and Bessie Liddle on behalf of the government, doing so in 1962 did show that the quantity of sugar the government issued was 'considerably higher', while the proportion of tea was 'considerably lower'. Rose also noted that, unlike before, when Bill Liddle issued them separately, tea and sugar were mixed together before being issued to Anangu in 1962. He was particularly interested in the government's issuing of flour to Anangu, noting that it had a 'revolutionary' influence on people's lives. Most strikingly, according to Rose, flour had replaced native foods, such as seeds and fruits, in the Anangu diet. He observed during his time there that Anangu women no longer carried out their customary role of gathering seeds and grinding native flour, and had come to rely almost solely on government rations.[22]

The book that resulted from Rose's fieldwork at Bloodwood Bore, *The Wind of Change in Central Australia: The Aborigines at Angas Downs, 1962*, was published in his adopted home of East Germany in 1965. His time on the station led him to conclude that the 'traditional way of life for the Aborigines was virtually gone', and that the speed with which Anangu were becoming 'detribalised' and 'acculturated'—which is to say assimilated into settler culture—was becoming increasingly rapid.[23] He drew the conclusion it was primarily economic factors that were responsible for the changes he had witnessed on Angas Downs.

A devout Marxist, Rose was both an intellectual and political outcast. His Marxist interpretation of social change that resulted from his fieldwork on Groote Eylandt was anathema to the prevailing anthropological paradigm. Rose's findings had drawn the ire of the then head of Anthropology at Sydney University, AP Elkin, who concluded that Rose didn't understand Australian Aboriginal kinship systems, and took measures to ensure that he would spend the rest of his days in Australia on the very margins of anthropology.[24]

However, it was Rose's politics that would see him eventually exiled from Australia. An ardent and active member of the Communist Party of Australia, he emigrated to the German Democratic Republic in 1956 in the midst of strident anti-communist sentiment in the Menzies government, and in the aftermath of being summoned in the Petrov Royal Commission into Espionage, under suspicion of his involvement in a Soviet spy ring. Rose undertook a doctorate that drew upon his earlier Groote Eylandt fieldwork, leading to his appointment as professor and head of the Social Anthropology department at Humboldt University in East Berlin.[25]

It was never Rose's intention to study the cultural encounter and change on a Central Australian cattle station. However, upon returning to Australia in 1962, to continue his earlier investigations into kinship, he found that, as a 'direct result of Government policy', Aboriginal people had been brought onto government settlements and missions, and that it was perhaps 'too late' to carry out his fieldwork. As he saw it, the 'disintegration of socio-economic relationships' of Aboriginal people had 'gone on apace' since the end of the war; as such, Rose felt he was in a 'race against time' to try to study Aboriginal people 'living under their original socio-economic conditions'.[26] Frustrating his sense of urgency, Rose's attempts to gain access to government settlements were blocked at every turn by the Menzies government and the Australian Security Intelligence Organisation. Furthermore, Elkin still wielded enough influence to weigh in and ensure Rose's research would be a non-starter.

Rose wrote to his friend Bill Harney, then park ranger at Ayers Rock, to tell him of his troubles gaining access to Aboriginal settlements, and Harney suggested he go to Central Australia:

> To hell with the settlements, there are quite a number of people outside these places ... Quite a number are out at a place called Angus [sic] Downs and some are at Ayers Rock ... This is a great study place for contact so come out my friend.[27]

As Harney's letter indicated, Angas Downs was hardly the place for studying people 'living under original conditions'. In his letter to Rose, he wrote that A<u>n</u>angu had been 'so pestered with tourists' that they had begun to 'cut crude weapons for sale' and demanded 'two bob' each time a tourist took their photo. Harney pointed out that this would work in Rose's favour, as he could give A<u>n</u>angu a price, take a photo and get their kinship information, and then move onto the next, adding 'when they find out what is afoot with your method, the others will come in'.[28]

Rose adhered to the Marxist theory that it was the mode of production, as the economic basis of society, that determined society's nature and development. Only 'incidentally' interested in what he called the 'the cult life' of A<u>n</u>angu, the 'acculturation' he witnessed at Angas Downs was analysed explicitly within a Marxist theory of historical change. As he understood it, history had an internal logic. A<u>n</u>angu at Angas Downs were moving through an inevitable sequence of economic structures and discrete modes of production. Rose believed that the change in the way of life for A<u>n</u>angu at Bloodwood Bore was a direct result of the introduction of rations, improvements in transport, the commodification of material culture, and the subsequent encounter with a cash economy.

8
THE WIND OF CHANGE

ROSE UNDERSTOOD THE 'wind of change' he observed at Angas Downs as having gathered momentum in the wake of World War II. Improvements in transport and communication as a result of the war set in motion a chain of events that brought notable change to the isolated southwest of the Northern Territory. The period witnessed unprecedented levels of money spent on technological advancement and infrastructure, including all-weather roads built between Alice Springs and Darwin. At war's end, a significant number of trucks of American origin had become redundant, and were offered for sale cheaply in and around Alice Springs. Many pastoralists acquired at least one for use on their stations. Rose argued that this influx of vehicles had two significant impacts—rendering camels and donkeys redundant to pastoralists, and increasing demands for roads to be graded and improved so that the newly acquired trucks could be utilised.[1]

Rose observed that with capital invested in the north at an unprecedented scale during the war:

> [I]t was not the Government's intention to allow the Northern Territory to relapse into its pre-war isolation and the demands for improved roads in Central Australia and elsewhere away from the main north-south and east-west arteries were acceded to.

> By the early 1950s a network of passable roads regularly graded by the Government reached even the most distant cattle stations in the west.[2]

As this network of passable roads penetrated the desert, the isolation that defined the 'early days' came to an end. That developments in technology, and subsequent improvements in transport, have been seen as significant turning points in the history of 'progress' in Central Australia is reflected in the titles of local histories, such as Bryan Bowman's *A History of Central Australia 1930–1980: From Horse and Camel to Motor Car, from Motor Car to Helicopter and Jet*, and Max Cartwright's *From Bush Tracks to Highway: An Account of Aborigine Footprints to the Horse and Camel Tracks of the Explorers, Followed by the Motor Tracks of Later Years: In the South Western Regions of Central Australia*.[3] Bowman notes that while roads were virtually non-existent before the war, some vehicles did make the journey over and into the sand hills of the southwest, and that they mostly belonged to scientific or prospecting parties. As the description in Chapter Five of Strehlow and McKinnon's journey by car into the southwest demonstrated, it was hard work getting vehicles through that country, but as Bowman observed, it was the tracks of these old cars that became the graded roads that 'opened up' Central Australia.[4]

However, it was not just an influx of vehicles that prompted increased spending on infrastructure in the Northern Territory. Anxieties about the 'empty north' had persisted well into the twentieth century.[5] A small white population, engaged in a highly mobile, domestic pastoral enterprise that was thoroughly dependent on A<u>n</u>angu labour, was considered evidence of the failure of settlers to adequately 'develop the north'. After the war, Prime Minister Curtin announced that 'developing the north' was essential for the future security of Australia. In 1945 the Northern Australia Development Committee was established—charged with increasing the population, improving the welfare and development of Aboriginal people, bolstering the value of production in the region, and ensuring maximum utilisation of the land and resources.[6] A report the committee prepared in 1947 highlighted the previous failures of the Commonwealth and settlers to develop the Territory 'beyond the pioneering stage', citing the inability or unwillingness of governments to finance transport and other public services as a significant factor.[7] The committee recommended funding for local medical services, education, transport and highways, airline subsidies, waters, stock routes, surveys and investigations, all of which were put into effect in the following years.[8]

Bloodwood Bore did not just mark a shift in location; it really was a 'New Angas Downs', as A_n_angu sometimes refer to it. Writing in my field journal about my first visit to Walara and first trip out bush with Tjuki Pumpjack in 2012, I reflected upon the way in which the different station sites emerged as different worlds in his memory that day. 'Old' and 'New' Angas Downs were two distinctly different places and phases in his life, as though his life were divided into two key episodes. On that first day, while we attempted to communicate with one another as best we could with limited English to draw upon, Bloodwood Bore was made manifest in his memory with the introduction of rations, the arrival of newcomers to Angas Downs, the first encounters with tourists who had come to see Uluru, and the money that they brought with them. I wrote at the time that it was truly difficult to imagine what each of these episodes meant to Tjuki because they weren't being spoken in the language that situates them and gives them meaning.

Although I had undertaken a three-week course in Pitjantjatjara at the University of Adelaide during the summer of 2012, I was unable to converse in Pitjantjatjara beyond simple sentences, and Tjuki's English was limited. Over the following four years, Linda Rive, Tjuki and I always travelled together—Linda the vital conduit for hearing and conceiving of Bloodwood Bore in the language and concepts that give it meaning. Tjuki recalled Bloodwood Bore on numerous occasions, adding new layers of detail with each remembrance. And yet, despite the rich and textured picture that emerged over that time, Bloodwood

Bore was always distilled in his memory in the symbols of rations, newcomers, tourists and cash money.

Tjuki Pumpjack says of the move to Bloodwood Bore:

> Three or four little houses were built for the whitefellas, but we were told, 'You lot live in wiltjas, around your fires. There are no houses for you.' So we didn't get housing. We did not live in houses. We lived there always, that was our home.[9]

The homestead was a modest affair pieced together with corrugated iron. In a 1960 inspection report, a patrol officer observed:

> Mr Liddle has no accommodation for his employees. He noted that huts had been built some time ago for accommodation but that they had been dismantled by the natives, who used the iron from them to construct wurlies ... Water is obtained from the station bore, approximately 200 yards south of the camp. The camp is situated about 180 yards north of the homestead and consists of about ten wurlies scattered over an area of about 80 yards.[10]

By 1962 Rose observed that much of the area around the homestead was completely void of vegetation, and that the A<u>n</u>angu camp and 'the immediate environment was also largely denuded of trees which had been used for firewood'.[11] The 'wurlies' in the patrol report are the wiltja in Rose's ethnography, and in 1962 he recorded thirty-nine of them in the A<u>n</u>angu 'camp'. Wiltja is the Pitjantjatjara word for 'shade', and is also the name of the shade shelter that A<u>n</u>angu use as a dwelling. Wiltja were customarily ephemeral in nature; the rhythms of the desert meant that this type of shelter, constructed from brush and branches, was only ever needed momentarily before moving on to the next camp. Rose observed that while the wiltja at Bloodwood Bore showed considerable variation, all made use of tarps or sheeting, bags and corrugated iron, to varying degrees, to make them weatherproof and windproof. Conveying a detached tone, Rose described the wiltja of the '"permanent" inmates' at Bloodwood

Bore as quite substantial structures that could be closed up while their owners were away. In contrast, those of the 'itinerants' had only sheets, and sometimes iron, to make them weatherproof.[12]

By comparison with the semi-nomadic existence at Walara, the changes in methods of and materials for building wiltja that Rose described reflect the increasingly sedentary lifestyle that became a feature at Bloodwood Bore. Rose's use of the term 'inmates' to describe 'permanent' residents of the camp, such as Tjuki, stands in marked contrast to Tjuki's own description of Bloodwood Bore as *home*. Sandra Armstrong's oral histories used in this research largely originate from four separate recordings, made with two different people, over a four-year period from 2009 to 2013. One of these oral histories was recorded during a single session in 2009 by Linda Rive for the Ara Irititja archive, while the other was recorded over three sessions in 2012–13 by Sam Osborne, who was researching ideas and understandings of education from an Anangu standpoint.[13] Sandra granted me permission to use the transcripts from each of these recordings.

Over the years I spent researching this book, I travelled widely with Sandra. The first time we found ourselves at Bloodwood Bore together was in June 2012. On that first day, after making cups of tea and being verbally ticked off by Sandra for bringing her an unsatisfactory quantity of paints and canvas from town, I pulled up a chair next to her and listened as she told stories, mapping the threads that tied her to that place. Sandra told me that she was from the place where we sat—that Bloodwood Bore was home.

During the time spent sitting or travelling with Sandra, she would tell stories, but I would also ask her to elaborate on certain points in the oral histories she had recorded with Linda and Sam, and sometimes to clarify them. These conversations would often result in the coming to light of additional information about life on Angas Downs that wasn't mentioned in the earlier recordings. For example, Sandra, aged approximately nineteen years old at the time of Rose's fieldwork, is the only Anangu I encountered in the four years of my own fieldwork who remembered Fred Rose clearly. I accompanied Sandra and her niece Teresa Mulla to the Mitchell Library in Sydney in 2013, to undertake a week of research in the Rose archive. While there, Sandra recalled certain aspects of his fieldwork methodology in detail, and said that, although she worked closely with Rose while he was at Bloodwood Bore, she didn't really know what he was going to do with all the information she was helping him to collect. She just thought 'he might take 'em away and do something'.[14]

The most striking feature of *The Wind of Change* is the 150 black-and-white portraits in the final pages of the book that capture Anangu living on Angas Downs at the time. Each portrait has a corresponding page of a matrix of data that maps each person's social relations. It also records their Aṉangu name, their English name, their sex, their age, their ancestral country, their totem and their immediate family members, and a footnote tells the reader every page of the book that they appear. As an appendix, Rose also included his fieldwork diaries in their entirety (minus personal details), which document in remarkable detail everyday life on Angas Downs between July and October 1962. These three features were the foundational pillars of Rose's methodological approach to fieldwork and anthropological enquiry. Sandra Armstrong recalled working with Fred Rose, saying that she helped him 'with the language and families', like 'This is my uncle, this is my auntie, father, mother.' Sandra says that she gave Rose the language names for relationships—that while sitting with him and looking at the photographs, he would ask her 'What do you call this one?' and that they worked together like this all the time.[15]

Sandra's descriptions of Bloodwood Bore also stand in contrast to Rose's use of the term 'inmates' to refer to her and her family. Despite the different circumstances in which they were recorded, the thread that connects all of her oral histories and memories is the strong sense that Bloodwood Bore is home. She says of this time:

> Aniwari Mitchell's father and mother, Melinda Mitchell's father and mother, my father and mother and Tjuki Pumpjack's father and mother, we were all family together that made up the Angas Downs community and we were collecting rations from there regularly.[16]

As each of the preceding chapters has illustrated, families living together and sharing resources is a fundamental social process in desert daily life, and, as such, is a significant element in the making of place for A<u>n</u>angu.[17] While Rose's language evokes the sense of Bloodwood Bore as being akin to a prison camp, Tjuki's and Sandra's memories reveal the ways in which the all-important nexus of food and family was making Angas Downs, according to their own sense of place.

By the time of Rose's fieldwork, Tjuki Pumpjack had been shepherding sheep, riding horses and learning the way of the cattle for two decades or more:

> I spent so long at Bloodwood Bore that I moved there as a man and I left as an old grey-haired tjilpi [old man, Elder]—well, almost anyway! I was a mature, grey-haired man. I was still riding horses, though, and still working the bullocks. I was still taking the bullocks all around, and still trucking them to Finke and Rumbalara and Deep Well, and also Alice Springs. So I worked for many, many years doing that, and so my life went along.
>
> I lived my life there, without leaving, in the same way that a true nguraritja would. I always thought to myself that I must be considered a nguraritja by now.[18]

To be nguraritja is to belong to a place. Tjuki described his becoming nguraritja, as it developed at Angas Downs, beginning with his family's arrival at Walara, and being reunited with his auntie Mimiya, his uncle Tjutjapayi and their family:

> We combined our camps, and we settled in to live there with them, and that is where I grew up and became a big boy. Right there. Time passed and we stayed and I became a young fella, and my whiskers grew, and I grew a beard there. I was a bearded man by then. Then I became a nyiinka (a pre-initiate)—a big boy—and so my mother and father took me up to Areyonga to go through Law and it was there I became a youngfella. I became a youngfella there, and when I returned, I started work. I worked on horseback, working the bullocks, and that's when I learned the ropes, where I learned how to ride horses, how to ride buckjumpers and stay in the saddle. My younger brother, Johnny Mulla, and I worked together.

> We started to work together and we grew up together and I became a man there, and then a senior man, and then an old man—in that same place. So I am like a nguraritja ... A nguraritja—a traditional owner—who lives their whole lives in one place and becomes an old grey man in the same place.[19]

Tjuki's evocation of his identification as nguraritja for Angas Downs is articulated in terms of his growing up there, being schooled in Law there, becoming a man there *and* learning the work of the pastoral industry. The transmission of knowledge that Tjuki describes not only differentiates older and younger generations, Elders and students, it maps a regional system of kinship that is inscribed in the Tjukurpa and made manifest in the landscape. Knowledge, too, as well as food, is fundamental to relationships of exchange; the sharing that is an integral part of the social processes creating relationships, connecting people to one another and to Country as kin.[20] In my reading of Tjuki's above statement, it appears that the rituals and knowledge of the pastoral industry had come to assume value in this significant social process at Angas Downs.

While it is true that there's much Tjuki couldn't share with me as a white woman, he did repeatedly emphasise that Bloodwood Bore was the place where he grew up and became a man. While anthropologists and historians have long ventured into the gendered cultural terrain of First Nations people, in the relentless pursuit to *know* the 'other', I am acutely aware that it isn't my place to delve any further into the domain of men. All we can know is what Tjuki chose to share. Once he returned from Law and started working with the cattle, it would seem that the process of learning the work of the pastoral industry became thoroughly entangled with the social process of acquiring knowledge and becoming a man at Bloodwood Bore.[21]

Anthropologist Arjun Appadurai has argued that much of the ethnographic record can be rewritten and reread from the point of view of the 'production of locality' as a social process.[22] Appadurai defines 'locality' as a 'complex phenomenological quality' that is primarily relational and contextual, rather than scalar or spatial. In other words, despite the common association of the word locality with the physical world, it is embedded in people, and realised in their relationships to one another and to place. According to Appadurai:

> [A] great deal of what has been termed *rites of passage* is concerned with the production of what we might call *local subjects*, actors who properly belong to a situated community of kin, neighbours, friends and enemies. Ceremonies of naming and tonsure, scarification and segregation, circumcision and deprivation are complex social techniques for the inscription of locality onto bodies. Looked at slightly differently, they are ways to embody locality as well as to locate bodies in socially and spatially defined communities.[23]

In my reading, Tjuki's above memory demonstrates that it was not just *rites of passage* but the *rites of the pastoral industry* that had come to assume significance in the creation of local subjects, which is to say, people who belong to a place.

Rose's observation that A<u>n</u>angu were in a rapid state of 'detribalisation' and 'acculturation' is symptomatic of the anthropological representations and systems of thought that emerged in the early twentieth century, and tended towards viewing Aboriginal relationships to place as being fixed in ritual knowledge and rooted in particular places. However, as Myers has noted, this view divorces relationships to place from the social practices—residing, sharing, loving, fighting and dying—in which they are made.[24] Rather than the anthropological standards of 'authenticity' and 'tradition' to which many Aboriginal people are still held accountable (none more so than in the realms of popular understanding, and legislative forms of recognition in land rights and native title), in both Tjuki and Sandra's oral histories it's the social practices linking people and place that emerge as central in continuing ways of placemaking. As the spatial dimensions of A<u>n</u>angu relationships to place were reorganised through migration and the encounter with white settlers, rations and cattle, A<u>n</u>angu were simultaneously producing locality and making a place for themselves.

9
A FORTUITOUS LOCATION

IMPROVED ROADS AND transport also 'opened up' Central Australia to tourism, and Bloodwood Bore just so happened to be located on the road to Uluru. Beginning in the early 1940s, images of Ayers Rock, as it was then known, began to appear in *Walkabout* magazine. By the late 1940s, there was an increasing interest in selling the 'outback' experience; as Michael Cathcart has observed, *essential* to the Rock's potency at this time was the idea of it as a symbol of *ancient* Aboriginality in a *timeless* land.[1] By the early 1950s, correspondence within the Welfare Branch indicates it was 'common knowledge' that truck driver Len Tuit was operating tours in the Southwest Reserve. In 1950 Tuit led a group of students from Knox Grammar School in Sydney. Those from the school were accompanied by a group of botanists, geologists, geographers and the anthropologist Charles Mountford, in something of a re-enactment of nineteenth-century colonial expeditions.[2]

Schools were the earliest organised tour groups to visit Central Australia. In 1946 Bill Liddle had acted as a tour guide for a group of Geelong College students who attempted to travel to Uluru. Travelling in ex-army Blitzwagons, the expedition was thwarted when they became bogged in weather damaged roads that forced them to turn back. A year later, Sidney Staines from Erldunda station successfully led the Geelong College students to Uluru. In the same year, Bill Liddle wrote to the Department of Works and Housing regarding the 'development of this part of the Northern Territory', and urging that the 'geological wonders' of Uluru and Kat̲a Tjuta be opened to the public.[3]

The correspondence from this time reflects the mounting pressure to excise Uluru and Kat̲a Tjuta, then known as the Olgas, from the reserve and declare the area a national park. In one 1951 letter, it's noted it was 'becoming abundantly clear' that Ayers Rock was attracting 'wider national interest' and that the 'existence of this most unusual geological feature' was 'considered to be common knowledge throughout Australia'.[4] The Director of Native Affairs noted that, although the time wasn't right to consider such an action, he was not opposed to the excision from the reserve 'providing it was retained for *National interest only*'.[5] The area around Uluru and Kat̲a Tjuta was declared a national park in 1958, and thus became a stage upon which nationalist narratives were to be projected.[6] For the tourist, the journey to the 'outback' became a national rite of passage. The quintessential tourist destination in Australia, it offered visitors the opportunity to travel back in time, and simultaneously experience modern Australia's frontier and settlement history in the 'prehistoric' and 'primitive' heart of the continent.[7]

The tourist route passed right through Bloodwood Bore. Tjuki Pumpjack says of the time that tourists arrived:

> Tourists [started] coming along that little old dirt road from a place called Mount Quinn. The road used to come past this side of Ukaka, a long time ago. That little old road is still there. The tourists would come down along that road, and come through here ... There was a different road that went from Bloodwood Bore to Ayers Rock. It used to come right through Bloodwood Bore. When the bitumen road was built, it was made into a very straight road, and now goes via a different route. But in the old days it was a winding little old road

> that went right through Bloodwood Bore and right past the homes of many An̲angu.[8]

The tourist season ran from April to September, and Rose noted that somewhere between four thousand to five thousand tourists passed through Angas Downs on their way to Uluru in 1962.[9] He recorded that the road carrying the tourist traffic to Uluru had bypassed Mount Quinn and Angas Downs since 1961, passing through Erldunda and Mount Ebenezer instead, which left Angas Downs sitting on a loop about 5 kilometres from the main road. Tour groups detoured onto the loop, specifically to visit Angas Downs. Sandra Armstrong recalls of the time:

> We were living there together when tourists first started to come through. They'd come from Alice Springs. They'd come through Henbury, from that turnoff, the turnoff to Kings Canyon. So that's the way tourists would come, through Mount Quinn and through Angas Downs. I was working there at the time cleaning dishes, as well as working with the stockmen ... on Angas Downs. I'd help with the bullocks. Bake bread and cook food. Serve the tourists. When the tourists came through, we'd be very busy, me, Elsie and Melinda ...
>
> So, anyway, there we were, all us young women working away in the kitchen, for the tourists. We would work for the tourists. We would start work, I would set everything, fork and knife, as I'd learned to do. I'd bake bread, then after baking it I'd cut it up and serve it up. I work from the kitchen. I'd look after the stove, make coals and get everything set up for the tourists' dinner ... They'd come in for their dinner with the driver and we'd sit and eat dinner together ... Pioneer Bus and TAA [Trans Australia Airlines] ... and Sundown Coach, and Bill Hann from Melbourne. Cobb and Co.[10]

Sandra and Tjuki told in the same way the story of tourists arriving in Central Australia—telling the listener how the tourists got to where they were going. They also orient the journey that tourists took in relation to current journeys and tracks. In my experience with An̲angu, I've found this is a common way for stories to begin. The tourist buses would stop to have a meal at Angas Downs in the 'chalet', described in detail by Rose:

> The Chalet was a new building erected at the beginning of 1962, consisting of a fly-proofed dining room with adjoining kitchen. Metal on the outside, it was lined with hardboard. With many louvered windows it was well adapted to the climactic conditions. Thirty yards to the south of the Chalet were toilets and showers for the tourists, but also used by the Liddles, but not by the Aborigines. It was in the Chalet, tastefully furnished with colourful plastic topped tables and appropriate chairs, that the tourists partook of their meals. Up to 40 people could be seated at any one time, so when two CATA buses arrived on one day, two sessions were necessary. The meals served to the tourists were substantial. They were always of the same pattern, with three courses – soup, meat and sweets.[11]

Rose noted that Arthur and Bessie Liddle cooked all the meals, and that the kitchen chores, preparation of vegetables, and washing up was done by 'the house girls Nos. 90, 91 and 107', who were Sandra Armstrong, Melinda Mitchell and Elsie Wanatjura respectively. Rose also observed that Sandra, Melinda and Elsie would clean up after the tourists had finished eating, and collect the leftover food in empty fruit or milk tins to take to the A<u>n</u>angu camp. Most of it, according to Rose, went to 'Nos. 77, 78 and 79', who were Sandra's mother and father, and her younger sister Rosie.[12]

However, tourist buses were not just stopping off at Angas Downs for a meal. A<u>n</u>angu were central to the tourist experience in the 'heart of the nation' and, like other sites of 'Aboriginal tourism' in Australia, Bloodwood Bore presented an opportunity for tourists to have a close encounter with the Aboriginal people who lived there. Tourism that focused on Aboriginal people and their culture originated in the nineteenth century in the southeast of Australia. From as early as the 1860s, daytrippers from Melbourne would visit Coranderrk Aboriginal Reserve and buy souvenirs made by the Aboriginal residents. In the 1880s La Perouse, in Sydney, emerged as a desirable destination for tourists seeking to experience both the 'birthplace' and the 'native essence' of the new nation, while, in the early twentieth century, visitors to Lakes Entrance in eastern Victoria would travel by boat to the nearby Lake Tyers mission, to buy souvenirs and take photographs of Aboriginal people who were residents there. In the more remote parts of the country, it was the extension of the north-south and trans-continental railways in the late 1920s that facilitated the early commodification of the 'primitive' world of the 'outback' for modern, urban-dwelling Australians. However, it was not until vehicles could travel along roads and penetrate deep into the desert heart of the continent that the *essential* tourist destination in Australia emerged.[13]

Despite this, it would appear that Anangu at Angas Downs didn't always satisfy the tourist desire for the 'authentic Aborigine'. Like the urban Aboriginal people of La Perouse in Maria Nugent's history *Botany Bay*, the cattle-station-dwelling people at Bloodwood Bore were considered by some tourists to be 'not sufficiently native' in appearance.[14] In a memoir of early tourism to Uluru, Edna Bradley describes getting off the bus at Angas Downs in 1957:

> As soon as we got off the bus the Aborigines crowded around and we got a good look at each other ... This was the first time I had been close to Aborigines and I was amazed at how dark and skinny they were, and their hair was matted. You could never put a comb through it I thought. I'd always imagined they would have been like the Aborigines I saw in my 'Dreamtime' books. Of course they were only photos or drawings and not the real thing, but these Aborigines were unkempt and their strong body odour was overpowering my senses. Their clothes were tatty and some women had layers of dresses on. Their appearance made me realise how different their lifestyle was to mine ...

Even the station itself was a disappointment—in her description, the buildings mirroring the 'unkempt' appearance of 'the natives':

> I have to say the homestead left a lot to be desired. I didn't know what the inside looked like, but from the outside, the flywire on the veranda was damaged in several places and there was no garden.

> No lawn, only red dust. There were used oil drums lying around, car tyres and bits of machinery scattered all over the area, giving the appearance of an old rubbish dump ... Everything was covered in dust. I wouldn't have fancied living there and was pleased to be boarding the bus to continue on.[15]

The 'Dreamtime Aborigine' Bradley came in search of eluded her. The station, too, was experienced as a poor imitation of the romanticised image of the northern cattle station that had been imprinted upon her imagination after reading about Elsey Station in Jeannie Gunn's classic colonial works *The Little Black Princess* and *We of the Never Never*. It was the image of Jeannie Gunn projected in those books—the white woman bringing virtue to the primeval north of the continent—that inspired Bradley to travel to Central Australia. In her own memoir, she likened herself to Gunn and felt that they were of the same 'ilk', writing: 'I was sure I could live in remote situations and survive just like Mrs Jeannie Gunn at Elsey Station'.[16]

Bradley was a member of the Petticoat Safari. Operated by Trans Australia Airlines (TAA) in 1957, it was one of the first 'official' guided tours to 'the Rock'. A women's-only tour to 'Alice and beyond', its purpose, as Bradley described it, was showing the rest of Australia 'that if women could travel to a far-off, inhospitable place, so could anyone else'. A thoroughly modern Australian woman, at the age of twenty Bradley had already 'seen most of Australia by ship, rail and air', and felt that the far reaches of Central Australia presented her with the kind of 'adventure' she was looking for.[17] The marketing strategy to entice white, modern, middle-class women to the Northern Territory worked. Frederick Rose observed in 1962 that one of the most surprising features of the tourist buses was that the percentage of women was very high, averaging about 70 per cent, but on occasions upwards of around 95 per cent. He described the 'representative tourist' as 'a woman, probably spinster, of either small independent means or with a profession – doctor or teacher – who living in a southern city' was lured to the Centre by its advertised 'glamour' and 'adventure'.[18]

Despite the overtly masculine nature of the myriad legends of the bush, women, too, had a role to play in the endeavour to write a frontier mythology into the heart of the modern Australian nation. The 'unsettled' and 'empty' north was to be discovered and possessed, but also tamed and domesticated. However, while the Red Centre was being marketed as the essential tourist destination in Australia, it would seem that for Bradley, the 'unkempt Aborigines' and dust at Angas Downs were somewhat disenchanting. The idealised image of the Australian outback constructed in Gunn's *We of the Never Never* eluded her. This is because the Never Never does not exist. Rather, as historian Mickey Dewar has observed, it's a creation of the white settler imagination: 'the dream of white occupation'.[19]

Rose observed in 1962 that the only reason the buses detoured onto the Angas Downs loop was to see and trade with A_n_angu. Art historian and curator Ruth B Phillips has described the tourist as both a consumer and a 'collector of tourist experiences' for which the 'souvenir' became an essential 'marker'.[20] As such, objects understood by the tourist as the archetypal utilitarian objects of the hunter–gather became increasingly popular commodities at Bloodwood Bore, purchased as tangible mementoes of their experience in the 'primitive' heart of the nation.

Sandra Armstrong recalls that when the tourists started to arrive:

> The old people started to make punu there ... At Angas Downs. The men would make boomerangs because of course they all knew how to make kali. Hunting kali [hunting boomerangs]. They also made piti tjukutjuku [small wooden dishes] and wira tjuta [wooden bowls] ... music sticks—and that's where it all started from. Nobody else knew how to do it at that stage. So we'd sell the things.[21]

Punu is the Pitjantjatjara word for 'wood' and is also the name given to objects that are carved out of wood for sale to tourists. The 'advent of the white man', and the impact of this encounter on material culture, as Rose described it, was threefold: changes to the subsistence economy rendered articles of material culture redundant;

the acquisition of iron led to the 'improvement or substitution' of tools used previously; and, most significantly:

> Economic change took place whereby tools etc. which previously were implements of production that enabled the Aborigines to obtain the wherewithal of living became commodities, in the modern sense of the word. And which could be exchanged for cash, by sale to tourists and others.

Rose noted that, although the first two conditions would appear to have been 'universal' in the Australian experience, the production of commodities for a tourist trade would only occur 'in restricted areas where conditions were appropriate', and that at Angas Downs, these 'conditions were fulfilled'.[22]

Rose observed that the majority of the trade with tourists at the time of his fieldwork was in customary tools, such as spears, boomerangs and dishes. He also noted that the arrival of tourists had impacted upon the production of these objects, as A<u>n</u>angu began to alter the dimensions of the tools to suit the market, with little regard for their traditional function.[23] Rose also documented the emergent form that he called 'wood carving in the round', which, as far as he had been able to ascertain, was a development 'indigenous to Angas Downs'. As part of his fieldwork, he collected 'specimens' of carved echidna, duck, kangaroo, turkey, marsupial rat, lizard, frog and snake, as well as a 'three pronged branch that had been modelled into an emu foot'.[24] Rose observed that the type of animal being carved at any one time followed a 'definite fashion'. When he first arrived at Bloodwood Bore, it was mainly blue-tongue lizards that were in production. However, Rose noted that the fashion changed almost overnight, when the 'leading figure in this art form', a man called Harry Brumby, made a ninu (native marsupial rat) that sold for one pound.[25]

Despite Sandra Armstrong's claim that no one else was doing anything like it at that time, the conditions that Rose described, while novel for A<u>n</u>angu in the southwest region, have occurred in earlier times at various sites of colonial encounter, both in Australia and further afield. Examples of Aboriginal people selling artefacts and crafts in the southeast of Australia emerged as early as the 1860s, at places such as Coranderrk, La Perouse and Lake Tyers.[26] Early in the twentieth century in the southeast, missionaries were important intermediaries in the sale of Aboriginal crafts and artefacts to outside markets;[27] by the 1930s and 1940s, this practice of 'mercantile evangelism',[28] as Rowse called it, had developed in the north of the continent, facilitated by missions in Arnhem Land, Hermannsburg and Ernabella.[29] Phillips analyses this type of commodity production in settler colonial societies outside of Australia by tracing the history of the 'souvenir arts' in North America in the nineteenth and twentieth centuries.[30] Her work in particular emphasises the importance of the economic value of objects in local economies where First Nations peoples were systematically marginalised from settler colonial economies through the expropriation of land, the establishment of reserves and processes of assimilation.[31] There is a comparable emerging body of scholarly literature highlighting the history of the economic value of Aboriginal artefact and craft production in nineteenth- and twentieth-century Australia.[32]

It's not only the tourists but the economic dimension of this encounter that are salient in the oral histories of Tjuki Pumpjack and Sandra Armstrong. During my research, I heard numerous stories about the A<u>n</u>angu encounter with tourists and the trade in punu at Angas Downs. What each of these stories has in common, apart from including the exchange of objects, are the words '*How much? Two bob! How much? Two bob!*' I heard this same phrase uttered over and over again. Sandra recalls the exchange in this way:

> My mother was still learning and she'd come to me and tell me that the tourists were always asking her, 'How much?' They were asking my mother, 'How much?', she'd tell me. She told me that they would ask my father, even while he was having a snooze, 'How much?' and he'd give the wrong price because he was actually going a bit blind by then, and they were hers to sell. 'How much?' they'd ask. None of them could understand English and so they'd sell their carvings for anything, really .... They'd say, 'One bob,' but we'd say, 'Mum, put the price up a bit!' I'd say that to Mum, 'Put the price up a bit! I'd say that

> to my mum! Ten bob! Twenty bob!' ... Those of us who had been to school and who knew a few things about numbers would be going 'Money pulka wangka!' [ask for more money] Because we knew they would be going and standing in front of the tourists and saying 'One bob! Two bob! Two bob! Two bob!' ... Poor things.[33]

Tjuki Pumpjack remembered these encounters in a remarkably similar way:

> The tourists would come down along that road, and come through here, and so the old women started cutting wood to make wooden carvings, nulla-nulla, coolamons and wira ... they'd all gather with their children, along the roadside when the tourists came through, and sell their punu to the tourists. The old men would be there as well, selling their wira and kali. The tourists would ask them, 'How much is this?' and the old women would say, 'Two bob.' 'How much?' 'Two bob.' The white people would be asking, 'How much is this?' 'How much?' 'Two bob.' 'How much?' 'Two bob.' They couldn't speak English and that's all they could say, those old women! ... They'd be there selling all their punu items ... They'd be collecting all these coins, lots of money, lots of silver ... They'd be making them out of mangata (quandong Santalum acuminatum) and selling them.[34]

It's currency and the question 'How much?' that are emphasised in both Tjuki's and Sandra's memories of exchanges with tourists. The unit of currency at Bloodwood Bore wasn't the penny nor the shilling but, rather, the 'florin' or two-shilling piece. Although the florin wasn't normally used as a unit of currency, goods purchased from the store, and prices A<u>n</u>angu asked for punu, were always in multiples of the florin, which A<u>n</u>angu referred to as 'two bob'.

Until the arrival of tourists, there was very little cash in circulation on the station. Rose noted during his fieldwork that Tjuki was the only person employed by pastoralism, and that he was paid a wage of ten shillings a day, the equivalent of two pounds, which he received in a lump sum when he went to Alice Springs. Sandra wasn't paid a wage, but given five pounds to spend when she visited Alice Springs. Rose noted that what Tjuki was being paid was slightly above the 'award' wage as declared in the *Wards Employment Ordinance, 1953–59*; however, what Tjuki was actually paid in hand, we don't know. Sandra was entitled to one pound per week but, again, we can't be sure that the amount of time she worked equated with the frequency she went into town with her five pounds. Rose made the observation that although Tjuki's and Sandra's wages may have seemed small by 1962 standards, it was the amount stipulated in the ordinance. Moreover, what he found most remarkable was the fact that they were being paid a wage at all. Rose noted that in many parts of the Northern Territory at that time, wages weren't being paid to Aboriginal people.[35]

Tjuki described, in English on this occasion, the practice of being paid when he went into town:

> We bin get paid right there, when you go to Alice Springs. We gettem paid on the road, somewhere on the road. We gettem money this side of Alice Springs, on the road, that's your pay. We gettem clothes then, good clothes. He takem from here, thinkin this man might lose money, gamble you know ... that's why we gotta takem Alice Springs. We get paid there, Alice Springs, we can gettem clothes then. Old Milton Liddle. Old Arthur, Arthur Liddle. We can get everything then. Cowboy shirt, cowboy hat.[36]

Little opportunity to spend cash on pastoral leases being a continuing circumstance in the postwar period, the system of paying wages when employees went to town was hardly unique. Rowse's research shows that across twenty stations in Central Australia around the mid-century, pastoralists determined the frequency with which people were paid, and that this was generally contingent upon the proximity of the pastoral lease to town and the frequency with which pastoralists made the trip.[37]

Tjuki links getting paid before going to town with concerns about A<u>n</u>angu gambling their wages in card games, which were very popular at Bloodwood Bore. The perception of gambling as both 'sinful' and facilitating the 'accumulation of cash without "thrift"' was common in Central Australia at this time, and, as Rowse has demonstrated, contributed in no small measure to the 'hinterland retailing' pioneered by Lutheran missionaries as a means to influence how Aṉangu spent their money.[38] In the late 1950s, Pastor Kaleski from Areyonga mission 'brought stores' to Angas Downs every six weeks to sell to Aṉangu. Rose noted the thirty-one items that Kaleski carried with him included flour, tea, tinned meat, biscuits, Salvital, Milo, plum pudding, and tinned herring and kippers. However, when Arthur Liddle opened a store on Angas Downs sometime around 1960, Liddle asked Kaleski to stop trading so as to not interfere with his business.[39] According to Rose, it was the opening of the store on Angas Downs that significantly transformed the economic exchange that was taking place between Aṉangu and tourists.

Prior to the store opening, Aṉangu had been accepting copper coins, or, preferably, material goods and food, in exchange for the carved wooden objects they made. The nature of these early exchanges led to assumptions 'the few shillings' that Aṉangu made from trade were trivial and amounted to begging. In a 1964 letter to tour companies that sought to discourage them from engaging Aṉangu in trade, the Assistant Director of Welfare, Les Penhall, wrote:

> The few shillings that the Aboriginals make in this way tends to undo the work of my officers who regularly visit the area to try and curb the growth of these rather unsavoury places ... I also believe it is common practice for tourists to hand out sweets or 'two bob' to Aboriginal children and adults to take their photograph. This sort of thing could have an adverse effect on our attempt to teach the Natives the principle of work for pay, and make them parasites on society.[40]

Penhall's letter reflects AP Elkin's description of this kind of economic exchange between Aboriginal people and tourists as an example of 'intelligent parasitism'. As he understood it, this act of begging was a deliberate performance; in the case of the trans-continental railway line, he observed that Aboriginal people took advantage with their 'well-developed art of preying' upon the passengers:

> Donning tattered garments, and borrowing babies if they have none of their own, groups of men and women visit the train stopping places to sell their own few artefacts, to amuse and to beg.

Elkin observed that the provision of ration depots and the work of the missions had failed to 'prevent this active, successful, interesting, and new form of hunting'.[41]

Assimilation policy sought to create self-sufficient citizens through education and domestication, and through the transformation from 'hunter–gather' to wage labourer within the settler capitalist economy. That the money earned from the sale of punu was written off as merely a 'few shillings', and seen as undermining attempts to teach A<u>n</u>angu the 'principle of work for pay', highlights the ways in which 'work' was understood primarily in material terms and within a wage labour paradigm. However, Rose argued that:

> To pass value judgement on the action of the Aborigines and describe them as parasitic on the white man in any way, [was] completely to miss the point.[42]

Once the store opened, and provided an opportunity to purchase items such as flour, tea, tinned meat, 'cool drink', fruit, sweets and bread, A<u>n</u>angu started refusing the tokens that tourists were offering and began 'demanding money instead'.[43]

Rose noted that the store, located inside the homestead, was entered through a padlocked door from the living room. To open the store, a 5-by-2-foot corrugated iron shutter on a wooden frame would be lowered, and this also served as the counter. Sandra Armstrong emphasises the importance of being able to purchase food as a motivating force behind making and trading punu with tourists:

> They'd get a lot of silver, and with that money they'd go to the store and buy a lot of food! Tinameat, tea, sugar ... They only had to do this once to learn to rush off and cut more wood![44]

Whereas missionaries had facilitated most artefact production in various locations around Australia until that point, A<u>n</u>angu at Bloodwood Bore were selling directly to tourists. In a December 1965 report from Angas Downs, a patrol officer named Stewart noted that A<u>n</u>angu there had 'a better comprehension of monetary values than Aboriginals on other stations'.[45] Furthermore, Rose wrote that at the time of his visit, it was the general rule that A<u>n</u>angu demanded cash payment for anything they did for a white person, and that the general attitude of A<u>n</u>angu at Bloodwood Bore 'to the white man was much more self-assured and militant'.[46] He observed that:

> The general attitude of the Aborigines in 1962 was that they endeavoured to obtain the highest price they were able from the tourists. Nevertheless, they knew the approximate value of the objects they produced and, even if there were no purchaser, they would not sell them at 'give away' prices.[47]

Rose described Mick[48] (No. 11) as an 'ardent trader', 'astute businessman', maker of the finest boomerangs at Bloodwood Bore, and enthusiastic gambler, who was unable to count and would come to Rose frequently to get him to count his money. Mick was particularly skilled in finishing off boomerangs to show the contrasting colours of the heart and sap of the mulga wood to best effect.[49] Sandra Armstrong, too, remembered Mick as a skilled craftsman and someone who made good money from selling punu at Bloodwood Bore.

On 4 September 1962 Rose wrote in his diary that Mick had done well at trading that day:

> He had 9 pound-5-3d wrapped up in a piece of rag although part of this money he won at cards. He sold a boomerang for 10/- and had his photograph taken 13 times for which he received 26/- ... Some of the tourists did not want to pay 2/- but the man who originally got No. 11 to pose said, 'fair crack of the whip: give him a go!' And the other tourists paid up. No. 11 did not have a single copper coin in his possession![50]

According to Rose, Anangu had completely rejected copper coins, due to their lack of purchasing power at the store, and he would find them lying on the ground and in the bins around the station. Two days later, he wrote in his field diary that he saw Mick had five nice boomerangs for sale and asked him how much he was going to sell them for, to which he replied 'a pound'. Rose saw Mick trading later that day, just before the buses left, and overheard a young woman approach him and point to the boomerang he had under his arm, saying, 'I'll give you one bob for that: there aren't any more tourists coming through today!' Mick's response to the young woman's offer was to walk 'away without saying a word, no doubt in disgust'.[51] Rose wrote that he often overheard Anangu describing tourists who didn't want to part with their money, or tried to get a lower price, as being 'hungry'.

Listening again to one of the earliest recordings made with Tjuki Pumpjack on the veranda of his house in Imanpa, some two years after it was created, I discovered a conversation at the end that hadn't been transcribed. Tjuki had finished his oral history telling, and he, Linda Rive and I continued to have a casual conversation while the tape recorder was still running, with Linda carrying on interpreting, as she always did. During this conversation, Tjuki Pumpjack told us that when Anangu gave tourists a price, sometimes the tourists would say that was too much. However, he felt that 'two bob' was like 'pocket money' and that some tourists weren't able to recognise the work that went into the carvings. He said that some old people at the time didn't properly understand the value of money, and would stand on the side of the road and say, 'Two bob, two bob,' to the tourists, and accept 'anything' for their punu. However, those people who were knowledgeable would ask for proper money for their work—for well-made boomerangs, for example—and they would get it, and tell the tourists they couldn't be cheated out of the money that their carvings deserved.[52]

There's a sense in Tjuki's oral histories from this time, as well as in Rose's observations, that the arrival of tourists, while providing Anangu with an important source of income, contributed to an emergent spatial order on Bloodwood Bore that separated the Aboriginal and white settler domains. It was white settlers who controlled the seemingly abundant supplies of food, cash and material goods. Until the arrival of tourists, it was also white settlers who determined the share that Anangu received. A sphere of encounter and exchange developed in the vicinity of the Chalet, and it was in this space that the value of punu as commodity was being constantly negotiated, as Anangu incorporated money into what anthropologist Basil Sansom has referred to as an already existing 'modality of exchange'.[53] Anangu had been exchanging material culture, ochre, 'bush tobacco', knowledge and marriage partners well before pastoralists, missionaries and tourists arrived.[54] Sansom observed that when money is incorporated into Aboriginal relationships of exchange, it ceases to exist purely in market terms. Rather, it is transformed into something else. In the Anangu camp at Bloodwood Bore, cash procured around the Chalet was transformed into a resource that was valued not just in terms of what it could purchase but in terms of the services of 'help, helping and helping out' among people who share history and a social relationship.[55] In this sense, punu can be understood not just as commodity, but as yet another technique, in a rapidly changing world, that Anangu incorporated into existing relationships of exchange, in order to make a place for themselves at Bloodwood Bore.

10
EMERGING ECONOMIES AND MAKING PLACE

AT A TIME of increasing government intervention in A<u>n</u>angu lives—and given the limited economic opportunities available to them—the immediacy of the punu exchange, the direct access to significant sums of cash, and the greatly enhanced circulation of material goods and resources at Bloodwood Bore were undoubtedly appealing to A<u>n</u>angu. Patrol reports from the late 1950s onwards reflect a significant increase in numbers living at Angas Downs, and also considerable movement between Bloodwood Bore and the mission settlements at Ernabella and Areyonga. The emergence of a commodity-driven market at Bloodwood Bore resulted in income from the sale of artefacts surpassing all other means. Rose estimated that 85 per cent of all money in circulation on the station came from the tourist trade.[1]

Anthropologist Nancy Munn recorded that A<u>n</u>angu at Areyonga in 1964–65 were paid fortnightly, and that payday was known as 'buyin' time', the time when money was spent at the store, while the week between was known as 'nothing-a-week'.[2] Furthermore, life on Ernabella and Areyonga missions was largely structured around routines of work and education, both religious and secular. The implementation of dormitories and communal feeding at Areyonga prevented people from preparing and sharing food according to their own kinship systems—a profoundly disruptive policy that

Rowse identifies as probably the most significant attempt by colonial authority to intervene in Aboriginal lives in Central Australia.[3]

In contrast, the only direct contact with Christianity and the missions at Bloodwood Bore was Reverend Kaleskis's four-to-six-weekly visits. Rose observed it was 'certain' that Anangu understood his primary role to be the selling of goods and the purchasing of dingo scalps. He also noted that although Christian ritual, primarily the singing of hymns, had great appeal among Anangu, 'Christian ideology and the associated code of morality' had had little effect at Angas Downs. Both gambling and chewing bush tobacco (two very popular pastimes at Bloodwood Bore) were considered to be immoral by the missionaries, and, according to Rose, Christian morality was 'treated with contempt' by the large majority of Anangu.[4] Arguably more important, Angas Downs, a cattle station owned by an Arrernte man and a Luritja woman, offered an opportunity for Anangu to camp relatively free from interference and according to their own cultural codes. During a visit to Bloodwood Bore in August 1960, Pastor Albrecht described the scene he encountered:

> When out there we found nearly 100 people at the place, many of whom were passing through on the way to Ernabella, others going back to Areyonga ... it appears that the whole atmosphere at the place attracts the people and they are a contented lot. Also, Mr Arthur Liddle is very sympathetic and prepared to help them. It appears the amount of meat he kills for their use is many times of what he uses himself. This is probably the main reason why most of them, with the exception of a few, are looking well and obviously not suffering.[5]

At a time of increasing interference in Anangu lives, as part of government attempts to assimilate them, Bloodwood Bore emerged as a relatively informal and unregulated space that became an important meeting place for Anangu in an era of assimilation and increasing surveillance.

Rose documented in detail the regular hunting of kangaroo, and the practice of dividing up and distributing the meat among families in the camp. He observed that the kangaroo was killed and cooked in a very particular way (never by a woman) and divided up among 'a considerable number' of people.[6] Despite not being able to formulate 'any definite kinship rule' for its division, he did note that the economic relations enacted were 'not individual, but collective' and 'certainly retained some features that stemmed from that [earlier tribal] condition'.[7] Similarly, the redistribution of rations and money was also an important part of daily life on Angas Downs, and Rose observed that time spent gambling, by both men and women either playing cards or the 'matchbox game', was the 'largest item for any single activity'.[8] Decks of cards were only available in Alice Springs, and Rose noted that A̲nangu played with a pack until they 'were literally falling to pieces, stained red with sand and the print half rubbed away'. Paper money was frequently used at card games on Bloodwood Bore, and big money could be won or lost this way. Rose wrote that one of his 'informants', No.142, a man called Timothy, brought him thirty pounds to count, which he had won at cards and left in Rose's possession in a dirty green sock. Rose noted that the sum was twice the weekly wage of a white man in Alice Springs. However, despite the significant sums of money changing hands on the station, because of the apparent lack of a relationship between this practice and an 'earlier tribal condition', in his study Rose directed little attention to gambling as a means of distributing resources at Bloodwood Bore.

The production and consumption of food and other resources is an integral social practice in A̲nangu culture that establishes and maintains relationships between wayltja, or kin. Rather than being grounded in an 'ethic of generosity' and unsolicited giving, anthropologist Nicolas Peterson posits the exchange of goods as a complex set of behaviours, not simply predicated upon need but bound up in relationships that have to be constantly produced and maintained, and understood in terms of hierarchy and authority, responsibility and obligation.[9] Punu—in particular, the money generated from the exchange and the subsequent access to a more diverse range of resources—assumed a significant role in the process of maintaining kinship networks at Bloodwood Bore.

Jon Altman and Nicolas Peterson have both shown how the availability of cash in Aboriginal economies led to the adaptation of gambling as a mode of redistribution to serve local needs and family obligations.[10] Furthermore, they have observed that although there were no strict rules for the distribution of cash, there are 'clear parallels' between the treatment of game and cash and the goods that the latter purchased.[11] While Rose viewed the hunting and distribution of the kangaroo as one of the last 'vestiges of earlier tribal economic relations', he wasn't able to see the gambling that was taking place all around him as an expression of the socioeconomic relations he believed to be disappearing. Rose perceived the encounter with settler capitalism at Angas Downs as the most significant factor contributing to the acceleration of 'detribalisation' and 'acculturation' of A<u>n</u>angu. Thus, while his archive is a rich record of the economic encounter at Bloodwood Bore, his analysis obscures the ways in which access to cash and goods for sale was incorporated into existing relationships of exchange, enabling A<u>n</u>angu to continue reproducing social relationships that were fundamental to their autonomy and identity. In seeking evidence to support his theories of historical change, and what he understood to be the inevitable transition from hunter–gatherer to absorption within the capitalist economy, Rose missed the subtle and complex ways that A<u>n</u>angu were drawing upon their existing cultural materials to embed themselves at Bloodwood Bore.

While the value of punu was determined in monetary terms in the exchange with tourists, the processes of distribution and redistribution at Bloodwood Bore demonstrate the ways in which economic objects 'circulate in different *regimes of value* in space and time',[12] and illustrate Arjun Appadurai's observation that a commodity is a 'thoroughly socialised thing'. Sandra Armstrong's oral histories from Bloodwood Bore emphasise the social dimensions of punu at Angas Downs:

> They'd go off on overnight trips to collect wood. They'd chop wood and cut and carve and carve and carve and make things. Meanwhile Mr and Mrs Liddle would be buying rasps and tomahawks and files and bringing them back to the store and of course they would be instantly snapped up! It was lovely really, what was going on and we were all learning.[13]

Punu as souvenir was not just about the exchange of goods and resources, but a vessel for the all-important transfer of knowledge between people. Sandra's memories from this period are replete with references to learning. The younger generation taught their parents about money and the value of their work in a changing socioeconomic landscape; the older generation taught their young people how to carve objects from wood:

> All the young people was learning from their parents. How to carve coolamon. Anything. Put wire in the fire and hot wire burn all this smoke. We was helping our parents.[14]

Rose took many photographs at Bloodwood Bore that captured family groups sitting around a campfire—'the social hearth of desert life'[15]—carving punu together. The sociality of souvenir production has emerged as significant in other places where the tourist trade provided local people with an important income source. The souvenir trade at La Perouse facilitated family camping trips to collect wood and raw materials, and the exchange of cultural knowledge and stories.[16] Ilaria Vanni describes the making of boomerangs and shell-work for tourists at La Perouse as being grounded in the handing down through generations of technical and local knowledge made manifest in a production process patterned by kinship relations. The souvenir became a vehicle for La Perouse families to secure the survival and transmission of local knowledge, and Vanni illustrates how they act as 'cultural markers of the community', which both represents and recognises itself in them.[17]

Similarly with the carved wooden objects made in La Perouse, the technique of using hot wire to burn a design into the surface of an object was used to embellish punu at Angas Downs. Rose observed that the technique was relatively new at Bloodwood Bore in 1962. Arthur Liddle had told him that it was he who first suggested that A<u>n</u>angu use the method, sometime around late 1960 or early 1961, and conversations with A<u>n</u>angu made him 'reasonably certain' that they had not used this method of ornamentation before then.[18] However, the method of branding artefacts was in use at Ernabella by the late 1950s, and Albert Namatjira at Hermannsburg has been cited as an influence on the innovation in the 1940s.[19] This technique emerged on Angas Downs with the movement of people between these places as part of a journey of knowledge that possibly originated in the southeast, where the technique was being used as early as the late nineteenth century.

The Pitjantjatjara term for any meaningful mark is walka—a practice Anangu have always used to mark objects, bodies and the physical landscape in sometimes enduring, at other times ephemeral, ways.[20] Rose took photographs of a young girl at Bloodwood Bore, who had a wire that Anangu call mani mani, making marks in the red dirt as part of a storytelling practice called milpatjunanyi, which involves drawing lines in the sand and beating the earth to establish the narrative's rhythm. This practice is evoked in a description of marking punu from the Amata community:

> And it is said in the olden times, beating the sand with a stick, they were telling stories. And now, thinking of these stories, we tell them and draw them. These stories are caused to rise in our work. And we work truly hard making these stories rise by drawing.[21]

Walka encoded punu with stories and knowledge. In *The Pitjantjatjara and Their Crafts*, Peter Brokensha noted there were arguments that artefacts being produced were 'non-traditional' due to the fact they were being 'made for money'. He argued that although the objects were no longer used for their traditional purpose, 'the tendency for change and adaption was more pronounced'; yet, the practice of branding objects with walka retained some 'traditionality' through the depiction of stories and myths.[22] Although Rose described the poker work used by Anangu as ornamentation, he did also note that Anangu stated 'quite emphatically' some designs were used only by women, while others were used only by men, indicating that the designs had cultural significance as well. Rose also observed that while the men sometimes used karku, or red ochre, to decorate their artefacts for sale, women never used karku because it was 'too dangerous for them'. Despite Rose's efforts to maintain a discrete distinction between 'sacred' and 'profane' art, the evidence at Bloodwood Bore showed punu to be capable of moving between domains, thus leading him to comment, somewhat ironically, 'so much for what one might call profane art'.[23]

Appadurai argues that space and time are 'socialised and localised through complex and deliberate practices of performance, representation, and action'.[24] Furthermore, he states that a tendency to focus on practices of localisation as being either *cosmological* or *ritual*, distracts us from their 'active, intentional, and productive character', and creates the 'dubious impression of mechanical reproduction'.[25] In my reading of Tjuki's and Sandra's oral histories, and Rose's ethnography and fieldwork diaries, the 'truly hard' work of making the stories rise in punu can be understood as a technique in the 'hard, often deliberate work of place making'.[26] Similar to the earlier nineteenth-century examples of tourism-inspired commodity production in the southeast of Australia and in North America, punu emerged in the midst of increasing economic marginalisation experienced by A̲nangu as a result of colonisation. Carved wooden objects continued to play an integral role in the local economy, metamorphosing from technologies produced to exploit the natural resources of the desert, to commodities that were exchanged for cash. More than just a commodity, punu provided A̲nangu with the raw materials for a vibrant social life; this merging of economies enabled them to continue to carve a place for themselves in the desert.

Bloodwood Bore really was a 'new' Angas Downs. The emergence of roads, bores, 'ration-times' and tourists heralded a new era in the cultural encounter on the station. At a time that is largely characterised as a period of increasing dependence, the punu trade at Bloodwood Bore provided people with significant economic freedoms. As money from the sale of punu was assimilated into existing modes of exchange, it acted alongside game, rations and other material goods as an essential conduit for the expression of kinship. As anthropologist Diane Austin-Broos has highlighted, for 'people who are economically marginal and pushed to the edge of the nation-state, these kind of relations have central importance'.[27] Bloodwood Bore's *locatedness* resulted in a set of circumstances that enabled Anangu to keep skills and knowledge in circulation. Punu afforded a greater degree of economic independence than on other stations or mission settlements at the time, and thus emerged as a vehicle for asserting and maintaining cultural identity during a period of marked change.

Despite the economic benefits that punu generated for Anangu, the emergence of tourism in the region presented the Northern Territory Welfare Branch with a new set of challenges. By the mid-1960s, the punu trade had extended from Bloodwood Bore to form a network of trading sites along the road between Angas Downs and Uluru. Combined with the trade in dingo scalps, and facilitated by the use of camels as a mode of transport, more frequent contact and new forms of social interaction between Anangu emerged. Travelling, trading and exchanging with family, Anangu wove a web of mobility in the southwest that persisted in frustrating Welfare Branch attempts to get them to 'settle' into wage labouring, and domesticated nuclear family units on the mission settlements at Areyonga and Ernabella. Anangu visibility, as well as their mobility, emerged as a significant problem for the Northern Territory administration, and, as such, Anangu are increasingly cast as 'the itinerants' in the records surviving from this period. In tracing the itineraries of 'the itinerants', the next section of this book pans out to situate Bloodwood Bore in the broader regional socioeconomic network, and shift the focus on practices of placemaking from cultures of economy to cultures of travel.

PART 4

ITINERARIES

11

'WE WERE ALWAYS TRAVELLING'

THE ALTERNATING RHYTHM of ananyi (travelling) and nyinanyi (camping) described in Chapter Two still characterises contemporary desert life. Anangu regularly journey along well-travelled roads that connect communities and kin in a dense network of relatedness spanning the southwest region. The 'Bush Bus' plays a central role in contemporary Anangu life, servicing over thirty-five remote communities spatially organised in several 'clusters' that lie to the north, south and west from Mparntwe (Alice Springs). The Docker River route leaves Mparntwe twice a week, stopping at Erldunda, Mount Ebenezer, Imanpa, Curtin Springs, Yulara and Mutitjulu along the 750-kilometre trip through the southwest.

Everybody 'out bush' knows the Bush Bus timetable—what day the bus is due to come through and what route it's following. It seemed as though Anangu always began talking about the bus's arrival not long before it got there, making sure to tell me it was coming and where it was going. People would begin milling around in anticipation. When it finally did arrive, there was always a flurry of activity and noise as people got off the bus and mingled, seeing who was on it, who was in community, and who was travelling where. Some people visited the shop, gathering supplies for the long journey, while others passed on things to give to people in other places. As I witnessed the various exchanges taking place along the Bush Bus itinerary, I began to realise that these encounters were more than just stopping-off points on a journey from A to B. These moments punctuate spatially and socially; they are an ongoing dialogue that connects people and place in a wider network of kinship. As I watched people come and go and intersect, I came to understand that mobility is a fundamental fact of desert life and, as Tim Ingold suggests, it is the path, not the place, that is the primary condition of *being-in place*.[1]

Geographer Tim Cresswell defines 'constellations of mobility' as patterns, representations and ways of moving that are not only interrelated but also specific to particular times and places.[2] In other words, he sees constellations of mobility as having broadly traceable histories and geographies. Through hearing Aṉangu stories in all of the communities along that Docker River Bush Bus route, I came to understand that the contemporary constellation of movement and meaning in which the bus travelled resonated with earlier patterns of movement, relations and exchange.

Although Angas Downs was the initial focal point for the oral histories we recorded together, Tjuki Pumpjack's memories often took us on journeys to places well beyond the station's boundaries. Sitting down at some old cattle yards at Wilpiya in March 2013, Tjuki seemed oblivious to the oppressive heat, and the clouds of flies that circled all around us. It was one of those days when the sun's rays were so hot, you could feel the thick atmosphere as you moved. The flies, too, were thick, forming in black patches on our bodies, and irritating my eyes, ears and nose. As Linda Rive and I sat sweating and swatting furiously, an unperturbed Tjuki told us that where we were sitting was the place he walked to with his family as a young child in search of his father's older sister. He told us that Wilpiya was on an old iwara, which is the Pitjantjatjara word for a track or travel route. Motioning southward along the iwara, Tjuki said that, a long time ago, Wilpiya spring, as well as others, used to carry water all along that iwara:

> People have been living beside this water since ancient times. The water would flow down this watercourse here. The spring was

> just over there, at that small spring area there. We had to jump over, or cross over, to the other side, stamping our feet as we landed on the pathway to the water, when the water was still here.
>
> The water is now long gone, since the wanampi left, probably he has gone much deeper inside the ground, and taken the water with him. Previously, however, there was a pond of water here, which flowed from the spring to that hill there. We would cross over the water to the other side. Naked people did this, landing on the other side, stamping their feet on the banks of the water. Later, we crossed over in cars and camels, as we travelled. We stepped over it, riding our camels, when we were on our way to Ernabella. We were always travelling.
>
> People have always come to this water, lighting their fires as they walked—all those naked people. We'd see them coming along, 'Fire's burning over there!'—and then some people would arrive. They would stay for a while, and then move on. This water was on a very important route that everybody used to take, on the way to Areyonga. For rations. By way of Ilara.[3]

Tjuki said that Aṉangu were always travelling. Petroglyphs and grinding stones, juxtaposed with the decaying remains of cattle yards and rusted-out troughs, are the material remains of past mobilities that continue to resonate at Wilpiya. Sitting in that place, Tjuki wanted to emphasise that Aṉangu had been living around Wilpiya and Walara since the beginning of time—that it has been a really bountiful area, abundant in kangaroos, goannas, lizards, quandongs, fruit, honey ants and springs. He wanted Linda and me to know that was how people lived for a really long time, making sure that we understood he wasn't talking about people he knew, but people who belonged to another time.[4]

Although the creation of the track and Wilpiya spring belong to deep time, this iwara is commonly evoked as the route that linked Areyonga mission—established to the west of Hermannsburg at a place known as Utju—with Ernabella mission, in the south at Pukatja. It constitutes a significant thread in the fabric of Anangu collective memory, as rendered in oral histories and other memory-making that is itself often produced during travel along the same route. This track was impressed upon my consciousness as a result of four years of talking with Anangu while recording oral histories for this research and simultaneously working for the Ara Irititja project in communities intimately connected to that iwara. This route was one of the most striking features to emerge throughout the course of this research and my work with Anangu, and one of the strongest themes I encountered in Anangu collective memory from the southwest region. For this reason, I use the names Areyonga and Ernabella throughout to reflect the particular time and place that I trace this iwara and the way in which Anangu collective memory speaks this history.

I think of this iwara as a 'story track'. Anthropologists David and Lesley Green define 'story tracks', in relation to their fieldwork for a public archaeology project in Arukwa, Brazil, as a mode of memory that represents a way of 'doing history' in everyday life.[5] Different from, but related to, 'story maps' that characteristically recount itineraries of travel by listing place names, 'story tracks' give form to a historical consciousness, in the sense that one was following a historical trail, but also to a temporal consciousness of multiple generations and species that have dwelled there.[6] 'Doing history' in this sense, they argue, is less a case of following lines through time than it is having a conversation with place. And more than just 'doing history' or demonstrating ecological knowledge, 'story tracks' reflect a way of knowing and living in a place by moving through it.[7]

Tracing the 'story track' between Areyonga and Ernabella missions in oral histories, noting the intersections and entanglements with other tracks and modes of memory-making, has illuminated which of the older rhythms of travel continue to resonate. The iwara connects Tjuki's travels recounted in his autobiographical narratives with the ecological times of the spring, the cosmological travels of the Wanampi, and historical times of camels, cars, rations and the missions. While the iwara was carved into the earth by the Ancestors in the Tjukurpa, Tjuki's memories reveal the new layers of meaning and values that came to be inscribed in places, and along lines of travel, deriving from their associations with human activities in the historical remembered past.[8]

In just one example of many iterations of the journey recorded by Tjuki Pumpjack, he describes travelling between Ernabella and Areyonga:

> We would bring them along that road, and I'd come from Walara, and we would leave Walara and go out along Wilpiya, and arrive halfway, fairly close to Atila. That's our old road, the old route we used to take. Nothing there now. People used to come up and follow that road right up to Areyonga. They would go to Areyonga for rations. And then they'd get those rations and put them on their shoulders, sometimes the tops of their head ... It was a long way to carry that much flour on the top of the head. We would go to Marutjura, and other people would go via Atila. Go via Anari. Some of the people, half of them, would have camels and the camels would carry stuff. The camels would carry the flour all the way back to Ernabella, and arrive back there. And they would have done that journey using the flour they got all the way from Areyonga.[9]

Niningka Lewis lived in Ernabella, but was born near Areyonga mission while her parents were visiting relatives there. She says that her parents would visit Areyonga for long stretches of time, but would always go back to Ernabella. Niningka recounts the itinerary in some detail:

> If you left Ernabella and camped halfway, the next day you'd arrive at Wanukulu. You'd spend a night at Wanukulu and then you'd walk for two days before you arrived at Tjulu. You'd leave Tjulu in the afternoon and then sleep halfway at a station windmill and then in the afternoon you'd get to Angas Downs or Bloods Bore [Bloodwood Bore]. You'd come to Bloods Bore. That was Mr Liddle's station. That was his station. He'd be there with his

> wife [Bessie Liddle] ... That's her place. That's where she used to live. She was nice, she'd give us rations ... She is a lovely woman. That's her country right there, Tempe Downs. Her husband had the station. The two of them lived there on that station ... From Angas Downs you walk to Walara, and sleep there one night. From Walara you would walk and finally arrive at Irawa Bore and you'd spend another night there. Then another days' walk with a sleep in between, and then finally the next day you would walk into Tempe Downs with your camels or your donkeys ... After one night sleep at Tempe Downs you would get up and walk the next day, and by the afternoon you'd be entering Areyonga ... Walking fairly slowly, with a string of donkeys, it was a good holiday.[10]

In this oral history, Niningka is travelling north. The places she recalls in the journey between Ernabella and Areyonga include a string of water sources that run like an artery in a north to south direction through the middle of southern Central Australia (**Map 3**). This string of water sources, and the pastoral stations and mission settlements that capitalised on them, provided a well-used corridor of mobility that continued to sustain A<u>n</u>angu socioeconomic life well into the postwar period. At various times and places across the earth, well-known and reliable water sources, such as springs, wells, rivers and mangroves, have provided the environmental and geographic foundations for rich and densely patterned travel and trade routes that Arturo Escobar refers to in a Colombian context as 'life corridors'.[11] Despite the stark contrast between the mangrove environments of Colombia and the arid rangelands of the interior, as 'life corridors' these logical lines of movement reveal 'routes' as rich sites for exploring cultures of economy and travel, and the cultural encounter in Australia.[12]

Sandra Armstrong went to school at Areyonga mission before she went to live at Bloodwood Bore when she was about eighteen years old. During that time, her parents lived on Angas Downs. When it

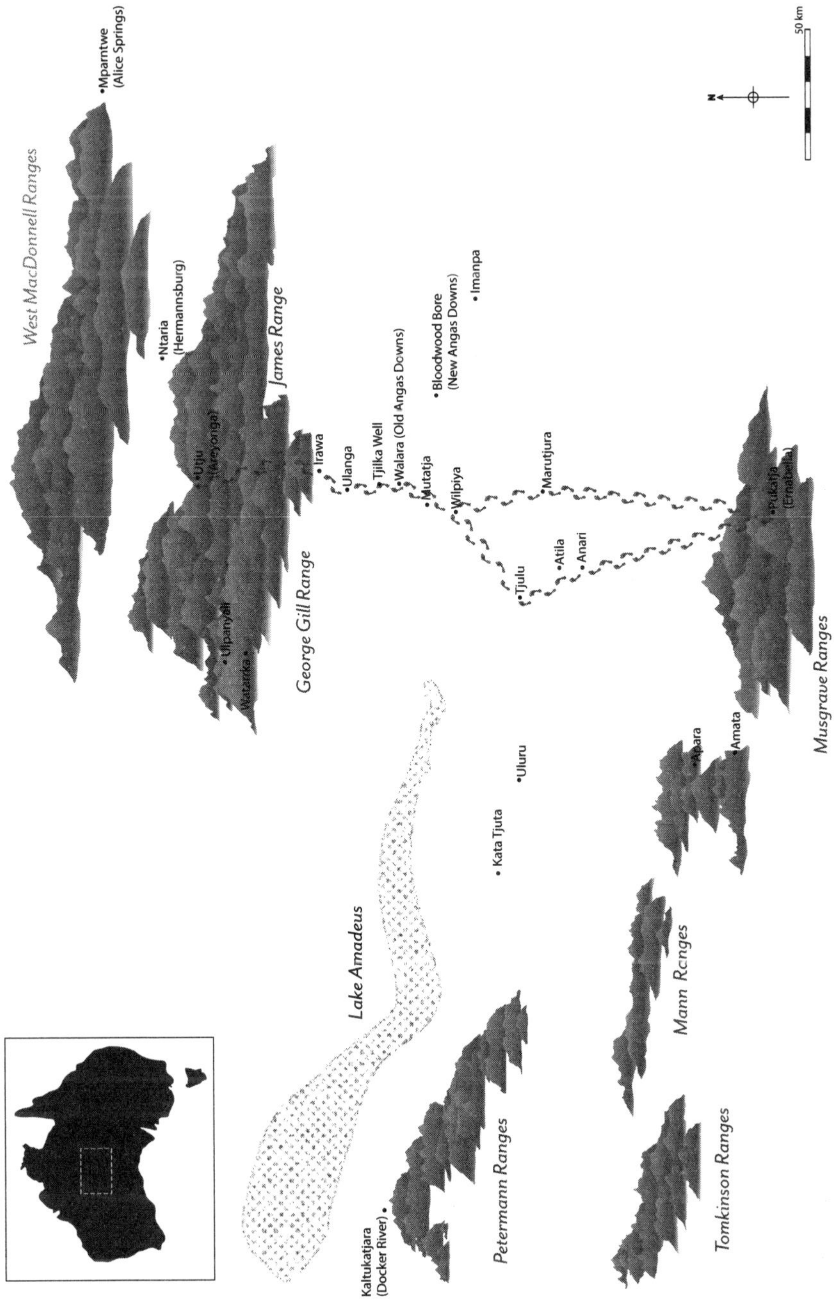

Map 3 is of the southwest, showing the 'story track' traced in A̲nangu oral histories recounting the journey between Areyonga and Ernabella missions. The places noted along the iwara are the water sources that form this Central Australian 'life corridor'. (Courtesy Felix Meyer)

was school holiday time, Sandra would travel to Bloodwood Bore and spend time on the station with her family:

> Yes, we used to go long distances from here for school. We would both travel without a second thought, any travelling, all of those relations. There were family here from Ernabella and when they travelled, they would visit different places and in turn would come to Areyonga; they'd travel to Areyonga, travel to Ernabella and I would see this. And a whitefella there (whose name I have forgotten) worked for the government and he would come and take us for school and find us when we would hide out at the station, all of those younger children, but we were able to see who was on board for school and we would get in with our family and go.[13]

Sandra's experience of going to school on the mission and walking to the station to be with family for the holidays is not unique. Across the broader body of Aṉangu oral histories, journeys made during 'holiday time' from Areyonga mission to Angas Downs and Tempe Downs stations emerge as an important theme. As part of my community engagement work with Aṟa Irititja, I worked in Uṯju, which was the site of Areyonga mission. I also worked in Imanpa, Mutitjulu and Docker River, and many people in these communities went to school at Areyonga. Throughout the course of my time in these places, working with Aṉangu and the archival materials held in Aṟa Irititja, I heard many Aṉangu talk about their travels between Areyonga mission and the stations that lay to the south, to visit family at holiday time. Collections that featured photographs from Areyonga mission in the postwar era were some of the most popular, and there are many oral histories held in Aṟa Irititja that recall this particular journey to and from school on the mission and the stations.

Education was a cornerstone of assimilation policy in the Northern Territory, and Welfare Branch employees were charged with the responsibility of gathering up children living with their families on stations and enforcing their attendance at school on one of the missions. Sandra Armstrong recalls patrol officers threatening parents with cutting off their rations if their school-age children were not in school:

> Government officials came and if any children on the bush stations were continually missing school, they'd come and talk (to the families) about taking them to school. The government came and took them to school but sometimes we'd hide, and they said, 'Your mother and father won't receive any rations,' and when they said that, we became afraid and we'd think, 'I'm going to school. I've been there before,' and we'd go to school when there were any visitors travelling from Ernabella to Areyonga.[14]

This policy of 'rounding up' and removing children to go to school was a significant factor in Areyonga and Ernabella emerging as pivotal hubs in A<u>n</u>angu itineraries. In a letter written to Frederick Rose before his arrival on Angas Downs, Bill Harney informed him that the Welfare Branch were 'ever around gathering up the children so that they can go to school on one of the settlements'.[15] His time at Bloodwood Bore led Rose to question the efficiency of the policy, on the grounds that the opportunities for using education were 'almost non-existent'. He also observed that the policy of placing children on mission settlements for schooling had had a 'profound effect on the pattern of movement of the itinerant Aborigines' and that journeys made to Areyonga were, in large part, to visit children at the settlement.[16] Rose noted, too, that the two main mission centres with a 'direct influence' on A<u>n</u>angu at Angas Downs were Ernabella and Areyonga. However, he wrote that it was by 'tacit agreement' Angas Downs fell within the sphere of influence of Areyonga.[17]

Sandra Armstrong emphasises the importance of food in her willingness to go to school away from her family. She says that she thought about school '*from a different angle*' from the government officials:

> [Y]es, it was going to where the food was, they would force us [to go] and to attend a good school and do good things, but I came to the view, 'Oh, there's good food to eat at school also and it's good to learn.'[18]

When asked why she went to school at Areyonga and not Ernabella, Sandra explained that the people who 'took us' would 'take us' through Angas Downs to Areyonga and that 'those South Australians are a different group'.[19] In her field notes from Areyonga in 1964–65, anthropologist Nancy Munn described the distinctions and connections between these two sites:

> Most of the Areyonga Pitjantjatjara come originally from the Petermann Range and bordering areas. They contrast themselves with people whom they also call Pitjantjatjara from the Musgrave, Mann and Tomkinson to the south by pointing out that the latter are 'south side' and can be labelled nyangapurunypatjara. In contrast, the northern peoples ('north side') are called nyangapinypatjara. Nyanga means 'this': puruny and piny are different terms for 'like' and here serve to symbolise a distinction between what my informants regarded as two different but closely related speech communities. Most of the southern people are now aggregated at Ernabella and the southern stations while the northern peoples have gravitated to Areyonga and the relatively northern stations ...
>
> While Areyongans usually recognised speech variations between northern and southern Pitjantjatjara, there were also occasions on which they insisted that the speech of Areyonga and Ernabella people was exactly the same. This variation in attitude is dependent upon context, and also reflects some informants' sense of a close association between themselves and the southern peoples with whom there was (and still is) considerable interaction.[20]

The sociocultural distinctions among people of the Western Desert were reflected in the constellations of people on particular mission settlements and stations in the southwest region. What Rose understood to be a 'tacit agreement' between Angas Downs and Areyonga was more a reflection of these strong sociocultural threads that tied the mission settlements to different geographic locations in the Western Deserts. However, while Sandra clearly sees the Pitjantjatjara at Ernabella as a 'different group', her oral histories, like the broader body of A<u>n</u>angu oral history and memory, demonstrate that even though 250 kilometres separate Areyonga and Ernabella, people living in these places kept in regular contact. These two mission settlements, and the stations that lay between them, became the knots that tied the threads of travel together in a network that took shape as A<u>n</u>angu incorporated new places into existing patterns of mobility.

12

THE ITINERANTS

THESE LINES OF travel not only feature in Anangu stories; they have left traces in the written archives. The 'story track' connecting Ernabella and Areyonga in Anangu oral history narratives also appears in Welfare Branch patrol reports and correspondence. In 1960 a Welfare Branch patrol officer was sent out with the purpose of surveying the southwest to 'ascertain the reasons for and the destination of the current movements of the Pitjantjatjara people and also the general route used by them'. Patrol officer Giddens noted that previous reports had indicated Curtin Springs and Angas Downs were most frequently visited and would prove the 'most fruitful field for inquiry'. The patrol officer reported thirty-eight Pitjantjatjara people camped at Angas Downs, noting that:

> The party was enroute from Ernabella to Areyonga and with the exception of the two Areyonga natives ... all were Ernabella people ... The two men from Areyonga stated that they had gone from Areyonga to Ernabella in recent weeks and it is assumed that they acted as messengers to invite and to conduct the party to a possible ceremony at Areyonga ... No other travellers to Areyonga were located at other centres but the various pastoralists reports indicate that an almost direct route from Ernabella to Areyonga is used taking advantage of what possible sources of water and food exist

including the station homesteads of Mulga Park, Curtin Springs, Angas Downs and Tempe Downs.

Giddens' patrol of the southwest led him to conclude in his report that the opportunity to attend ceremony was 'irresistible' and, as such, the Pitjantjatjara migrations would prove difficult to keep in check. The report noted that any action to discourage movements from Areyonga or Ernabella would have to be in the form of the deprivation of rations, but Giddens felt that could prove too harsh a measure to mete out during the dry conditions that prevailed at the time. He recommended that a closer relationship be established with the pastoral stations on the general travel route, to 'prevent such undesirable congregations'.[1]

Anangu are constantly referred to as being 'itinerant' in the correspondence, and the subject line of patrol reports and directives was often 'The Itinerant Aborigines':

> The itinerant Aboriginals presently at Victory Downs have come mainly from Musgrave Park, Mount Davies and the Giles area, and those at Angas Downs seem to be continually on the move between Areyonga and Ernabella and the cattle stations in between. Efforts are continually being made to try and persuade them to either return to Areyonga where their children can attend school or to Ernabella mission. However, they are very independent and spend a large amount of their time wandering around Angas Downs, Mount Ebenezer, Victory Downs and Mulga Park.[2]

'Itinerant' describes a person who wanders from place to place. However, in the Welfare Branch correspondence the use of the term 'itinerant' to describe groups of travelling Anangu refers to more than just habitual wandering. Rather, 'itinerant' emerges in the correspondence files as shorthand for 'unemployed' and 'idle natives'.[3] The prevailing policy in the 1960s sought to assimilate Aboriginal people through education, domestication and the transformation of the 'hunter–gather' to wage labourer within the settler capitalist economy. Within this political economy, Anangu mobility was understood as inherently problematic.

This mobile mode of engagement with the world, and the challenges it presented to assimilationist objectives of social reform, is not unique to this time and place. The construction of the category of 'vagrant', and the criminalisation of 'vagrancy', emerged in early modern Europe—in particular, those places that entered earliest into the period of mercantile capitalism, such as Holland and England in the late sixteenth century.[4] Angus Bancroft's study of Roma and Gypsy-Travellers in Europe notes that the construction of the 'vagrant' illustrated two developments, which combined to 'produce a modern idea of spatial order and control'.[5] The first was the establishment of the nation-state guaranteeing property rights. The other:

> [W]as the emergence of the work ethic and the reviling of those nomadic individuals who appeared to reject it, and so were a threat to its legitimacy.

Bancroft writes that Gypsy-Travellers in the early modern period were subsumed into the general category of vagrants, and, in some parts of Europe, were subject to severe repression, punishment and segregation, which served to authenticate the emerging European social order and work ethic. In this sense, Bancroft argues, the construction of the vagrant was important in the construction of 'a settled European identity', whereby 'work ethic, the morality of property, and civility, were set off against the vagrant, the vagabond and wandering Gypsy'. Coinciding with the emergence of the modern bureaucratic nation-state in the eighteenth century, governmental responses to itinerant travellers, Bancroft notes, changed from a position of repression and punishment to policies of *forcible incorporation* within the nation-state.[6]

Anthropologist Liisa Malkki has argued that ideas about countries, cultures, roots, nations and national identities are associated with a 'powerful sedentarism' representing a way of thinking that is 'taken for granted to such an extent that it is nearly invisible'.[7] Ideas of land and possession are central to the creation and maintenance of the nation-state and, as Malkki observes, the ways in which nation-states are constructed as natural, or normal, rest upon the idea of mobility as a problem—an anomaly requiring correction.[8] James Scott's research into modern state crafting was the result of wanting to 'understand why the state has always seemed to be the enemy of "people who move around"'.[9] Originally focused on Southeast Asia, Scott noted that the question transcended regional geography:

> Nomads and pastoralists (such as Berbers and Bedouins), hunter-gatherers, Gypsies, vagrants, homeless people, itinerants, runaway slaves, and serfs have always been a thorn in the side of nation states.[10]

Inspired by these analyses of the relationship between mobility and sedentarism, I read 'the itinerants' as they emerge in the Northern Territory Welfare Branch's correspondence files within this broader geographical and historical context that is the Australian settler state's colonial inheritance.

'The itinerants' is just one of many ways in which Aboriginal mobility has been imagined and constructed within colonial power relations since Europeans arrived in Australia in 1788. Branding Aboriginal people as 'nomads' and misrepresenting their mobility as the aimless wandering of the hunter–gather were discursive strategies that underwrote the British possession of the continent and denied recognition of Aboriginal rights to land.[11] Civilising and domesticating both land and people in an effort to make them productive in the settler capitalist economy has been pursued primarily through ideas of sedentarisation. Bain Attwood observed of the so-called 'habitual wanderers' of the Gippsland region in Victoria in the late nineteenth century that Aboriginal mobility at the time was understood by missionaries at Lake Tyres and Ramahyuck missions 'as incompatible with proper control of them',[12] and undermined their efforts towards re-socialising Aboriginal people as sedentary agriculturalists. Attwood illustrated how the sojourns of the 'habitual wanderers' of the Gippsland region in the late nineteenth century were problematic not just because they made the Brabralung hard to control but because their 'excursions' discredited the missions and undermined their 'hard-won reputations'.[13] Despite efforts to civilise the local people and enforce the ethic that 'able-bodied' men should 'work for their bread', as Attwood noted, 'classic problems of economic underdevelopment' meant that an

Aboriginal sense of place persisted, frustrating missionary attempts to convert people to the work and time rhythms of industry capitalism.[14] In this regard, there's little to distinguish twentieth-century assimilation policy from earlier colonial attempts to absorb Aboriginal society into a capitalist wage labour framework. The similarity in the language used, and the objective of resocialisation it conveys, reflects historian Russell McGregor's observation that, rather than articulate a singular meaning, assimilation policy after the 1930s represented a re-emergence of a 'discourse that runs throughout the history of Aboriginal-European interactions'.[15]

The normalisation of sedentarisim in the national, or natural, order of things, has resulted in the pathologisation of mobility. The missionaries at Lake Tyers and Ramahyuck pathologised Aboriginal mobility, claiming that itinerant behaviour led to the people squandering money, drinking and associating with 'depraved' white men, which inevitably resulted in the 'habitual wanderers' returning to the mission 'unwell in mind and body'.[16] This moral pathologisation of mobility has been a similarly powerful force in the desert.

The preoccupation with 'the itinerants' in the southwest in the 1960s was nothing new. As earlier chapters have demonstrated, movement of peoples in the region, both Aboriginal people and white pastoralists, emerged as a 'problem' for the prevailing social order. Despite concerted efforts to 'settle' and 'civilise' both the landscape and the population, sedentarising the nomadic people of the so-called 'hinterlands' continued to elude and frustrate the administration in the postwar period. Correspondence and reports generated over the years following Giddens' 1960 patrol reveal the Welfare Branch preoccupation with stemming the flow of 'idle' and 'unemployed' 'itinerants' as something of an obsession. This fixation is evidenced in hundreds of pages of census taking and report making, documenting attempts to 'settle' A̲nangu at either Ernabella or Areyonga mission and place them into 'permanent employment'. More than an account of A̲nangu mobility, the Welfare Branch's documents, both in the construction of A̲nangu as 'the itinerants' and in the records that tracked their movements, reveal the value of the archive as an artefact of white settler colonial ways of constructing the world. In this sense, I read this documentary archive not to discover facts about the past but to understand what the Welfare Branch wanted to do, what its patrol officers thought they were doing and what was actually happening on the ground.

The Aṉangu way of moving in the world was understood by the Welfare Branch as antithetical to the work ethic. The fixation on sedentarising Aṉangu, and fostering the transformation from subsistence lifestyle to wage labourer, is reflective of a regime of values, tightly woven into the very fabric of settler capitalism. This system of values rendered patrol officers and administrators largely ignorant of the ways in which Aṉangu were incorporating the limited economic opportunities available to them into existing social and ecological itineraries. When the punu trade came to the attention of the Welfare Branch, 'the few shillings' that Aṉangu made was understood as undermining attempts to teach them the principle of 'work for pay', while encouraging them to be 'parasites' on society. However, there are traces in the correspondence files that reveal the anxieties surrounding the trade in artefacts to be about more than parasitism. When it was brought to his attention, the Director of Welfare, Harry Giese, viewed the punu trade as resulting in 'the undesirable situation of large numbers of unemployed and idle natives' congregating in camps outside of stations and mission settlements.[17] In a letter to the Assistant Director of the Southern branch, Giese noted:

> The congregation of itinerant Aboriginals ... will need to be carefully watched. You will appreciate that groups such as these can do considerable harm to the public image of the work we are attempting to do and therefore all possible steps should be taken to reduce their number and their assemblies as much as possible.[18]

The emergence of tourism in the region presented the Welfare Branch with a new set of challenges and, as such, it was Aṉangu visibility, as much as their mobility, that posed a problem.

In a letter accompanying a patrol report, Assistant Director of Welfare Les Penhall wrote to Giese and acknowledged that Aṉangu, 'like many people in the Northern Territory' at the time, were 'out to make what they can while the tourist season' was on. However, he noted that their 'bedraggled and neglected appearance' presented a problem from a 'public relations' perspective:

> The public relations aspect is important if the policy of the Government is to succeed and there is no doubt that these camps are undesirable from a Health, Education and Social Advancement point of view.

Penhall issued a directive requesting that regular patrols be carried out. Patrol officers were instructed not to pay maintenance to station owners for the provision of rations to 'itinerants', in the hope that hunger would force them onto the settlements. Station owners were told to inform the branch of 'any unusual accumulation of Natives on their properties'; patrol officers were to seek the cooperation of tourism companies in order to stop tourists engaging with camps of 'itinerants'.[19] Penhall's instructions reveal the irony of a situation that required patrol officers to be highly mobile in order to stop Anangu from interacting with groups of mobile tourists, in an attempt to get them to settle.

In October 1965 patrol officer DA Stewart was sent out to investigate:

> [T]he sale of artefacts by Aboriginals to tourists travelling the roads to and from Ayers Rock and the approach and appearance of Aboriginals as seen by the tourists.

Stewart reported learning of 'several perturbing activities'. While visiting Mulga Park station, he 'heard' of the 'methods being used by Aboriginals to stop tourists':

> The usual method adopted is for a group of children to run out and flag down a car or a bus and then those adults with artefacts to sell converge on the tourists. Some of the aboriginal women deliberately remove a clean dress and have a dirty torn one on underneath and this is to give the tourist the impression that they

> are in distressed circumstances, and that nobody, especially this Branch, has done anything to provide for them.[20]

Constant references in the records to the encounter between A<u>n</u>angu and tourists as a threat to the 'public image' of the Welfare Branch's work shed light on the very real anxieties that, despite appearances, all was not as it should be—and, even worse, that word might get out. To complicate matters further, A<u>n</u>angu were not the only group of 'itinerants' proving difficult to control:

> Those of us who come into contact with tourists in Central Australia invariably find that they wish to see Aboriginals in their primitive state and whether they are interested in the work that is being done on Settlements or not, they are forever asking whether they can find groups such as this ... Tourist bus drivers are quite aware of this and naturally they are pleased to see itinerant groups so that they can cater for the needs of their clients.[21]

Despite concerted efforts to discourage and prevent the encounter between A<u>n</u>angu and tourists, the branch found it difficult to oppose the tourist desire for encounters of the 'primitive' kind. Furthermore, patrol officers were reporting that the policy of not paying maintenance for those A<u>n</u>angu who refused to relocate permanently at one of the mission settlements had 'done little to solve the problem'.[22]

It was apparent to the Welfare Branch that the artefact trade had given rise to an emergent local economy and was playing a significant role in A<u>n</u>angu migrations. Numerous references in the correspondence files that acknowledge the role of punu in supplementing a subsistence lifestyle are accompanied by statements that the policy of withholding rations was failing to discourage itinerant behaviour. A<u>n</u>angu were able to obtain sufficient food for themselves by selling artefacts or trading in dingo scalps, as well as sharing in the rations of permanent station residents, which was being complemented with 'bush tucker'.[23] In conceding that the policy of the Welfare Branch was failing, patrol officer Stewart lamented that another 'form of control' was proving difficult to determine:[24]

> The itinerant aboriginals in the area have become quite independent of the Government aid although they will accept it whenever it is offered. It seems that their main object of being in the area is to carry out rituals that are important to them and in view of the fact that this Branch is not prepared to maintain them, they have maintained themselves by living off country to some extent, but like many other people in the Territory these days, supplementing their other means of subsistence by exploiting the tourist industry ... I am sure that they are not the least bit concerned about the harm which they may do to themselves or to this Branch so far as the public image is concerned.[25]

Despite coercive policy aimed at forcing people onto settlements, the Welfare Branch was faced with the reality that A_n_angu moved, as Assistant Director Les Penhall described it, 'of their own free will and not usually at the instigation of anyone in particular'.[26] Patrol officers reported that, in response to being asked to relocate to a settlement or mission, A_n_angu would be most agreeable, often saying that they would be moving on 'next Monday', but in reality moving when they were 'good and ready', and returning to the area as soon as they felt the need.[27]

Reading A_n_angu itineraries alongside the Welfare Branch's construction of them as 'the itinerants' in the written archives, it's possible to see how A_n_angu mobility and ways of being-in-the-world were imagined and understood by the Northern Territory Administration. The Welfare Branch correspondence is marked by tension and uncertainty, which makes it a productive site for comprehending the ways in which the settler capitalist state both sought and struggled to *forcibly incorporate* A_n_angu into its cultural and economic order. From the perspective of the Welfare Branch and patrol officers, the transformation of the itinerant A_n_angu into domestic family units, provided for by 'able-bodied' wage labourers, would teach them the principle of individual effort for individual gain and make them responsible citizens of the nation. If only they could get them to stay in one place long enough.

13

THE WALKABOUT LEADERS

THE WELFARE BRANCH was acutely aware that A<u>n</u>angu mobility was linked to cultural objectives as well as economic ones, and that patrol officers were largely powerless in their attempts to curb people's movement.[1] Writing to the Director of Welfare some four years after first commencing the patrols to investigate 'the itinerants' in the southwest, Assistant Director Lovegrove conceded:

> I don't think the situation has changed at all since we first commenced these visits and the Aboriginals in this area have their own very definite ideas on when they will travel there, what they will do while they are there, and when they will return.[2]

While the documents record the difficulties the Welfare Branch encountered in stopping itinerant behaviour, there's no serious consideration of how the rules that were being made might be understood, or what the people who were subject to them may have wanted.

The intransigence that was undermining Welfare Branch attempts to get A<u>n</u>angu to 'settle' was embodied in the men the branch referred to as the 'Walkabout leaders'. Widely known in the present-day communities of the southwest (and most likely beyond, in places such as Hermannsburg, Haasts Bluff and Papunya), Harry Brumby, Captain No. 1 and Nipper Winmati were named in numerous patrol reports as the leaders of the 'itinerants'. Many of the encounters between patrol officers and A<u>n</u>angu appear in reports as a conversation with one of these three men:

> On my return from Docker River on the 14th September, I contacted a fairly large group of Aboriginals who were temporarily camped at the Mulga Park turnoff from Ayers Rock road. There was about 30 Aboriginals in this group and they informed me that they were travelling to Areyonga. They intended to join up with the group camped at Angas Downs turnoff. All of these people were travelling by means of camels and they expected to be at Areyonga in about a weeks time. This group was lead by the well-known 'Walkabout' leader, Nipper ... It is now becoming fairly obvious that this particular group of Aboriginals do not intend settling anywhere.[3]

References to the 'Walkabout leaders' in the documents are thoroughly entangled with accounts of ceremonial activities, the punu trade, 'puppy dogging' and 'holidays'. Mention of their names is generally accompanied by an acknowledgement of their persistent refusal to settle, despite the repeated requests of the patrol officers for them to do so. In almost all instances of reported contact with these men, patrol officers recorded the use of camels as an essential means of transport.

In *To Ayers Rock and Beyond*, Bill Harney describes the camel as an integral part of the A<u>n</u>angu resistance to white settler ways:

> [L]ooking over the whole party I felt that I was in the presence of a people who were masters of their tribal lands. The camels too were somehow part of the picture. Having once opened this country they were now the chattels of a nomad race who refused to be bondsmen for white people who think they are free but are slaves to a convention that keeps them working to survive ... What history has been made with the camels?[4]

Far more suited to the arid environment than horses, camels played an important role in the colonisation of the region. Explorers, Afghan traders, pastoralists, missionaries, doggers, police and anthropologists all relied on camels to facilitate their movement through the desert landscape.[5] However, they also played a significant role in the changing A<u>n</u>angu socioeconomic itineraries.[6] In describing A<u>n</u>angu mobility in 1962, Frederick Rose observed that A<u>n</u>angu at Angas Downs journeyed to Areyonga in the north, Uluru and the Petermann Ranges in the west, and to Erldunda in the east, and that they 'were largely dependent on camels for transport'. Rose argued the excess army trucks that became available for purchase at the end of World War II had resulted in a rapid transition from camels to motor vehicles on pastoral stations, which left many pastoralists with 'teams of useless camels on their hands'. The camels were, in turn, given, or sold cheaply, to A<u>n</u>angu to use as they wished, which Rose argued completely 'revolutionised' the ways in which A<u>n</u>angu travelled, particularly in regard to the significantly increased capacity for carrying supplies and belongings.[7]

Rose took great interest in how A<u>n</u>angu had come to incorporate camels into their socioeconomic itineraries and documented in detail, both in writing and photographs, the particular ways that people packed their camels, as well as the reasons for, and the various destinations of, their travel. While at Bloodwood Bore, he documented the contents of the camel pack of No. 45, a Wintalyka man named Jimmy Walkabout. He photographed all the gear in the pack, which included:

- two large ground sheets
- a bundle of clothes, including a shirt, singlet, a pair of trousers and an old coat-tails jacket
- a pillow
- a gallon tin for water
- two leather belts
- a piece of rope
- a 25-pound bag of flour
- a bag of tea and sugar
- a bag of money

Jimmy had also packed a 0.22-inch rifle and apologised to Rose that his wife hadn't yet put her belongings, except for her swag, on the camel. Nipper Winmati, one of the so-called 'Walkabout Leaders', told Rose that he had inherited his camels from his father, and there had originally been seven but three had gone bush. He had recently travelled from Uluru to Angas Downs with nine others, and it had taken four days; he was about to travel to Areyonga, which would take him five days. According to Rose, Nipper emphasised that he didn't travel by the bitumen road tourists used, but through the 'bush using native wells and rock holes for water'.[8]

Rose grouped all of the A<u>n</u>angu living at Angas Downs into 'family units'. He then divided these family units according to whether they were 'permanent' or 'non-permanent' residents at Angas Downs. Rose observed that nine of the eleven 'permanent' family units had no transport facilities, while eight out of the eighteen units that were 'non-permanent' had camels or donkeys. He noted that seven out of the remaining ten 'non-permanent' residents 'were directly attached to other units possessing transport facilities'.[9] Rose's observations are a rich resource for understanding the extent to which camels impacted on changing patterns of travel, and the significant role that these animals played in the persistent travel along the Areyonga–Ernabella route. However, Rose's distinctions between 'permanent' and 'non-permanent' should be treated with some caution. He noted that those A<u>n</u>angu he considered to be 'permanent' were almost entirely dependent on government rations and had given up their 'nomadic way of life'. And yet, he also observed that these 'permanent' family units would sometimes leave the camp for weeks at a time, indicating that 'permanent' did not mean entirely sedentary.

Anthropologist Robert Layton has noted that in the period following the establishment of Ernabella and Areyonga, A<u>n</u>angu greatly increased their mobility by adopting camels as transport.[10] This is borne out by Tjuki Pumpjack's oral histories, which emphasise the significant role that these animals came to play along this travel route:

> A very long time ago we used to live at Areyonga. We used to sit down at Areyonga. From there we started out on our journey, on

> camels. We travelled through Mount Connor, and from there we went to Tjulu. From Atila, Mount Connor, we travelled along the road, right down to Ernabella. We arrived in Ernabella and there we stayed for quite a reasonable length of time. After that, we returned. Many people went back to Areyonga again, but I didn't. I stayed on at Old Walara then. I used to go around with camels. My own camels. We used to go very speedily, moving fast through the country.[11]

Layton also noted that camels not only enhanced Aṉangu mobility but were important in transporting and guiding white travellers such as HH Finlayson, Arthur Groom, Charles Mountford and Bill Harney.[12] In *To Ayers Rock and Beyond*, Bill Harney wrote of an encounter with Nipper Winmati and Paddy Uluru at 'the rock', where they told him their methods for catching and breaking in wild camels:

> Naked hunters for ages, they had now adapted themselves to camel transport after the Afghans and Arab camel-men had been pushed off the roads by motor transport. I asked one of the men where he got his camels from. 'Some we buy from 'nother one blackfellow ... pay with puppy-dog scalp ... some we catch in bush where mob run wild'.
>
> 'How you catch them?' I asked him, and he replied 'easy catch camel with nother one camel ... just follow them up all day like dingo when they follow kangaroo ... no-more-long-time camel knock up from follow-business then we throw rope on leg and they lay down on ground just like when man put pack on their back.'
>
> 'They quiet then?' I questioned.
>
> They laughed at my question then Winmati answered, 'camel proper cheeky when caught, but we tie him'.[13]

Harney then negotiated with the men that he would pay them cash to take him into the country west of Uluru with their camels. His recollections reveal that Aṉangu had not only mastered camel husbandry; camels were a potential source of income, as well as a mode of transport.

According to Rose, in 1962 a cow camel was worth ten pounds, while a bull was worth sixteen pounds ten shillings. He noted that

Nipper Winmati's camels were all cows; while Rose was at Bloodwood Bore, Nipper sold a baby camel for ten pounds. His father, who died the year before, also had a baby camel, which he sold to Tjuki Pumpjack's younger brother Johnny Mulla, for ten pounds. When Rose asked Nipper if he would charge for travelling with him and his camels, he said that he would charge Mick (No. 11) two pounds ten shillings to travel from Uluru to Angas Downs, but he wouldn't charge Tjuki Pumpjack, as he was walytja.[14] The average weekly wage for a white male settler in Alice Springs at the time was approximately fourteen pounds, so it isn't surprising that A<u>n</u>angu who owned camels were perceived as being 'rich'.[15]

The A<u>n</u>angu grasp of camel husbandry is also evidenced in the 1969 ethnographic film *Camels and the Pitjantjatjara*. Made by anthropologists Roger Sandall and Nicolas Peterson, the film documents A<u>n</u>angu as they travel from Areyonga, down through Tempe Gap into the mulga and sandhill country to the south, just north of Angas Downs, where they catch and then 'smoke' a wild camel to 'make him quiet'. A man known as Captain No. 1 leads the group.[16] Captain No. 1 is named in the Welfare Branch reports as one of the 'Walkabout leaders'. In a 1966 report, patrol officer Stewart wrote:

> On route between Mulga Park and Curtin Springs I came across a group of twenty Areyonga aboriginals on walkabout. Captain No. 1 who was in charge told me they were going to look for camels and also hunt 'puppy dog'. The group consisted of 9 men, 3 youths, 5 women and 3 children (only one child of school age). On every occasion I have visited this area over the past three years I always seem to strike Captain No. 1 and his group on 'holiday' for one or two weeks. This is probably his method of satisfying a patrol officer, however, it is obvious he has little intention of staying in one place and will continue to 'walkabout' as he wishes.[17]

As the reports of encounters with the 'Walkabout leaders' Nipper Winmati and Captain No. 1 suggest, camels had value beyond that for which they could be sold or exchanged. The animals not only revolutionised the way that A<u>n</u>angu could travel but were an essential means to the trade and exchange of dingo scalps, and the important 'holidays' to Country that 'dogging' trips facilitated.

The trade in dingo scalps was bound up with the business of travelling with camels in the southwest, which A<u>n</u>angu referred to as going 'puppy dogging'. As Chapter One illustrated, 'dogging' was responsible for many of the earliest encounters and economic exchanges between A<u>n</u>angu and white settlers in and around the Musgrave and Petermann Ranges. In 1935 HH Finlayson observed that dingo scalps had become a form of 'currency' exchanged between A<u>n</u>angu and the white man for rations.[18] In 1937 Ernabella mission introduced a policy to pay A<u>n</u>angu the full bounty for dingo scalps, instead of the rations they received from white settlers; this effectively drove the white doggers out of the area, making dingo skins a significant source of cash income for A<u>n</u>angu.[19] Dingo skins remained valuable commodities and continued to play an important role in A<u>n</u>angu socioeconomic itineraries for the next three decades.[20]

Tjuki Pumpjack describes 'puppy dogging' in some detail:

> We were riding our camels and so off we went, right up towards Docker River. We went to Docker River. We were out there to hunt dingoes. Papa tjuta [many dingoes]. Young ones and grown up ones. After we got the dingoes we skinned them and got the skin parts that we could sell. Pangki [skins]. We got all those pangki, a big bag full. We brought our big bag of pangki back with us, as we started to turn back for home. We travelled in a big circle, right around from the Docker River area, turning back for home at that point, and starting to head back towards Ayers Rock again, travelling by way of Mantarur. We came back via a place called Mantarur.
>
> Eventually we arrived back at Ayers Rock at the tourist camp ... The tourists gave us all sorts of things like lollies and so on. Biscuits, food and so on. We started to organise our camels to go. Some people gave us new trousers. We were getting ready to depart on our camels, when some people came up with trousers for us.

> Other people were already getting ready to go so they took our camels, and the tourists helped us by giving us a ride in their tourist vehicle back to Tjulu [Curtin Springs].
>
> At Tjulu we all got out and started to sort through our dingo skins, where we sold them all for brand-new trousers and clothes. Good trousers! Money, $100! We got all sorts of nice new clothes and then we arrived at Walara all clean and smart.
>
> So that was what we did going out to get dingo skins. We went out. Right up towards Docker River and then turned back in a big circle, via Ernabella way. Ernabella was halfway on our big journey and then we went back up to Ayers Rock. There were lots of white people at Ayers Rock, all tourists. After that we went to Tjulu by truck. The other people continued on the three camels while we went to Tjulu by truck.[21]

Over the period that we worked together recording his life history, Tjuki Pumpjack told a number of stories like this one. These dogging trips were always recalled fondly by Tjuki, and in the telling often took on the quality of a travelling epic, as they recounted in detail the journey to the west, and into the Petermann Ranges.

Frederick Rose's fieldwork diaries are filled with references to A<u>n</u>angu coming and going from Angas Downs on dogging trips, none more so than Harry Brumby. Harry Brumby's A<u>n</u>angu name was Tjuwiri, and he was one of the Wintaylka (Mulga Seed) men from the Petermann Ranges who were recorded in William Liddle's daybook as being employed by him in 1939.[22] Tjuki Pumpjack said of Brumby that they had all 'sat down together' at Angas Downs from the 'early days' and that 'he was our kin'.[23] Rose observed that while Brumby had clearly been associated with Angas Downs for a long time:

> He was not one of the 'permanents' and received neither Age Pension nor Sustenance from the Government. He was a man who obviously did not like remaining too long in the camp at Angas Downs.[24]

Furthermore, even though Brumby had been in contact with white people for as long as anyone at Bloodwood Bore, Rose noted he displayed a dislike for remaining in the station camp, 'as if he had an antipathy to remaining too long in contact with the white man'.[25] Brumby appears time and again in Welfare Branch reports as the 'Walkabout leader' who refused to 'settle':

> There are included in this group of about 25 who are led by an aboriginal known as Harry Brumby who is from the Angas Downs, Curtin Springs area. This is the last group who are not really settled at a station or settlement. I have spoken often to Harry about this and he keeps assuring me he will go to Areyonga. I have made it quite clear to him that he will not receive rations at Mulga Park, Curtin Springs or Angas Downs and have told these stations I am not prepared to certify any future maintenance claims which show him and his group.[26]

Despite patrol officers' confidence that refusing to ration Brumby would force him to relocate to Areyonga once it became difficult to obtain food,[27] Rose's fieldwork diaries demonstrate that he had been living relatively independently of the government, and travelling continuously, for years.

On 23 August 1962 Rose noted that Brumby had six pounds ten shillings 'stowed away in a filthy old flour bag'. A week later, he observed that Brumby brought in six dingo scalps, five pups and an adult female, for which Pastor Kaleski from Areyonga paid him five pounds ten shillings. Brumby then left Angas Downs for three weeks, returning on 25 September with fourteen dingo scalps, which, Rose noted, he sold elsewhere—most likely, Curtin Springs. Brumby was also regularly earning cash from selling punu, so, compared with the ten shillings a day that Tjuki Pumpjack was being paid as a stockman (in a lump sum when he went to town), this was not an insignificant amount of money for A<u>n</u>angu.[28]

Evidence suggests that 'puppy dogging' continued to be of significant value in socioeconomic itineraries in the southwest throughout the 1960s. Patrol reports indicate that when conditions permitted, A<u>n</u>angu chose to go 'puppy dogging', forgoing the opportunity to trade punu at the height of the tourist season. In June and July 1966 patrol officer DA Stewart carried out a census in the southwest, paying particular attention to numbers and movements of 'itinerants' in the area. Although the tourist season was 'in full swing', Stewart observed that Anangu were 'not nearly as interested in selling artefacts to tourists as in previous years'. There were several occasions of rain in the first six months of 1966. Stewart recorded that the rains had brought with them plenty of surface water, wildlife and bush foods, and thus the main interest for the 'walkabout' movement that year was 'puppy dog time'. Stewart encountered no itinerants at Mount Ebenezer, Erldunda, Victory Downs or Mulga Park, and only small groups at Curtin Springs, Wilpiya and Angas Downs, all of whom said that they were on 'holiday' and had an interest in hunting 'puppy dog'.[29] For A<u>n</u>angu in the southwest, whose homelands lay in the Western Desert, 'dogging' provided the all-important opportunity to combine earning an income with visiting Country with kin.[30]

While dingo scalps had value in monetary terms, like punu, they were 'thoroughly socialised thing[s]' that circulated in different regimes of value for A<u>n</u>angu.[31] 'Puppy dogging' trips provided the opportunity to hunt for the purpose of economic exchange, while travelling with family and continuing the crucial exchange of knowledge—in story, song and ceremony—among kin in Country. For some who had grown up on mission settlements, or stations, 'puppy dogging holidays' led them to the homelands of their parents and grandparents, some of them for the first time.

The A<u>n</u>angu use of the word 'holidays' in relation to 'puppy dogging' needs to be understood in the broader context of colonial relations at the time. Life on the settlements, particularly on the missions such at Ernabella and Areyonga, was more rigidly controlled than that on the station at Angas Downs. 'Puppy dogging' not only presented an opportunity to travel with family, visiting Country and sharing knowledge, but was a response to the highly ordered regimes on the mission settlements. 'Puppy dogging' trips gave A<u>n</u>angu an opportunity to earn an income, while moving around and experiencing the world in ways that they were accustomed to, free from the imposed order and structure of the settlements, and the Welfare Branch's overt efforts to make them settle. The country to the west was known for plentiful supplies of dingoes, and had always been difficult for white settlers to travel, so while out there, A_n_angu really were on 'holiday'.

The enhanced mobility of travelling with camels, coupled with the money or goods acquired from the exchange of dingo scalps and punu, as well as rations supplied to 'permanent' residents on the stations and mission settlements, gave large groups of A_n_angu significant freedoms during the 1950s and 1960s. In the web of mobility and meaning traced in the southwest throughout this period, it wasn't just homelands in the Western Desert that emerged as significant sites; the stations and mission settlements were also important nodes in the constellation of mobility that emerged. The settlements at Angas Downs, Mulga Park, Victory Downs, Musgrave Park, Ernabella and Areyonga are cited consistently throughout the Welfare Branch correspondence files, particularly in relation to ceremonial activities.

Before the emergence of pastoralists and missionaries, and their abundant supplies of food, large ceremonial gatherings in the Western Desert and Central Australian Ranges would have been infrequent, made possible only during times of ecological abundance. By the 1960s it was apparent that the emergence of ration depots had worked to alter the ceremonial migration of people. The provision of a stable and consistent food supply allowed for an increase in the frequency and duration of rituals, as well as the numbers of people who could be supported at any one time.[32] As with regions in other parts of Australia, it was pastoral stations, and both their ability and need to support small communities of Aboriginal people, that 'sewed the knots of the social and ceremonial network' in the late nineteenth and early twentieth centuries.[33]

In June 1965 patrol officer Grimwade reported encountering Harry Brumby at Angas Downs and trying to obtain information from him about the 'Red Ochre Corroboree', which had come to the Welfare Branch's attention. Grimwade noted that he was able to 'find out very little about the Red Ochre corroborees, apart from the route followed' and that it was 'highly secret'. He observed that the ritual had originated in Ooldea in South Australia, and that the ceremonies taking place in the Northern Territory involved people from Warburton and Blackstone in Western Australia, Ernabella and Musgrave Park in South Australia, as well as Aṉangu from Areyonga, and the local stations and settlements as far north as Yuendumu.[34] Four months later, patrol officer Stewart reported encountering a large congregation at Mulga Park station, noting that the reason for the gathering was for 'ceremonials to be held so that important tribal beliefs and rituals could be passed on from the Elders' to up and coming men. He said that some 250 people had been present at the 'peak of the ceremonials', which had been going for about three weeks. Stewart wrote that Mulga Park and Angas Downs had 'fair sized permanent camps', and that it was at these two places that Aṉangu usually congregated for their ceremonies. He concluded that it was going to be difficult to 'reduce the number of ceremonials', as Aṉangu knew that they could 'obtain sufficient food by the sale of artefacts, and also by the sharing of food with permanent residents' on the stations.[35]

In 1966 District Welfare Officer Lovegrove reported encountering a 'big Aboriginal ceremony' at Musgrave Park. As many as 500 Aṉangu—200 men and 250 to 300 women and children—had gathered for the purpose of ceremony from late June through until at least the third week of July. Lovegrove noted that the 'exodus' from both Ernabella and Areyonga was the biggest for many years, and it was likely due to the 'favourable' conditions that ceremonies had increased in importance and encouraged 'whole families' to migrate to the important areas.[36] Anthropologist Aram Yengoyan recorded 150–200 ceremonial activities at Musgrave Park over a sixteen-month period between 1966 and 1967, arguing that the impact of settlements on the ability to support larger populations for longer periods of time, coupled with enhanced mobility, had given rise to ritual ceremonies being performed with a much greater frequency than in the past.[37] Furthermore, Yengoyan contended that this ritual realm was critical in establishing and maintaining distance and difference: Aṉangu used terms like 'blackfella' and 'whitefella' not only to distinguish between Aboriginal and white settler worlds but to show that Aṉangu dwelled in, and are defined by, a cultural realm that white Australians can never understand, let alone possess.[38]

Larger settlements created for A<u>n</u>angu a significantly expanded social universe, which, despite a rapidly changing socioeconomic landscape, provided the necessary elements for a dynamic social life. Shaped by economic, social and geographical isolation, there emerged distinct social and spatial spheres, or domains, to differentiate between 'blackfellas' and 'whitefellas'.[39] While these separate spheres have been a product of both A<u>n</u>angu and white settler desires at different times, 'puppy dogging holidays' and the expansion of the 'Red Ochre Cult' can be understood in terms of efforts to maintain, and strengthen, the A<u>n</u>angu lifeworld and relationships of exchange—as distinct from white settler culture that sought to absorb and assimilate them into the settler capitalist worldview.

It's also possible to read the intensification and expansion of ritual practice as yet another mode for making place in the wake of dislocation.[40] Mobility, enabled and enhanced by camels, and later by motor vehicles, was a crucial element in this particular expression of autonomy.[41] Ceremonial activity in the region is reported frequently in Welfare Branch correspondence between 1964 and 1968, and even as late as 1972. Despite attempts made to learn more about the rituals, and to put a stop to the unsatisfactory situation of large congregations of A<u>n</u>angu, the archive demonstrates the limits of the branch's authority in the realm of the 'Red Ochre' ceremonies. While it made distinctions between what was seen to be permissible and 'unsightly' or 'undesirable' congregations, in reality it was beyond the branch's knowledge and power to enforce such a distinction. The little that was known of the region's 'travelling cults' suggests that ceremonial leaders had fearsome reputations and an authority the Welfare Branch could hardly match.[42]

Reading of the 'Red Ochre Cult' in the archive while living in Mparntwe, I was struck by the ways in which this particular constellation of mobility continued to resonate in the present. As a white settler living in Central Australia and working 'out bush', I soon learned that as the weather gets warmer and summer draws nearer, 'business time' approaches. Always palpable, the sense of distinct blackfella and whitefella worlds feels especially acute at this time. The deep distance and whispers impressed upon me the tacit understanding that white settlers shouldn't ask questions; men's business is not whitefella business and certainly not a white woman's business. Like the patrol officers of the 1960s, present-day white misfits, missionaries and mercenaries, myself included, can't know what happens during business time. We are prohibited from travelling throughout large swathes of the desert for undetermined periods, to prevent any encounters with the large groups of travelling men. No one really knows when it begins and when it will end. All you can know is that business is happening and not to ask any questions.

What struck me the most at this time was that the power and authority of the settler colonial state were entirely impotent in this realm. In conversation with other white settlers who have lived in Central Australia for some time, many observed that with each passing year, business extended for longer and longer periods of time. There was a shared sense that this prolonging of business time served a particular purpose. Whereas the ritual ceremonies of the 'Red Ochre Cult' in the 1960s and 1970s were observed to take place with much greater frequency than they had in the past, it would seem that today it's concentrated into an extended period of time. Now, as then, it seems that perhaps this all-important business serves not just to make boys into men but to reinforce the distance and difference between black and white worlds, and to emphasise a robust cultural sphere that the settler colonial state can't comprehend, nor possess.

In 1965 it came to the Welfare Branch's attention that a number of the 'itinerants' would relocate to the Petermann Ranges when a rations depot was established there.[43] As a result, Director of Welfare Giese instructed staff in the Southern Branch 'to press on with all speed with the Petermanns project'.[44] The settlement at Docker River in the Petermann Ranges was finally established in 1967, on one of the sites that TGH Strehlow had suggested thirty years earlier, in an effort to stem the flow of Anangu migrating out of the desert.[45]

In April 1968 District Welfare Officer Cooke met with Nipper Winmati and Harry Brumby at Curtin Springs, and reported that although they were 'very keen' to move to Docker River, they were 'adamant about taking a means of transport with them'. Cooke advised the men to leave their 'normal means of transport', which was camels and an old truck, at Curtin Springs. In his report, he noted that there was a strong possibility Winmati and Brumby would insist on taking their own means of transport to Docker River, and if that was the case, there was little that could be done to prevent it. Despite this, Cooke felt it was 'most desirable that this group be stabilised' and that 'every effort should be made to locate them permanently at Docker River'.[46] Four months later, patrol officer Stewart travelled to Angas Downs and Curtin Springs, with the 'purpose of moving part of the Aboriginal population to Docker River settlement'. He reported that at the time of his visit, there was a 'Red Ochre' ceremonial gathering at Angas Downs involving 200 Aṉangu from Areyonga and Angas Downs, and that the men didn't want to depart for Docker River until the rituals were complete. Stewart also noted that the men 'were quite adamant they were going to take their camels to Docker River', and that he gave them 'fair warning' that if they insisted, their camels may be 'destroyed'.[47]

In August 1968 there were 134 people recorded as living at Docker River.[48] On a trip to the new settlement, District Welfare Officer Cooke intended on speaking with the men at Angas Downs who declined to relocate while 'business' was still going, to discuss the 'case for and against the use of camels as a mode of transport'. On the way out to Docker River, Cooke encountered Captain No. 1, and a group of approximately twelve Aṉangu and 'at least 100 dogs', camped between the Angas Downs turn-offs. He reported that they were 'being supplied with rations by an Angas Downs vehicle', and would return to Areyonga in one week's time when a large group of Aṉangu at Mulga Park returned to Angas Downs. On his return trip from Docker River a week later, Cooke encountered camped at the Mulga Park turn-off a group of approximately thirty Aṉangu, who intended on meeting up with the group at the Angas Downs turn-off. Led by the 'well known "Walkabout" leader Nipper', they were travelling with camels and horses, and expected to be in Areyonga in 'about a weeks time', Cooke noted.[49] He concluded that it was:

> Becoming fairly obvious that this particular group of Aboriginals do not intend settling anywhere. They seem to be almost constantly on the move between Areyonga, Angas Downs, Mulga Park and Curtin Springs, with the occasional foray to Musgrave Park and Ernabella. Their most permanent centre seems to be Angas Downs and if any attempt is to be made to stabilise this group I think that the only place they will regard as 'home' will be Angas Downs.[50]

The tensions and fissures of the white settler colonial imaginary, and the resilience of Aṉangu social life, can both be read 'along the grain' of the Welfare Branch correspondence files.[51] In their persistent efforts to curb the socioeconomic activities that were encouraging Aṉangu mobility, the uncommon sense of the deeply contradictory assimilationist agenda is revealed, as reflected in the observations of patrol officer Lovegrove:

> On one hand it is good to see people who are self reliant, and are no expense to the Government but on the other hand it is unfortunate that this way of life does a considerable amount of harm to their own image and to the branch public image.[52]

Aṉangu capitalised on the very few opportunities available to them in the economically underdeveloped north. They did so in a way that enabled the expansion of their existing social universe, while simultaneously distancing themselves from whitefellas and the dominant social order they represented. However, demonstrating relative economic independence, in ways that enabled the maintenance of their own social sphere, was seen to be incommensurable with the settler capitalist story that assimilation policy would make Aboriginal people 'more like us'. It was Aṉangu mobility—and, by extension, their visibility—that undermined the administrative pretence that all was in order and as it should be.

The 'story track' that connects Areyonga, Ernabella and the stations that lay in between is significant not just because it sheds light on the historical importance of the route but because it illuminates mobilities that lay at the heart of an Anangu engagement with the world. Following this 'story track', noting the clusters of camps and the roads that connect them, reveals how existing patterns of mobility and kinship incorporated new technologies of travel and resources to create new geographies and expanded social networks. Furthermore, it shows us that places, rather than bounded and fixed, are relational and made through intersecting travels, encounters and exchanges.

As Jane Carey and Jane Lydon have argued, a focus on Aboriginal networks of travel and exchange reveals 'a range of new histories "from below"', but also 'sharpens our appreciation of the limits and contradictions of imperial power, authority and legitimacy'.[53] The construction of some Anangu as 'the itinerants' in the Welfare Branch's correspondence files reveals the deeply contradictory architecture of an assimilation agenda that sought to sedentarise and transform Anangu into the kind of human material suitable for a capitalist system, in the economically underdeveloped north.[54] Reading 'the itinerants' alongside the itineraries that mark Anangu memory exposes the ways in which mobility was structured by different knowledge traditions, undermining the normalisation of sedentarist thinking, and reflecting it as a projection of bureaucratic policy objectives.[55]

Despite the establishment of the settlement at Docker River as a means to 'stabilise' the itinerant groups, Anangu brought their own interpretations to bear on the new settlement. The establishment of Docker River in 1967–68 coincided with a suite of other factors around that time that contributed to continuing mobilities, and yet another significant reconfiguration of Anangu socioeconomic constellations. Furthermore, despite the above report arguing that the only hope of 'stabilising' the remaining itinerants would be to establish a 'permanent centre' at Bloodwood Bore, these changing circumstances of the late 1960s and 1970s would instead result in the eventual demise of Angas Downs.

PART 5

UNMAKING ANGAS DOWNS

14

RETURN

THE LATE 1960S AND 1970S in northern Australia witnessed significant migrations of Aboriginal people away from pastoral stations. These movements marked the end of the interdependency that had characterised the pastoral industry in the region throughout the twentieth century. The event of the 'equal wage' has become symbolic of this significant period of change in the history of colonialism and cultural encounter in the north of Australia. Despite the assumed emancipation of Aboriginal labour following the decision, the extension of equal wages to Aboriginal stockmen coincided with movements of large numbers of Aboriginal people off the pastoral stations. While this historical moment has divided opinion as to whether it heralded the end of an era of exploitation, or brought about mass evictions and the subsequent collapse of socioeconomic relations in the northern regions, as a number of historians have demonstrated, it was but one event among many in a larger process of change.[1]

Just as there was no one reason for A<u>n</u>angu to migrate out of the Western Desert towards mission settlements and pastoral stations, there is no one reason why, decades later, A<u>n</u>angu left Angas Downs. Arguably the most significant period of change since A<u>n</u>angu first began walking out of the desert, the complexity of this moment can't be apprehended in singular cause-and-effect narratives. The late 1960s and 1970s were marked by flux, and complex processes of transformation, in the northern regions of the continent. Multiple factors in a rapidly changing national social, political and economic landscape resulted in a recalibration of relationships between A_n_angu and the state, and a reconfiguration of the regional system in the south-west of Central Australia. Some places ceased to exist, as new places emerged, in a changing A_n_angu constellation of sociocultural mobility.

The Director of Welfare, Harry Giese, urged the southern division of the Welfare Branch to establish a new settlement at Docker River in 1965.[2] However, the suggestion for the establishment of a settlement in the Petermann Ranges had re-emerged earlier, in 1961, when the Research Officer for the Welfare Branch, Jeremy Long, reported that 'developing the Petermann Ranges area offered much better prospects' than what was then on offer at Areyonga. Long's reasoning at the time was that the people at Areyonga were 'markedly more mobile than those in other settlements', that there was little opportunity to develop a cattle project, and that the water supply might prove inadequate for the growing population.

It was around this time that the capacities of mission and government settlements were emerging as yet another problem for the Welfare Branch and its assimilation agenda. In March 1961 Long submitted a report that outlined the prospects for 'accelerated development' to meet the needs of the growing populations at the western settlements of Papunyna, Yuendumu and Haasts Bluff. Long reported at the time that the 'settled areas' in the region weren't able to provide enough work. Furthermore, he noted that the hope the settlements might 'serve their purposes as "staging camps" and "training centres"', and that Aboriginal people would then 'disappear' into the general population, seemed unrealistic. He suggested sinking several bores and establishing 'outpost stations', comparable to those that had been established at Fregon and Amata in South Australia in 1961, to relieve the pressure of the growing population on firewood and water supplies at Ernabella mission. Establishing an 'outstation' in the Petermanns, as Long imagined it, would be a move towards ensuring a future for

A<u>n</u>angu, as well as reducing the number of them 'moving round the stations and sitting down on the Ayers Rock road'.[3]

Despite the assumption within the Welfare Branch that establishing a settlement at Docker River would solve the problem of 'the itinerants', patrol reports reveal an underlying anxiety that, in reality, this was not the case. Although the number of people at Docker River was increasing—a population of eighty was recorded at the new settlement in May of 1968[4]—similar numbers were reported as living at Bloodwood Bore and Wilpiya on Angas Downs at around the same time. In April 1968 District Welfare Officer Cooke noted that the group at Wilpiya was 'opposed strongly' to his suggestion that they move to Areyonga. They also resisted a move to the newly established Docker River:

> This group wish to remain at Angas Downs and I can therefore make no recommendation to provide for their welfare other than a concentration of welfare activity at a centre on the Angas Downs lease.
>
> The owner of Angas Downs is willing for a settlement to be established on the lease and action has already commenced to start a school. I recommend therefore that the school be extended to include a settlement complex so that full provision can be made for the welfare of Angas Downs Aboriginals. If something is not done along these lines urgently we can expect numerous critical reports from travellers during the forth-coming tourist season … I would suggest that urgent negotiations take place to establish a permanent settlement for these people at Wilbia Bore … I would like to see a school established at Wilbia Bore or in the near vicinity with a view to expanding the centre to settlement proportions. I feel that the Angas Downs population could then be stabilised and the centre could avail itself of any benefits obtainable from the tourist industry. Some gardening and farming could be carried out and labour could be supplied on a casual basis to Angas Downs and other surrounding stations.[5]

The primary objective of assimilation was 'waged citizenship', and, as Rowse has observed, two decades of efforts to implement assimilation had made the state increasingly aware of connection to Country as a continuing determinant of A<u>n</u>angu actions, and also an obstacle to wage labour.[6] A waged citizenry rested upon the stabilisation of the population, and the travelling mode in which A<u>n</u>angu made their way in the world was antithetical to the social transformation that the Welfare Branch desired. Despite assumptions that Docker River would be a panacea for the problem of 'the itinerants', A<u>n</u>angu kept moving, and Angas Downs became the focal point for the Welfare Branch's sedentary visions.

Assimilation policy was collapsing under the weight of its internal contradictions. Cooke's report is brimming with tension; the chimera of a settled group of A<u>n</u>angu, tending gardens, farming and partaking in casual labour, is at risk of being subsumed by a sense of 'urgency', and the foreboding of a 'critical' condition. In a patrol report five months later, Cooke observed that the 'itinerants' displayed no intention of settling anywhere and that if an attempt to 'stabilise' the constantly wandering A<u>n</u>angu was to be made, 'the only place they would regard as "home" would be Angas Downs'.[7] Late in 1968, presumably sometime after September, five large caravans were placed on Angas Downs. One was to be used as a schoolroom, two as ablutions vans; one was to be a kitchen, and one was to be a three-bedroom flat for the teacher.

Less than a year later, in August 1969, Cooke wrote to the Assistant Director of the Welfare Branch recommending that the mobile units be removed from Angas Downs, as he felt that the:

> Aborigines are unlikely to congregate there in any numbers in future and it would not be advisable to give them any encouragement to do so.[8]

It was recommended that the units be moved to Docker River. Cooke noted that the decision was motivated by a visit to Angas Downs by Reverend George Hardy from the Presbyterian Synod in Sydney, who later wrote to the Director of Welfare to complain about the 'apparent abandonment of the expensive units' on the station. In 1969 Arthur Liddle complained to Reverend Jim Downing that he had fought hard and long to get a mobile school, ablution facilities and a house for a teacher from the Welfare Branch. Liddle told Downing it was not long after the mobile units had been delivered to Angas Downs that a patrol officer turned up with trucks and urged people to go to Docker River.

This episode raises a number of questions. What happened at Bloodwood Bore that could have brought about such a dramatic change in circumstances in the course of less than a year? Why was the 'urgent' and possibly 'critical' condition of the 'itinerants' around Angas Downs no longer an issue for the Welfare Branch? If, as reported, Angas Downs had been abandoned, where had An̲angu gone? Perhaps more pertinently, why did they leave a place where they had adamantly expressed a desire to stay?

When I asked Sandra Armstrong why they took the caravans away from Bloodwood Bore, she said that it had happened around the time everyone started to leave. Docker River had been established and many people decided to make the journey home:[9]

> They brought the caravans here but all of Anangu were beginning to disperse to their own country, thinking to return to various sites for cultural reasons and they were leaving. There were people at Wingelina, there was probably a bore there for them and Docker River people, and others were leaving for Amata, which was a new settlement. There were many new (communities) at that time: Fregon, Amata, Wingelina, Blackstone and others. Warakurna and others were somewhat later but the main ones people were living at were Fregon, Amata, and other people were also living at the homelands and we were the only ones (left) living at the station.[10]

Sandra didn't talk about movements away from Angas Downs in terms of An̲angu being forced off the station. Rather, as she tells it, these migrations were motivated by cultural reasons, primary among them the desire to return home. The term 'homelands movement' has come to characterise this particular moment of Aboriginal mobility in the north of the continent. This return to Country has largely been understood as a phenomenon resulting from an assertion and affirmation of Aboriginal autonomy, the origins of which are assumed to be the dramatic changes taking place in the Aboriginal policy landscape of the 1970s. However, a number of the places that Sandra cites as enabling A̲nangu to return to Country emerged as early as 1961; in the case of Docker River, Fregon and Amata, they were not ancestral homelands as such but, rather, new government and mission settlements.

Not all movements away from settlements and stations at this time were to ancestral homelands. Despite assumptions that the homelands movement represents the moment the Aboriginal desire to move away from larger government settlements was made manifest, outstations have emerged at various times and locations throughout the twentieth century, many predating the so-called 'movement'.[11] Outstations are small, decentralised communities of kin established by Aboriginal people on land that is significant to them. The term first emerged within the context of the pastoral industry, and refers to the camps or dwellings that were more than a day's return travel from the main homestead. In contrast, in the Aboriginal context, outstations have emerged as manifestations of the desires of Aboriginal people to live independently of the state, and according to their own cultural logic and way of being-in-the-world.[12] Like 'puppy dogging holidays' and the 'Red Ochre Cult', outstations can be understood as an effort to reinforce the distinctions that had emerged in the preceding decades between the separate spheres, and spatially assert their independence from the dominant white settler domain. However, creating distance between themselves and white settlers was not the only reason that A̲nangu sought to move away from larger government settlements and stations. Rather, as Sandra describes it, outstations reflect the ways in which Aboriginal people might align themselves with various 'outsiders' in order to pursue their own values and concerns.[13]

This entanglement of objectives is critical in understanding A̲nangu movements away from existing settlements and pastoral stations in South Australia, the Northern Territory and Western Australia throughout the 1960s—movements predating both the implementation of equal wages and the phenomenon of the homeland movement. While the settlements at Fregon, Amata and Docker River were 'outsider' initiatives intended to relieve the pressure of increasing populations at Ernabella and Areyonga missions, many A<u>n</u>angu who moved to these new settlements did so because they saw it as an opportunity to live on, or closer to, their Country, as Sandra explains. The settlement at Fregon was established in 1961, as an outstation of Ernabella mission, implemented with the aim of relieving the mounting pressure that the increasing population was placing on available resources. Bill Edwards supervised the establishment of the new settlement at Fregon, and noted that at the time the South Australian Aborigines Protection Board was critical of Ernabella's policies of education in the Pitjantjatjara language and respect for A<u>n</u>angu culture. Frustrated by the distinct lack of assimilation taking place on the mission, it established a government settlement at Amata in the same year.[14] Whatever the rationale was for the establishment of these new settlements, for A<u>n</u>angu they presented an opportunity for people to move closer to their homelands. The people who moved from Ernabella to Fregon, approximately 50 kilometres to the south of the mission, were primarily 'pilatja' or plains people, whereas those who moved to Amata, at the western end of the Musgrave Ranges, were 'api mirrputja' people from the hills of the ranges.[15]

Regardless of the official logic as outlined by the likes of Director of Welfare Giese and patrol officer Jeremy Long, from an A<u>n</u>angu perspective the establishment of Docker River was understood as the government's acknowledgement of and support for their intrinsic relatedness to that land.[16] Recalling when A<u>n</u>angu began to move from Areyonga to Docker River, A<u>n</u>angu man Sandy Willie said that this was the time 'Welfare been shifting [people back to] their own country', and that when they got to the new settlement, A<u>n</u>angu were saying, '"Oh, my country that way" or "My country that way"—"I got to go to my place"…"I got to go to my place."'[17] Sandy Willie was part of the small group of men from Areyonga who worked on the clearing of the airstrip to service the settlement at Docker River,[18] which commenced in December 1967. By February 1968 the population was beginning to grow, the first manager of the 'outpost', Max Cartwright, reporting at the time that some people were arriving 'by any means possible'.[19] By August 1968 there were 134 people living at Docker River,[20] having travelled there from various locations in the Northern Territory, South Australia and Western Australia. All of them considered Docker River to be their Country, or part of their Country, or closer to their Country in the Petermann Ranges than where they had been living previously.[21]

Despite administrative intentions to limit settlement at Docker River to those people who were 'from' the area, or who had previously resided in the Northern Territory, A<u>n</u>angu had different ideas about who had the right to live there. Claims to a relationship with Docker River were continually subject to dispute and negotiation within the new settlement. Administratively defined 'areas' were very different from A<u>n</u>angu definitions of the area; this is understandable, given that Docker River is only 10 kilometres from the Western Australian border, and the Petermann Ranges are closely connected to the Rawlinson Ranges, which lay fully within the Western Australian administrative area. Anthropologist Susan Tod Woenne observed during fieldwork at Docker River in the 1970s that distinctions such as 'Western Australian people' versus 'Northern Territory people', or 'Areyonga people' versus 'Warburton people', were 'frequently used by settlement staff and taken up by Aborigines themselves when rights to settlement services and privileges were contested'.[22] As Woenne described it, Docker River became a crucial link in the widespread network of social and territorial relationships.[23] This reconfiguration of relationships to place is reflected in A<u>n</u>angu woman Tjukupati James's statement that the 'traditional Ngaatjatjarra people left this [Docker River] area, intending it be only temporary, but they died while they were away'. Tjukupati says that A<u>n</u>angu who live there now are 'keeping' the land, and are from 'the same big extended family'.[24] It wasn't simply a return journey home—in making the move to Docker River, A<u>n</u>angu were seeking to assert and maintain their relationship to Country, while simultaneously securing their place in yet another new home.

Angas Downs had always been intimately connected to the Docker River area. Tjuki Pumpjack's oral histories, and the historical evidence that survived in the photographs and diaries of HH Finlayson and Frederick Rose, and in TGH Strehlow's early correspondence and patrol reports, point to the Wintaylka, or Mulga Seed Dreaming, as

What kind of place is Angas Downs? The journey to understand the history of this place began with an assumption of this cattle station as a product of colonial (dis)possession and myth making in the Northern Territory. It ended with an understanding of Angas Downs as a deeply storied place—not only lived in, but (un)made by the A<u>n</u>angu who lived there. Remains of an Angas Downs vehicle (2014) and windmill (2012), Bloodwore Bore, Angas Downs. *Shannyn Palmer*.

Tjuki Tjukanku Pumpjack on the veranda of his house, Imanpa community, 2013. *Rhett Hammerton.*

Tjuki Tjukanku Pumpjack, Bloodwood Bore, Angas Downs, 1962. This photograph is 'No. 1' in Frederick Rose's book, *The Wind of Change in Central Australia: The Aborigines at Angas Downs, 1962*. Placing Tjuki as No.1 reflected Rose's recognition of Tjuki's senior status at Angas Downs. Sandra Armstrong too said of Tjuki's authority: 'Old Tjuki Tjukanku was really ninti [knowledgeable], he was number one.' *SLNSW Frederick Rose Papers Box 8.*

Sandra Armstrong holding a photograph of herself from the Frederick Rose archive during a research trip to the Mitchell Library in 2013. *Shannyn Palmer*.

Sandra Armstrong, Bloodwood Bore, Angas Downs, 1962. Sandra was 'No. 90' in Frederick Rose's portraits. Sandra said that she worked with Rose and would sit with him looking through his photographs and he would ask her, 'What do you call this one?' and she would tell him the language names for kin relationships. *SLNSW Frederick Rose Papers Box 8*.

Doggers' camp in the Musgrave Ranges, circa 1928–30. The arrival of 'doggers' presented the earliest instances of regular contact between A<u>n</u>angu and white men in the Western Desert. The superior hunting skills of the A<u>n</u>angu meant they were of great benefit to doggers, while A<u>n</u>angu valued the flour, sugar and tea that they could get in exchange for dingo scalps. *A<u>r</u>a Irititja, Ramon Brown Collection AI-0035182, photograph taken by Allan Ferguson Brumby.*

'Everybody was thinking about the whitefellas living in Ernabella!' Ernabella mission was a significant site in the first encounters between A<u>n</u>angu, whitefellas and their food. Ernabella Mission, circa 1946–8. *A<u>r</u>a Irititja, Barbara Bills Collection AI-0004822.*

William 'Old Bill' Liddle, 1935. Legend has it that sometime around 1928–9, after purchasing 2000 head of sheep in South Australia, Liddle returned to a soak that he had come across during his travels into the Western Desert and set up camp there. He called the place Angas Downs. *SLSA, Charles Mountford Collection PRG 1218/34/124.*

The place where Bill Liddle established Angas Downs station was called Walara. Tjuki Pumpjack said that when he and his family arrived at Walara, 'We combined our camps and we settled in to live there with them, and that is where I grew up.' Walara, 2012. *Shannyn Palmer.*

Clay pan at Mutatja, Angas Downs, 2013. In the arid rangelands pastoralism met with the ecological limitations of the desert, resulting in constant movement between a network of sites. The unpredictable 'pulse-reserve' model of rainfall meant that Liddle could move from the relatively reliable water source at Walara to the more ephemeral water sources like the clay pans at Mutatja. *Shannyn Palmer*.

Remains of the sheep camp at Mutatja, 2013. A mere three to four years after establishing the sheep run at Walara, the sheep had turned the country into a dusty sand drift. *Shannyn Palmer*.

The Bloodwood and the bore, 1962. The move to Bloodwood Bore marked the beginning of a new era in the history of the colonial encounter on Angas Downs station. *SLNSW Frederick Rose Papers Box 8.*

Frederick Rose in the A<u>n</u>angu camp at Bloodwood Bore, 1962. Rose lived at Bloodwood Bore between July and October 1962. He observed that much of the area around the homestead was completely void of vegetation and that the A<u>n</u>angu camp was 'largely denuded of trees, which had been used for firewood'. *SLNSW Frederick Rose Papers Box 8.*

The homestead at Bloodwood Bore was a modest affair pieced together with corrugated iron. *SLNSW Frederick Rose Papers Box 8.*

Wiltja in the An̲angu camp at Bloodwood Bore, 1962. Wiltja is the Pitjantjatjara word for shade and is also the name of the shade shelter that An̲angu use as a dwelling. Rose recorded thirty-nine of them in the An̲angu camp. *SLNSW Frederick Rose Papers Box 8.*

‘I became a young fella there … I worked on horseback, working the bullocks, and that’s when I learned the ropes, where I learned how to ride horses, how to ride buckjumpers and stay in the saddle.’ Tjuki Pumpjack demonstrating spear throwing at Bloodwood Bore, circa 1956–8. *A<u>r</u>a Irititja, Leo Quin Collection AI-0026034.*

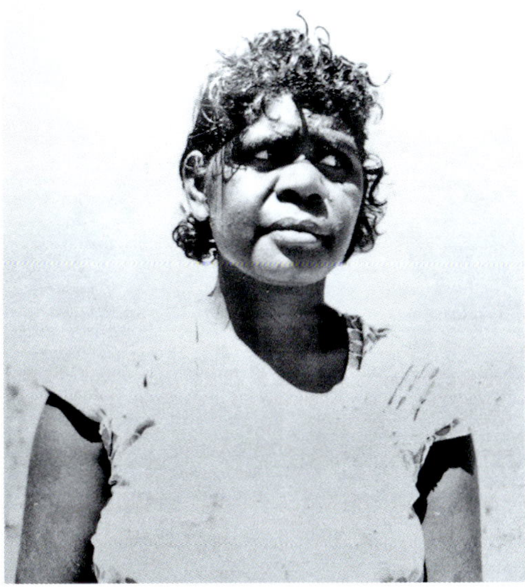

Sandra Armstrong, Bloodwood Bore, 1962. On the back of this image, Frederick Rose wrote ‘House girl Sandra’. Sandra recalled, ‘there we were, all us young women working away in the kitchen for the tourists. We would work for the tourists … I would work from the kitchen … and get everything set up for the tourist’s dinner.’ *SLNSW Frederick Rose Papers Box 8.*

‘The Chalet’, 1962. Tourist buses would stop to have a meal at Angas Downs in the building known as ‘the chalet’. Rose described the chalet as being ‘tastefully furnished with colourful plastic topped tables and appropriate chairs’, which could seat up to forty people at any one time. Rose noted that somewhere between four to five thousand tourists passed through Angas Downs on their way to Uluru in 1962. *SLNSW Frederick Rose Papers Box 8.*

A<u>n</u>angu trading with tourists at Bloodwood Bore, 1962. Rose observed that the only reason the buses detoured onto the Angas Downs loop was to see and to trade with A<u>n</u>angu. Mick is in front at the right with his back to the camera. Rose described Mick as an ‘ardent trader’, ‘astute businessman’ and ‘maker of the finest boomerangs at Bloodwood Bore’. *SLNSW Frederick Rose Papers Box 8.*

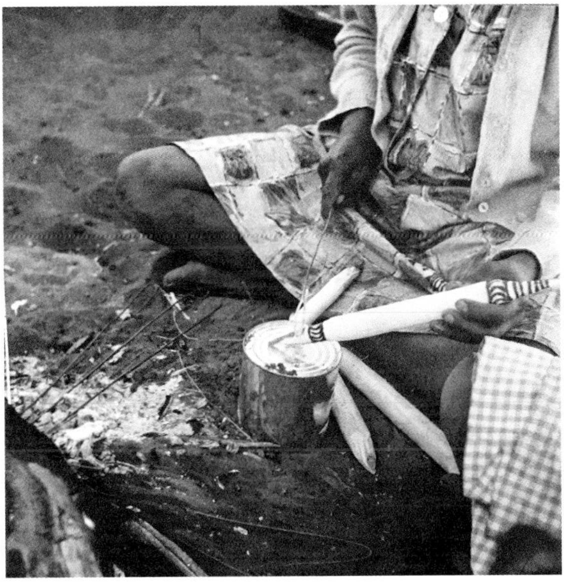

Decorating punu at Bloodwood Bore, 1962. A<u>n</u>angu used hot wire to burn designs into the surface of the punu. The practice of branding objects was not just about ornamentation for tourists, it encoded punu with stories and knowledge. *SLNSW Frederick Rose Papers Box 8.*

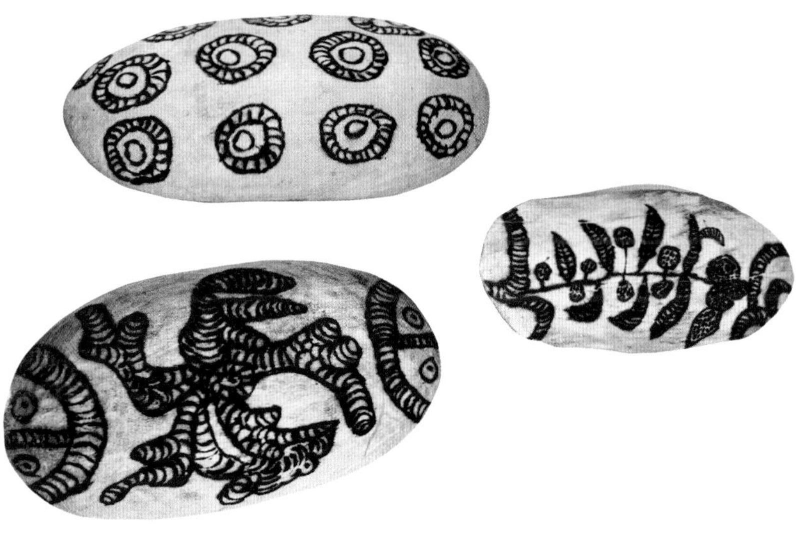

Branded piti dishes collected by Rose at Bloodwood Bore, 1962. While the value of punu was determined in monetary terms in the exchange with tourists, these objects also became critical vessels for the transfer of knowledge between generations that enabled A<u>n</u>angu to assert and maintain their cultural knowledge and identity during a period of significant change. *SLNSW Frederick Rose Papers Box 8.*

'We were always travelling.' Iwara is the Pitjantjatjara word for track, or travel route. This is a section of the iwara that is commonly evoked in Anangu oral histories as the route that linked Areyonga and Ernabella missions. Angas Downs, 2011. *Shannyn Palmer*.

Tjuki Pumpjack said that 'people have always come to this water' and that it was an important stopping off place along the iwara that ran between Ernabella and Areyonga missions. Wilpiya Spring, 2011. *Shannyn Palmer*.

'People have been living beside this water since ancient times.' Petroglyphs are some of the traces of travels past along the iwara that runs between Areyonga and Ernabella missions. Angas Downs, 2014. *Shannyn Palmer.*

Areyonga mission, 1970. Education was a cornerstone of assimilation policy in the Northern Territory and the Welfare Branch was responsible for gathering up children like Sandra Armstrong and enforcing their attendance at school on Areyonga and Ernabella missions. *Ara̲ Irititja, Margaret and David Hewitt Collection AI-0038513.*

Ernabella mission, 1963. The policy of 'rounding up' and removing children to go to school was a significant factor in Areyonga and Ernabella missions emerging as important hubs in An̲angu itineraries of travel. This travel between the stations and missions led to the Welfare Branch casting An̲angu as 'the itinerants'. *Ara̲ Irititja, Allan Wilson Collection AI- 0023794.*

Following WWII, camels completely revolutionised the ways in which A<u>n</u>angu travelled, particularly in regard to the increased capacity to carry supplies and belongings. Family group travelling west with camels, 1962. *A<u>r</u>a Irititja, Bill Edwards Collection AI-0013332.*

Camels not only revolutionised the way that A<u>n</u>angu could travel, but were an essential means to the trade and exchange of dingo scalps and the important 'holidays' to Country in the Western Desert that 'puppy dogging' trips facilitated. Dingo skins laid out at Ernabella, circa 1957. *A<u>r</u>a Irititja, Bill and Allison Elliot Collection AI-0018038.*

'There is nothing at Angas Downs, only the place itself, but it is still our place.' Tjuki Tjukanku Pumpjack and the remains of Angas Downs station at Walara, 2012. *Shannyn Palmer*.

the thread that spanned approximately 500 kilometres, and half a century, to connect these two places. The establishment of the settlement at Docker River had a significant impact on the population at Angas Downs, as Anangu seized the opportunity to re-people the places they thought of as home. Sandra Armstrong recalls her mother getting homesick for her Country:

> My mother would tell me the stories. Perhaps my mother was very knowledgeable, greatly so. For that side (west, towards and including Ngaanyatjarra region). My mother got homesick for (her) Country and I asked her, 'Why are you so homesick for your Country? Do you want to go back?' ...
>
> 'Kutipitja-pitjala ngura tjantu-kutu.' This is how she spoke and I'd say, 'No, you can't go now, you're talking about places with ini kura kura [ordinary or made-up, names that are not the real thing] this Country is no good!' She'd spoken about those places and she'd say, 'They're living in no good country, living in other people's Country ... I want to go back to my own Country ...
>
> I want to go back to my relations and live in my Country.' After talking about it and talking about it, she snuck off; she really went and she left her family behind. She took her parents and my younger sister, the youngest one, since she had grown, having raised her to the age of a young teenager, she took her but I was still living (at Angas Downs) by myself.[25]

Sandra Armstrong was a baby when her parents left the Ngaanyatjarra Country near present-day Irrunytju (Wingelina) community in Western Australia and walked to Walara. For her, like many of her generation, mission settlements and pastoral stations had *always* been there and had *always* constituted some part of her everyday social life. Unable to relate to the placenames evoked with such yearning by her mother, it was Angas Downs that was Sandra's place. Reflecting the generational differences in experience, her historical remembrance demonstrates that, despite the fact the *physical* Country around Irrunytju is Sandra's ancestral homelands on her mother's side, it is Bloodwood Bore that is *meaningful* to her.

In a July 1969 census report, Tjuki Pumpjack's widowed father, Sandra's mother and father, Tjuki, his wife Dolly, daughter Edith and son Rover, and his brother Johnny Mulla and his wife, Sandra's older sister Ada, and their family, were all recorded as living at Angas Downs. Sandra is adamant that even though people were starting to leave the stations and places like Areyonga and Ernabella to live closer to their homelands, she and Tjuki and their families wanted to continue living on Angas Downs.[26] However, at around the time that they took the caravans away, Tjuki's older brother passed away. Just as the death of Tjuki's grandfather near Amata over three decades earlier had compelled their move from the area, marking the beginning of the journey that eventually led them to Angas Downs, his older brother's death compelled a move from the station; this marked the beginning of a journey that appears to have led, in one sense, to the end of Angas Downs. Tjuki recalled:

> We lost my number one brother. That's why we cleared out a little bit. We shifted away. We moved to Mulga Park, and we went there via Ernabella. We lost my brother, my oldest brother. That's why we got out, you know? Like early days people.[27]

Tjuki and his wife and children, and his brother Johnny Mulla and his family, travelled to Ernabella, to Amata and right up to Pipalyatjara, his mother's and grandmother's country in South Australia. It would seem that they were gone for a considerable length of time. When asked how long, Tjuki replied, 'we walked around for two years. It could have been one year, we don't know'.[28] Sandra went to Amata too. By this time, she was married, and Sandra says that she and her husband Esky were there for a few years, but she felt homesick for Angas Downs:

> I didn't really know that place. (I said) 'Hey no, let's go, I'm getting homesick because this is their place (not ours).' So we both got a car after working and we snuck off and left.[29]

Tjuki recalled about their return to Angas Downs:

> We came back again and things had changed here. 'Where is everyone living now?'[30]

A letter from a patrol officer named Weber in September 1969, a month after patrol officer Cooke recommended the removal of the caravans from Angas Downs, noted he had visited the station a few days previously and that:

> There were no Aborigines present at the time of my visit and the Aborigines that were resident there, have in the main, shifted to Mt. Ebenezer.[31]

By the time Tjuki and Sandra returned to Angas Downs sometime in the early 1970s, Mount Ebenezer roadhouse had become the main locus of A<u>n</u>angu activity in the area. Given its location on the Lasseter Highway, the direct tourist route to Uluru, Mount Ebenezer was a popular place for A<u>n</u>angu to sell punu to tourists. When the remaining families at Bloodwood Bore left the station on sorry business, it would seem that the tourist buses no longer had a reason to detour onto the Angas Downs loop; this redirected both the punu trade and the income generated by the Liddles from catering to the tourists to Mount Ebenezer roadhouse. Sandra Armstrong says that while many people were leaving and returning to their Country: 'other families had learned to drink and went to Ebenezer'.[32]

A number of factors coincided around the latter half of the 1960s and early 1970s that contributed to increasing migrations away from pastoral stations and missions, towards new places. The *Social Welfare Ordinance 1964* ended the restrictions that had prevented A<u>n</u>angu access to alcohol. The availability of alcohol, combined with access to the punu trade, meant that Mount Ebenezer roadhouse became a popular place for A<u>n</u>angu. Coupled with the increased access to cash, via aged pensions and unemployment benefits, A<u>n</u>angu mobility was further enhanced. Sandra Armstrong says that while they were living at Ebenezer, people were talking about the new settlements at Amata and Docker River:

> When we were at Ebenezer, we would hear (stories), 'Hey, there's a settlement at Amata and a settlement at Docker River but we were forever going on the road to Amata, of course, 'sit-down money' (unemployment benefits) and the pension had been established. And that got me thinking, 'Hey, we should do that [start our own community] in our own country.' That's what I was thinking about.[33]

The increased access to cash via aged pensions was a significant factor in the disintegration of pastoral paternalism in the north of the continent. While the pastoral award didn't come into effect until 1968 in the Northern Territory, and 1969 in Western Australia, and was made available only to men, aged pensions had been extended to Aboriginal people in these regions in 1959 and 1960.[34] While, in both regions, eligible people only received a 'pocket money' portion of their benefits, the rest going to the stations or settlements that rationed them, it signalled the eventual transition from rations to cash.[35] Although Aboriginal people were only receiving a portion of their benefits for much of the 1960s, as the punu trade and 'puppy dogging' demonstrated, the increased amount of cash in circulation undermined the ability of the stations and settlements to hold people in the hinterlands.

As direct access to cash through pension payments enhanced Aboriginal freedoms, it simultaneously began to erode what had been a not insignificant source of income for pastoralists. Having been in receipt of government payments for the 'maintenance of dependents' on their stations since 1947, Charles Rowley noted that in the 1960s Northern Territory pastoralists were known to joke that they made more money from Aboriginal people than they did from cattle.[36] Following the Equal Wages decision in 1966, and the 1967 Referendum that voted overwhelmingly in favour of removing two references in the Australian Constitution that discriminated against Aboriginal people,[37] from 1968 onwards in the Northern Territory, and 1969 in the Kimberley, social security benefits were paid directly to Aboriginal people. While these factors combined to form an economic blow to some pastoralists, they also, as Sandra's recollection demonstrates, served as a stimulus to Anangu desires to assert their autonomy and establish outstations.

The extension of most social service payments in cash from 1968 onwards, followed by unemployment benefits in 1974, largely eliminated the need to sell labour to survive and created a new threshold of possibility for the establishment of outstations. Nicolas Peterson has referred to this moment as something of a 'watershed', arguing that it was the direct access to cash that resulted in the Anangu abandonment of camels, and a 'greatly increased involvement with cars'.[38] This enhanced access to motor vehicles worked to further transform Anangu mobility and played a significant role in the gathering momentum of the outstation movement.[39]

As growing numbers of people expressed their desire to live in smaller, decentralised camps located on or near their homelands, settler state plans for the transformation of the Aboriginal situation in the wake of assimilation had to come to terms with the 'structural constraints of isolation and radical cultural difference'.[40] The prevailing political paradigm of the 'absorption' and 'incorporation' of Aboriginal culture into settler society was thus necessarily eclipsed by an emergent policy era articulated in the language of 'rights', 'cultural difference' and 'self-determination'. While this shift in policy is largely attributed to the election of the Gough Whitlam Labor government in 1972, it was the Liberal prime minister William McMahon who declared in his Australia Day speech at the beginning of that year that Aboriginal people should be supported in maintaining their culture, language and traditions, and encouraged to exercise 'effective choice about the degree to which, they come to identity themselves with ... [the wider Australian] society'.[41] It was, however, the Whitlam government that called this sentiment 'self-determination'.

The shift in policy rhetoric from 'assimilation' to 'self-determination' served to legitimise outstations in the eyes of the settler state, which sought to make them examples of the genuine commitment to self-determination.[42] The decision to financially assist groups who wished to move, coupled with the establishment of the Royal Commission into Aboriginal Land Rights in 1973, provided significant stimulus to the creation of outstations, marking the beginning of what became known as the 'homelands movement'.[43] Throughout the 1970s, in the 'first wave' of the Pitjantjatjara 'homelands movement', outstations were established at Pipalyatjarra, Kunamata, Yaluyalu and Walinya (Cave Hill) in South Australia, and Irrunytju (Wingelina), Papulankutja (Blackstone), Warakurna (Giles Weather Station) and Mantamaru (Jamieson) in Western Australia. All of this contributed significantly to the reconfiguration of the populations of pastoral stations and settlements in the southwest.[44] According to Reverend Jim Downing, the 'first wave' of Pitjantjatjara movements radiated out from Amata in the first half of the 1970s, while the 'second wave' extended from Ernabella in the second half of the 1970s. Downing, writing of the enthusiasm for the policy of self-determination at the time, claimed that 'extravagant help was given, and some rash promises made, [that] rais[ed] people's expectations high'.[45]

Sandra Armstrong recalls that it was while she was living at Mount Ebenezer that a whitefella came looking around and asking A<u>n</u>angu, '*Do you people want a job? ... Do you mob like to sit down with Aboriginal people separately?*' Sandra says that she thought to herself, '*Uwa [yes]! We might think about that ... [to] make a new community.*'[46] In the Angas Downs archive from this period, there's significant correspondence written by Department of Aboriginal Affairs Community Advisor Bruce Tilmouth, a man more commonly known as 'Tracker'. A member of the Stolen Generations, Tracker was taken in by Arthur and Bess Liddle on Angas Downs in 1970. He grew very close to Arthur and Bess during his time there and, as John Liddle recalls in Alexis Wright's 2017 book *Tracker*, he worked with and got to know all the 'old fellows and the old women' on the station.[47]

An agreement in the correspondence files reads:

> The Community known as Muntawarra may reside upon Angas Downs near Centenary Bore three miles in from the Mt. Ebenezer Boundary for a period of two years ... After the expiration of this

> Agreement negotiations can take place for a permanent excision over said area for the purposes of Aboriginal communal living.[48]

In a letter to the Department of Aboriginal Affairs (DAA) in January 1979, Arthur Liddle wrote that he agreed in principle. However, he wished to add that he'd like to receive rent for the land, compensation for maintenance and running costs of the water supply, and requested that the community supply their own pumping equipment, noting:

> After such an agreement is reached between Muntawarra Community, DAA and myself, I agree to allow the community to reside on this bore ... We welcome this community and will continue to assist them in every way possible. We look forward to their future development and success in this venture.[49]

Bruce 'Tracker' Tilmouth held meetings with Tjuki Pumpjack, Sandra Armstrong and Johnny Mulla to discuss the establishment of the community. In the correspondence, Tjuki, Sandra and their families are referred to as 'the Muntawarra people', and Tilmouth proposes the establishment of a community garden, as well as a chicken run and provision of a tractor. Tilmouth reported that the camp at Centenary Bore was 'spotlessly clean and garbage put into a tidy heap', and recommended that the 'community should be given as much assistance as possible'.[50] By April 1979 a tractor had been delivered, goat pens and chicken yards had been constructed, and a garden cleared.[51]

Sandra says that they established the outstation at Centenary Bore because they wanted to get away from the drinkers and problems at Mount Ebenezer and the Imanpa community recently established at a place called Perentie Bore. This was in 1978, after the owner of Mount Ebenezer station, Ted Kunoth, excised a portion of it, likely in an attempt to draw A̲nangu from the nearby Mount Ebenezer Roadhouse.

This was not a unique situation: as early as 1974 the then Chief Government Advisor on Aboriginal policy, HC ('Nugget') Coombs, observed that as well as wanting to assert and maintain a special relationship to the land, Aboriginal people sought to relocate to outstations to avoid the tensions associated with living in large communities, and to minimise white people's influence in their lives, including the alcohol they were associated with.[52] Similar motivations have been expressed regarding the desire to establish outstations away from other desert settlements, such as Papunya, Yuendumu and Balgo.[53]

Despite Tilmouth's April 1979 report stating that 'the community at Muntawarra [was] running quite smoothly', six months later he relayed that Arthur Liddle said he wouldn't grant an excision for the 'community', and wanted 'them moved back to Ebenezer or Imanpa as soon as possible'.[54] Tilmouth noted that people visited the area from Amata and other communities frequently, and Sandra Armstrong says that Arthur Liddle changed his mind because:

> Well, too many drinkers was coming to his boundary. We was in the boundary of Angas Downs, Centenary's Angas Downs. And people, you know when they drink too much grog, and they lookin' for us all the time and he [Arthur Liddle] don't like people from drinkers.[55]

Despite wanting to avoid the problems encountered at Mount Ebenezer and Imanpa, it would seem that they surfaced at Muntawarra too. It is probable, as Sandra suggests, that it was the heavy drinking and fighting crossing over his boundary and onto his property that discouraged Arthur Liddle from assisting A<u>n</u>angu in their desire to continue living on Angas Downs. There is a strong sense in Wright's book *Tracker* that the Liddles and their extended family network valued kin, language and culture deeply. Perhaps, as Sandra suggests, this incursion of people from other communities and the drinking that took place there threatened to destabilise the home that the Liddles had built and nurtured on the station.

In August 1981 the Imanpa Community Advisor, a Mr G Langford, wrote to the DAA on behalf of Tjuki Pumpjack, regarding the 'Muntawarra land problem'. The letter stated that Arthur Liddle:

> [S]aid he would give land to Tjuki Pumpjack not to the government. This issue has been going on for a long time. Could you please tell us what you can do to help.[56]

Correspondence between the DAA, the Community Advisor at Imanpa, Tjuki Pumpjack, Arthur Liddle and the Aboriginal Development Commission paints a vivid picture of the administrative labyrinth that had to be navigated in order to secure a sublease on Angas Downs. In a two-page letter to Tjuki, the DAA informed him that they needed to receive written confirmation from Liddle as to the area of land to be leased, as well as permission from the Northern Territory Government to drill for water in the area negotiated. Upon written confirmation from Liddle, Tjuki would then need to meet with the DAA and apply to the Northern Territory Department of Land for a sublease. The land also had to be surveyed, after which, Tjuki was informed, there would be 'numerous forms to be filled in and agreements reached', and that the 'main problem' would be:

> The final negotiations of an area of land and equipping of a suitable water supply. As these issues involve two sections of government and the provision of money the finalisation of a lease takes time. In respect to the money issue this is even more serious (for yourselves) when it is remembered there are many groups pushing for their own areas of land over the Northern Territory.[57]

Tjuki couldn't read or write, so it's probable that the information in the letter was relayed to him through the Imanpa Community Advisor. Langford also received a letter from the DAA. Written on the same day, it requested that Langford visit when next in Alice Springs, so that they could discuss 'in greater detail the problems that do beset us in obtaining land tenure for people in similar circumstances to the Muntawarra group'.[58]

In addition to the increasing demand for outstations, the passing into legislation of the *Aboriginal Land Rights (Northern Territory) Act 1976* allowed for Aboriginal people in the Northern Territory to make claims upon unalienated Crown land. Claims were to be made on the basis of 'traditional' Aboriginal rights to land, which would be judged by a Land Commissioner whose job it was to ascertain whether those making the claim were the land's rightful 'traditional owners'. Although the legal interpretation of what constitutes a 'traditional owner' under the Act has evolved and expanded over the forty years since it first emerged, in its infancy the legal definition of traditional ownership was largely based upon the orthodox model of Aboriginal land tenure first posited by yet another 'white expert', AR Radcliffe-Brown, in the early twentieth century.[59] Although from the earliest claims heard in the Northern Territory in the late 1970s none of the evidence presented upheld Radcliffe-Brown's narrow definition of the socially and spatially fixed 'patrilineal horde',[60] in 1981 judgements of rights to land would almost certainly have been made with this narrow definition in mind.[61]

The nature of Aboriginal social organisation and land tenure has been long and hotly debated among 'white experts' in the discipline of anthropology. This is particularly the case in relation to the so-called 'enigma' of Western Desert land tenure.[62] The unusual flexibility of identification, and the fluidity of relationships to land among the Western Desert cultural bloc, has resulted in different conceptualisations of land tenure and conflicting interpretations among anthropologists as to what constitutes a traditional owner. A war of words has waged over categories and concepts such as 'hordes', 'bands', 'clans' and 'estates'. While there has been much ethnographic fieldwork since the 1950s that's challenged the orthodox model of Aboriginal land tenure, the highly circumscribed ideas of 'white experts' had significant influence on definitions of 'traditional ownership' in the early days of the Land Rights Act (NT).

It's highly likely that the problems the DAA anticipated in 'obtaining land tenure for people in similar circumstances' to Tjuki and Sandra related to the apparent futility of seeking land tenure for a cattle station mob who had ancestral homelands several hundred kilometres to the south or west. However, these conflicts about what constitutes a traditional owner were not only debated among the 'white experts' of anthropology, or between Aboriginal and white settler conceptualisations of law. Tracker Tilmouth recalled that all the land claims at this time were also marked by 'arguments' and 'misunderstanding' of ownership among Aboriginal people; there is a sense in his recollections that these conflicts were a result of colonisation and subsequent migrations and removal of people from their Country.[63]

Francesca Merlan has argued in relation to Aboriginal speech about 'getting the land back' that the 'getting' is not understood by Aboriginal people as gaining formal title but, rather, taken to 'signify an active process of reasserting practical relationships to it'.[64] In light of this, it's possible to read Tjuki's letter to the DAA seeking help in 'getting' the land from Arthur Liddle as an attempt at maintaining a practical relationship with Angas Downs. In the four years that we recorded his life story together, Tjuki Pumpjack never talked to me about Muntawarra and the failed attempt to secure an outstation at Centenary Bore. When I brought it up with him, he wasn't much interested in talking about it. We visited the abandoned outstation at his granddaughters' suggestion, but standing among the ruins of a windmill and pieces of a rusted, decaying boring plant, his mood seemed to reflect the day itself, which was sombre and overcast. We didn't stay long and never spoke of Muntawarra again.

While I don't know exactly how the meetings about it played out, I imagine that the bureaucratic process to secure land tenure on Angas Downs, as outlined above, would have been unfamiliar to Tjuki Pumpjack. Four months after Tjuki wrote to the DAA seeking help, the area officer wrote to Arthur Liddle, informing him that:

> After due consultation with Tjuki and other members of the community it became evident that the Muntawarra group does not at this stage wish to move to Angas Downs.[65]

Sandra Armstrong says that they left Centenary Bore because they had to travel to Imanpa every day to take the kids to school, so it made more sense to live there.[66] Access to resources such as water and vehicles, and the provision of services such as education and health care, were significant in the establishment of outstations, and often constrained people's aspirations to live in smaller, decentralised communities. Muntawarra, with not so much as an adequate bore, lacked even the most basic resources, and thus the raw materials for social life.

Pastoral stations like Angas Downs were sites where people had lived, worked, shared, fought and died for three decades or more by the time a movement away from them began. In this sense, they were no different from mission and government settlements, no matter the administrative policy or development rationale behind them.[67] Movements away from Angas Downs during the 1960s and 1970s can't be understood in isolation, or solely in relation to the collapse of the relationship between Aṉangu and pastoralism. Rather, they must be examined in the context of the broader regional changes and migrations taking place at the time. Furthermore, these regional shifts, which resulted in yet another phase of spatial reorganisation, must be understood with a longer-term view, and as part of a continuous historical process of transformation that began with the earliest encounters with white settlers and 'settlements'.

From here, the history of Angas Downs gets infinitely more complicated. It moves into territory that lies beyond the scope of this book—territory that was a whole new world order, with radically different meanings, that requires a book of its own. The shift in rhetoric to a language of 'rights' and 'self-determination', and the subsequent funding for autonomous 'outstations' and 'communities', began to rapidly recalibrate social practices and relationships of exchange among Aṉangu, yet again. It's likely that 'the Muntawarra group' were encouraged to move to Imanpa, due to the probability of their failing to secure land tenure on Angas Downs, just as they were simultaneously drawn to it to avail themselves of the resources and services that had been concentrated there. Although the station continued to be a focus for both Tjuki and Sandra in various contexts, they were never able to 'get it back', in terms of reasserting the practical relationships that had *made* Angas Downs.

15

'THERE'S NOTHING THERE NOW, BUT IT'S STILL OUR PLACE'

IN RESPONSE TO my question 'Why did A<u>n</u>angu leave Angas Downs?', Tjuki Pumpjack provided a very different narrative from Sandra's:

> A long time ago we were living on Angas Downs. A long time passed and then we all moved to New Angas Downs. A long time passed ... Arthur Liddle was our boss for a long time. One day Arthur Liddle became ill and died. Bessie Liddle's husband died. After that we had no idea what we were to do. We said, 'What are we to do now?' 'Where should we go?' We decided, 'Let's all move to Imanpa, Imanpa is very close.' We all moved out of our houses, left those buildings and moved to Imanpa. This was because our boss Arthur Liddle had died. If he had not died we would still be there today.[1]

Tjuki Pumpjack and Sandra Armstrong began living at Imanpa community sometime around 1980–81. Despite Tjuki's statement that they moved away from Angas Downs because their boss died, Arthur Liddle was still alive at the time. In a history of the pastoral development at Angas Downs, historian Dick Kimber noted:

> Arthur Liddle continued to run Angas Downs as a cattle station during the 1980s and 1990s, but was under increasing pressure, as were many pastoral enterprises and was eventually taken over by

> the mortgagee. In 1994 the property was advertised for sale by the Commonwealth Bank and on 2 May 1994 it was purchased by the Imanpa community.[2]

Arthur Liddle lived for at least a decade after Aṉangu moved away from Centenary Bore. For ten years or more after Tjuki and Sandra moved to Imanpa, he persisted in trying to eke out a living on the marginal pastoral lands of Angas Downs; yet, Tjuki Pumpjack's oral history tells us that the cause of Aṉangu leaving the station was Liddle's death, stating matter-of-factly that if he hadn't died, they would still be living there today. What could this utterance mean?

Arthur Liddle's death wasn't the cause of Angas Downs' demise, but that Tjuki remembered it as such makes this episode in his memory rich with meaning. Sandra's memories of the same period—the desire of many Aṉangu to return to their Country; increased access to cash via pensions and 'sit-down money'; the emergent social problems of settlement life; the resulting aspirations of autonomy in smaller, decentralised communities; and the difficulties encountered in realising those objectives—articulate more squarely with the broader social, political and economic forces exerting an influence at the time. Congruent with the archival evidence and the various threads of historical and anthropological arguments woven since then, her memories lend themselves to the framing of this complex period of change in a somewhat 'faithful' and linear historical narrative. In contrast, Tjuki's remembrance illuminates the ways in which memory actively and creatively manipulates the past in an effort to make sense of the present.

In the essay 'The Death of Luigi Trastulli: Memory and the Event', oral historian Alessandro Portelli explores the death of Luigi Trastulli, a 21-year-old steel worker from Terni in Central Italy, and how it was 'elaborated, changed and interpreted in the *longue duree* of memory and culture'. Portelli illuminated the ways in which memory manipulated the dynamics, causes and chronology of Trastulli's death, in order to *heal the historical wounds* inflicted by circumstance and the event.[3] He argued that sometimes it is the 'dubious reliability' of oral histories that makes them valuable, and that the causes of 'faulty memories':

> [M]ust be sought, rather than in the event itself, in the meaning which it derived from the actors' state of mind at the time; from its relation to subsequent historical developments; and from the activity of memory and imagination.[4]

Confronted with Tjuki's 'faulty memory' of Arthur Liddle's death, Portelli's work encouraged me to focus my attention beyond the content of Tjuki's oral histories, and towards questions of why he remembered the end of Angas Downs the way he did.[5]

According to Portelli, memory manipulates factual detail and chronological sequence to serve symbolic, psychological and formal functions.[6] Guided by Portelli, in my reading it 'makes sense' to understand the collapse of the pastoral era as a traumatic experience for Tjuki Pumpjack, and to interpret the death of Arthur Liddle as an attempt, conscious or otherwise, at seeking adequate causation for an otherwise incomprehensible event. However, while the death of Arthur Liddle seems to suggest a psychological interpretation, there's much in Tjuki's oral histories that suggests more than individual psychology is required to understand his insistence that when Arthur Liddle died, '*everything changed for good*'.[7] Thinking deeply about the shifting and layered meanings of ngura, within the context of the momentous change that came with white settlers, sheep, cattle, bores and settlements, is necessary to understand Tjuki's interpretation of this period, and to speculate upon the broader spheres of place, sovereignty and recognition his memory might be interpreted as speaking to.

The half-century traced over the course of this book saw A<u>n</u>angu migrate to Angas Downs, set up camp there, and begin to translate existing social relations, made up of expectations and obligations, into the new pastoral context in which they found themselves. Bill Liddle sought to transform Walara into a sheep run he called Angas Downs, and from the moment A<u>n</u>angu arrived, in an open-ended system of exchange among kin, they set about transforming that sheep run into ngura. As A<u>n</u>angu relationships to place were reorganised through the act of migration, and the encounter with rations and work, A<u>n</u>angu simultaneously set about mobilising existing social and cultural practices to make a place for themselves at Angas Downs.

To be nguraritja is to belong to a place. Tjuki Pumpjack recalled that it was while he was living at Bloodwood Bore he began to think that he was nguraritja for that place:

> I lived my life here, without leaving, in the same way a true nguraritja would. I always thought to myself that I must be considered a nguraritja by now. I've been here my whole life, and I am now a tjilpi [Elder]. So here I am—a nguraritja. I married here, all my children were born here, my grandchildren were born here. I have granddaughters. Because I have been here for so long, I have to be considered to be a nguraritja. I got old here. I am a nguraritja, and I have no feeling or desire to be any other place. This is where I belong.[8]

Over the course of a life, Tjuki and others like him, now deceased, hunted, shared food, exchanged knowledge, performed ceremonies, got married, had children, fought and died, and these social events are both memorialised in the places they occurred and made the basis for claims of identification with particular places. Tjuki Pumpjack articulated his identification with Angas Downs in terms of a lifetime of embodied experience in that place. Over the period of time that we recorded together, it's the significant relationships he formed there that he repeatedly cited as justification for his claim of being nguraritja at that place, and, as he described it, he had 'no feeling, or desire to be any other place'.

Tjuki Pumpjack recalled that when they moved from Walara to Bloodwood Bore, 'ration times' started and many A<u>n</u>angu began arriving at the station. According to Tjuki, they came to Bloodwood Bore looking for rations and, because of this, A<u>n</u>angu who arrived at that time:

> They were visitors really, just visiting. They were people just visiting, coming to ask for rations. All visiting. However, people like me were the real nguraritja who had been there all our lives.[9]

Having walked to Walara with his family as a young child, Tjuki's sense of belonging to Angas Downs as nguraritja at around this time when others were arriving is made explicit, demonstrating the ways in which the cattle station was being incorporated into an intimate knowledge of place and relatedness. Frederick Rose carried out ethnographic fieldwork at Bloodwood Bore, the place where Tjuki said that he first began to feel like he was nguraritja. Tjuki is 'No. 1' in the 150 portraits that make up the final pages of Rose's ethnography. Rose spelled his name as Chuki and made the observation that:

> No. 1 appears as Chukumba in William Liddle's Day Book as being employed by him. He clearly has had considerable experience in the pastoral industry. He wore elastic sided boots and a wide brimmed hat, but there was nothing of the lair about him.[10]

The 150 photographs are arranged in family groups, and Tjuki, his two brothers and their respective families are the first families to appear. Rose's observation that Tjuki had appeared in Liddle's daybook and was clearly knowledgeable about the pastoral industry indicates Rose's awareness that Tjuki had been with the Liddles and worked on Angas Downs for a considerable period of time. Situating Tjuki as 'No. 1' in his visual record of the station community would appear to reflect Rose's recognition of Tjuki's senior status at Bloodwood Bore at the time of his fieldwork. A̲nangu acknowledged this too. Sandra Armstrong says of the time that she began working at Bloodwood Bore:

> Old Tjuki Tjukanku was really ninti, he was the number one, and he would be there. Old Tjuki Tjukanku.[11]

The word ninti in Pitjantjatjara means to *know* or be *knowledgeable*. To be knowledgeable in the A̲nangu social universe is to carry authority, and Sandra's use of the term to describe Tjuki, referring to him as 'number one', indicates recognition of the authority he held at Bloodwood Bore.

I, too, encountered this recognition of Tjuki's authority to speak for Angas Downs. I first visited Imanpa community in 2011. Rose's ethnography in hand, I was keen to learn more about the station and the people who lived there. I was told by numerous people that if I was interested in learning more about Angas Downs, I should speak to Tjuki Pumpjack—it was his place. I first met Tjuki Tjukanku Pumpjack in Imanpa in 2012. Standing out the front of the store as Tjuki and his wife Rosie approached, I said hello and introduced myself in awkward Pitjantjatjara. Rose's book in hand, I told Tjuki that I had something from Angas Downs I would like to show him, to which he replied in English, 'Angie Downs, that my Country.'

My arrival presented Tjuki with an opportunity to document his deep connection to Angas Downs as ngararitja for that place. I would keep returning to record his stories and knowledge, and, as such, I would also bear witness to his claim. The analysis offered in this book has been shaped in profound ways by this relationship. Regardless of the nature of my interest in Angas Downs, Tjuki had his own message that he wanted recorded. The act of 'witnessing' is of critical importance in the relationship between speaker and listener, and necessarily shapes the way that historians produce their histories. It automatically brings an oral historian close to their 'sources', and raises the challenge of how to respond, both ethically and critically, to voices in the present, as a means to understanding the past.[12]

The half-century traced in Tjuki Pumpjack's life history was in many ways focused upon a very present dilemma. He enjoyed that I kept turning up at Imanpa wanting to *know* more, and that I went to him to learn. He always made sure to emphasise when he was saying something that he considered to be important, while also stressing his authority to do so. It's significant that much of his oral history featuring in this chapter was recorded in our first two sessions together. Although he would go on to record various aspects of his life in detail over the following four years, at the time we recorded these memories he couldn't have been certain we would build a relationship that lasted as long as it did. The knowledge we recorded over those two days on

19 and 20 September 2012 is, I believe, what he considered to be the most important:

> I always stayed in the one place and I grew old and grey in that place, never leaving. I became the nguraku mayatja [boss for that place]—living my entire life in that one place, looking after it, managing it. It was there that I became an old man ... I grew up there from a little boy to an old man, in that one single place. I am now a nguraritja of that place. I have been there my whole life. This is an important detail, which is why I am mentioning it. Everyone says I am one of the most important people around here. White people always come and consult me. They always ask me where I am from and I always tell them, 'I have spent my entire life right here!' I grew up at Walara. I became a man here. I married here. I lost my wife here. As time went by I decided to get myself a second wife, a second companion, and so I married Rosie Tjapakula who comes from here ... I became a tjilpi [old man, Elder] here! By then, of course, I would always think to myself—surely I am nguraritja of this place? I must be a nguraritja. I never moved from here. I have lived here my entire life. I must be nguraritja. This is what I thinking. It was a fact that could not be denied. I would think to myself, 'I have lived my entire life here, working this land, caring for this place, and never left. Ngayulu nguraritja. I am an owner for this land now. I am just like a proper nguraritja, fulfilling all of the duties required by a proper nguraritja, living here my entire life, so I must be a nguraritja.
>
> So, even though I was born elsewhere, from the point in my life when my father announced we were all moving to where his older sister was living, we came here, and settled here, and never lived anywhere else.[13]

Tjuki Pumpjack lived a kind of life on Angas Downs that left him in no doubt he truly belonged to this place. That he was nguraritja was not just something he felt deeply but, as he makes a point of emphasising, carried an authority others recognised.

However, it is not only between A<u>n</u>angu that claims of identification are assessed. With the emergence of the *Aboriginal Land Rights*

(NT) Act 1976, and the *Native Title Act 1993*, the Australian state has made judgements whether First Nations people are who they say they are, and whether or not they conform to the legal discourse of 'authenticity' that has developed with these legislative frameworks for the legal 'recognition' of ownership.[14] Unchanging relationships between people and place lie at the heart of this settler-state-conceded notion of authentic Aboriginality, and First Nations people in Australia are required to perform this static criteria of authenticity in exchange for the state's recognition.[15] The settler colonial state's construction of peoples and identity in this way has impacted upon the politics of First Nations representation.

I understand Tjuki Pumpjack's statement as a reflection of the expectations that state-conceded 'recognition' places upon First Nations people. Ngura, and his sense of himself as nguraritja, as evoked in his oral histories, is somewhat self-conscious, as evidenced in his statement '*I think to myself, I must be the traditional owner, what else can I be?*'[16] Tjuki shifts between stating '*I am nguraritja of that place*' to questioning '*surely I am nguraritja of this place?*'; to saying he is '*nguraritja pu̱runypa*', which translates to *like* or *similar* to a nguraritja. Tjuki *felt* deeply that he was nguraritja, that Angas Downs was his ngura, and yet, there is much in his oral histories that indicates he was cautious about making such claims. The term nguraritja has been codified in land rights and native title legislation as 'traditional owner'. Anthropologist Peter Sutton notes that in native title legislation:

> '[T]raditional owners' are deemed to have rights to assert a relationship with their country as a matter of origin there, whether they live there or not. They 'really come from' or 'properly belong to' their country in an intrinsic sense ... 'Historical people' are living where they are because of historical factors such as migration and deportation, and do not 'really come from' their current location.[17]

The 2000–01 De Rose Hill native title claim in South Australia hinged upon the development of a definition of nguraritja that was 'stable' and 'law-like'. However, as anthropologist Paul Burke noted, the Anangu evidence of what constituted a nguraritja was indicative of the 'multiple pathways to "country" in the Western Desert', and in a number of cases asserted a more impenetrable, metaphysical assessment of nguraritja. In response to a question about his not being born on De Rose Hill station, Burke noted that Whisky Tjukanku responded, 'no I didn't born there but I am a nguraritja. The land tells me I'm a nguraritja'.[18] Whether or not Tjuki was, or would ever be, recognised as a 'traditional owner' by the state is not the concern here. Rather, I'm interested in illuminating the ways I think he came to internalise the paradoxes of place and belonging in the wake of colonial 'settlement'. Tjuki Pumpjack's evocation of his status as nguraritja seems to indicate great awareness of the consequences of history—emphasised in his utterance that even though he was born 'elsewhere', he considered himself nguraritja for Angas Downs.

Both Tjuki Pumpjack and Sandra Armstrong's oral histories have been rich source material, not just for charting the history of Angas Downs station over the course of the twentieth century but for the important insights they provide into changing relationships between people and place. Like Tjuki, Sandra Armstrong articulates her identification with Angas Downs in terms of her hard work and the process of learning that she underwent on the station. Although she grew up at Areyonga mission, where she went to school, it was to Angas Downs she always returned. Bloodwood Bore was where she learned the way of the cattle, the tourists, money and punu. It was also the site where her children were born, and the place where she took her older sister to die because she was afraid she would die in the wrong place.[19] Angas Downs is the place she returned to daily, in memory and in speech, as the primary locus of her identity, forged in the everyday intimacies of living, sharing and learning among kin. In the time that we spent together, there wasn't a single occasion Sandra didn't discuss Angas Downs, and express her sense of ownership of the place and raise the issue of 'getting it back'. There was no question in her mind that Bloodwood Bore was her place and, like Tjuki, she lived a kind of life there that made her sure of that.

Tjuki's and Sandra's memories have highlighted how the ways in which meaning was made changed as Anangu lives were lived under very different conditions of being-in-place, which emerged within the colonial context and were shaped by the cultural encounter.[20] Perhaps most significantly, even as Angas Downs reorganised A<u>n</u>angu relationships to place through migration, rations and work, as Tjuki's and Sandra's oral histories demonstrate, A<u>n</u>angu simultaneously began to transform the cattle station into 'camp', and, in turn, into Country.

Country isn't only a source of identity—it's passed down from one generation to the next. Those who 'hold' the Country are obliged to teach the next generation and *replace* themselves as holders of the Country.[21]Approaching the age of fifty, Tjuki Pumpjack was a senior man when the social order of Angas Downs began disintegrating. As Sandra said, he was ninti, and had reached the time in his life when the responsibility had fallen to him to hand down to the next generation the knowledge he'd accumulated and valued. However, the world in which he'd become a knowledgeable man disappeared.

Tjuki Pumpjack could not have seen coming the collapse of the world in which he saw himself as nguraritja. Writing of Plenty Coups, the last great Chief of the Crow nation, and of the moment the Crow moved onto a reservation in Montana in the early 1880s, philosopher Jonathan Lear observed the Crow had no conscious understanding of the 'breakdown of happenings' that were about to occur, and nor were they 'in a position to understand the significance of what it was they were about to endure'. Lear writes that the Crow did not 'self-consciously formulate laws of logic' but, rather, they lived in a way that 'manifested certain basic commitments' that opened out onto a 'field of possibilities'. Lear notes that when the Crow moved onto the reservation, the field of possibilities broke down. In his book *Radical Hope: Ethics in the Face of Cultural Devastation*, Lear asks the question 'what happens to the subject when the possibilities of living according to its associated ideals collapses?' It's impossible to know how Tjuki Pumpjack experienced the unravelling of life on Angas Downs. However, guided by Lear, it's possible to interpret his memory of Arthur Liddle's death as being witness 'to a loss that is not itself a happening but is the breakdown of that in terms of which happenings occur'. [22]

It must have perplexed the old people who had grown up on the stations when the opportunity to pass down the way of the horses, bullocks and managers disappeared.[23] Tjuki stated unequivocally that they left Bloodwood Bore because their 'boss' had died, and that if he hadn't died, they would have still been living there today. The death of Arthur Liddle in Tjuki's memory suggests a psychological interpretation—it seems to make sense to interpret the collapse of the pastoral era as traumatic for Tjuki Pumpjack:

> When [Arthur Liddle] died everything changed for good ... We were thinking, 'Oh, we got nothing! We'll have to go back to Imanpa! We have no boss man now!' So we had to move to Imanpa and this is where we stayed after that. And our old place went to nothing.[24]

The world he knew had given way to a new social order. In the wake of the failed attempt to keep living on Angas Downs, Tjuki surely felt powerless in the midst of such dramatic change. However, there are other possibilities when interpreting what the death of Arthur Liddle in Tjuki's memory might mean.

Lear's book *Radical Hope* is a philosophical enquiry into Crow chief Plenty Coups' statement:

> But when the buffalo went away the hearts of my people fell to the ground, and they could not lift them up again. After this nothing happened.[25]

At the outset, Lear argues that although it makes sense to interpret this statement as meaning the Crow became depressed after moving onto the reservation, the psychological interpretation is 'in too much of a rush'. Tjuki Pumpjack's oral histories indicate that the demise of Angas Downs struck at the core of his sense of self as nguraritja in that place. What if Arthur Liddle's death went deeper than traumatic response? What if, as Lear suggests, his memory provides insight into a particular point—the demise of Angas Downs—where things stopped happening?[26]

There was no decisive moment that brought the end of life on Angas Downs for A<u>n</u>angu. Rather, life gradually ebbed away over more than a decade, some thirteen years passing between the establishment of Docker River towards the end of 1967 and the move to Imanpa around 1981. While some may choose to look upon A<u>n</u>angu migrations to Angas Downs as representative of displacement, it's the demise of the station that emerges in Tjuki's oral histories as an experience of being displaced.[27] In my reading, this sense of displacement underpins a politics to his remembrance, which isn't just symptomatic of the trauma of past events but, rather, speaks directly to a politics and ethics of the present. In Tjuki's oral history, Liddle's death perhaps not only served to condense a complex and confounding period of change into a coherent story that made meaning out of that moment but also sought to endow the moment as a marker of time.[28] The death of Arthur Liddle signified a turning point in Tjuki's life history and he stated unequivocally that when Liddle died '*everything changed for good*'. The imaginative act of singling out Liddle's death as momentous marked the eclipse of 'ration times', with which Liddle was intimately associated, and the beginning of 'sit-down times'. 'Sit-down times' refers to the period characterised in Tjuki's memory by the distribution of cash in the form of welfare payments—or 'sit-down money', as A<u>n</u>angu call it. Perhaps more significantly, beyond the literal association with the extension of unemployment benefits to A<u>n</u>angu, the symbolism of 'sit-down times' in Tjuki's memory also points to the transformation of a social world understood in terms of travelling, sharing, learning and working into a social condition articulated in terms of immobility.

Rather than referring solely to the distribution of welfare payments, or to immobility in a literal sense, it's possible to read Tjuki's 'sit-down times' as reflective of a shift to conditions that were unknown, representing a 'gap' in his life story, reflective of an experience of (dis)placement. Reflecting upon recording the life story of Darwin man Roy Kelly, anthropologist Basil Sansom wrote that there are two things to note about a life story: one is sequence, and the other is 'gaps'. Sansom observed that 'Army Time' was a gap in Kelly's life story, as was his time served as a police tracker. Sansom wrote that it was a required gap:

> A time without story, consigned with good reason to the backward abyss of deliberately relegated experience. Things beyond recall are not unremembered, but are rather things deliberately to be put away.[29]

Tjuki Pumpjack relayed his oral histories as a series of journeys made over a lifetime of travelling. In his retelling, these journeys stopped short with the beginning of 'sit-down times'. In recounting his life, he never ventured into territory beyond this time and, sensing that this 'time' had been 'put away', I never asked him to.[30]

Similar to Plenty Coup's statement '[a]fter this nothing happened', Tjuki Pumpjack's remembering ended with Angas Downs. In his memory, 'sit-down times' was a place without story, and this was most likely an implicit critique of that era. As ngararitja for that place, there was nothing left for him to do, and, insofar as he was ngararitja, in practical terms he ceased to be.[31] There was a sense, not just in Tjuki's oral histories but also in his perspective on the world and his demeanour, that after Angas Downs, life lacked order and meaning:

> They are seeking new ways of life. They are moving around and tasting the white man's ways. They want to drink white man's wine. They want to smoke white man's drugs ... They want all these things and they are prepared to travel widely in search of them ... A lot of A<u>n</u>angu live like that nowadays. That's their choice. They have made their own lifestyle choice. I think they should all go home and stay home and look after their homes. But that is not their idea. That's not what they want. But their lifestyle choice leads to tears. I think they should stop, forget about the drinking and come back home.[32]

As Lear's interpretation of Plenty Coups' statement 'after that nothing happened' suggests, witnessing such a breakdown of happenings might well lead someone like Tjuki Pumpjack to say something enigmatic, like that when Arthur Liddle died, '*everything changed for good*'.

The various explanations traced here for the demise of Angas Downs illustrate Appadurai's observation that 'locality is a fragile social achievement':

> Even in the most intimate, spatially confined, geographically isolated situations, locality must be maintained carefully against various kinds of odds ... ecology and technology dictate that houses and inhabited spaces are forever shifting, thus contributing to an endemic sense of anxiety and instability to social life.[33]

Approximately ninety years old when he passed away in September 2015, the scale of the change Tjuki Tjukanku Pumpjack witnessed over nearly a century is impossible for me to fully comprehend. Over the course of his life, ecology, technology and government policy did, indeed, dictate that places would be 'forever shifting'. Against various kinds of odds, Tjuki Tjukanku Pumpjack, and A<u>n</u>angu generally, drew upon the raw materials of social life to negotiate what was imposed upon them by white settlers, and create new techniques and technologies of making place that would enable them to accommodate a constantly changing world.

For reasons beyond his control, Tjuki Pumpjack never got the opportunity to socialise the next generation and replace himself as nguraritja at Angas Downs. He had witnessed the collapse of a way of life and the passing into a time of no story. Towards the end of his life, he seemed troubled by the reality that he was unable to pass on his place. When recording at Walara, he would often say that the Country was dying because he was the last one left, and after him there was no one to 'hold' it. It seemed as though when he died, Angas Downs would die with him. This underpinned the four-year process of talking, travelling and recording oral histories with me—he was on a mission to have his knowledge, and his relationship to his place, recorded. Tjuki Pumpjack had lived a life on Angas Downs that left him in no doubt it was *his place*. Articulated in terms of nurturance, authority and life-long residence, he evinced the self-assurance of a person who truly *knows* a place.[34] Tjuki wasn't interested in the role of 'informant'; he had his own message and his own way of telling it. He told his story to preserve it, and did so with the hope that, one day, future generations of his family would find it, and learn about who they are and '*come back home*'.

However, Tjuki himself had not lived on Angas Downs for thirty or more years when I met him. While it's often assumed that the kinds of migrations that brought people like Tjuki Pumpjack to places like Angas Downs were representative of 'dislocation', it was clearly Angas Downs that he felt dislocated from. My turning up served as a catalyst for thinking and talking at length about the place. Tjuki was also keenly aware that others might end up reading this, and in showing us his Country, he's telling us who he was, and what his rightful place in it was. Having recorded his knowledge, I believe he left this earth with some sense that Angas Downs would remain ngura—which is to say a named and enduring place.

> There is nothing at Angas Downs, only the place itself, but it is still our place. – Tjuki Tjukanku Pumpjack

EPILOGUE: PALIMPSEST

THE PALIMPSEST—A TEXT having been overwritten, or erased to make way for another text—is an apt metaphor for Angas Downs. Describing Bulman pastoral station in the Northern Territory, anthropologist Gillian Cowlishaw wrote that the pastoral station as palimpsest is not about texts but rather:

> [E]ntails the lives of disparate people engaged in shaping their own worlds. Those being overwritten find that their images and texts, their relationships with their place, begin to merge with the imported ones and can no longer be expressed unchanged. The new surfaces are moulded to what was already there and one form of meaning can graft itself onto another, using the contours of an earlier text to establish its own shape. If shaken together they might combine, only to separate when left alone. In some places the new surface will never 'take'.[1]

Pastoral colonialism in Central Australia never really 'took' to the arid geographies that it sought to transform. This book ends in 1980, a decade or so after the pastoral paradigm collapsed, when the layers that made this place finally separated, and Aṉangu who remained moved from Angas Downs to Imanpa community. The story of Angas Downs gets more complex as it moves into the era that

Tjuki Pumpjack referred to as 'sit-down times'. It's a different world from the one in this book, and one that presents a starkly different set of circumstances in terms of the relationship between A<u>n</u>angu and the settler state, and people and place. It's very difficult to write a history of the present. Perhaps with time, it will be easier to make sense of what became of Angas Downs.

Despite the significant shift in experience that came with the end of Angas Downs, there are sentiments that, nevertheless, remained constant. In an article in the *Alice Springs News* in 2002, both Tjuki Pumpjack and Sandra Armstrong were quoted as saying that a proposed tourism business on Angas Downs was about 'keeping' the land, so that their children and grandchildren could 'hold' it forever. Tjuki Pumpjack is quoted in the article as a resident of Angas Downs and senior Traditional Owner:

> We're making a tourism business to make money for the children. We are keeping this land as A<u>n</u>angu land and the children can hold it forever ... these are our ideas, not the Government's idea or other people's ideas. We have to take care of our land so that when we pass away, somebody doesn't come and take it over.[2]

Sandra Armstrong said:

> We need Aboriginal businesses, so that the children can work when they finish school. We are making the business on Angas Downs now and when we finish up, then our children and grandchildren will run the businesses and manage the land forever. The kids are going to Nyangatjatjara College now and then later they will work at the new roadhouse and animal sanctuary on Angas Downs.[3]

The tourism business on Angas Downs never eventuated. Ten years after that interview, I sat in on a recording with Sandra and Sam Osborne, and listened as she expressed the same ideas about Angas Downs. In this sense, it's possible to understand Angas Downs, in Sandra's evocation of the place, as a symbol of what Lear describes as 'radical hope':

> But I'm thinking I need to settle down now at Angas Downs and do what they want, all of the younger generation. That's what I'm looking at. And this is what I'm talking about here (pulls out papers with a business plan for Angas Downs) ... I need to look at Angas Downs. That's all I need to do ... They first need to learn from Angas Downs, how to run a business for themselves, that's what I think. I'll be leaving this here and what will they think afterwards? And I'll be watching them like a spirit. That's what I think and I'm talking to them about this in advance, I don't know when I will pass away, (only) God knows my (time) ... From all my (affairs), they're all preparing, that's what I'm looking at, 'and you will all run (the) business on your own for the future generations, through your children, through your grandchildren'. That's what I can see into the future, not looking back.[4]

Lear writes that for a vibrant culture, it's the 'task of the older generation to adapt the culture's ideals to current challenges and to pass on those ideals to the next generation'.[5] In Sandra's statement, it's possible to read Angas Downs as symbolising that ideal and the hope for future generations of her family. A generation or more of absence from Angas Downs had passed, and yet I didn't spend a day in her company when Sandra didn't speak about 'getting Angas Downs back'. However, her talk of getting the land back shouldn't be understood solely in terms of state-conceded land rights or native title.[6] Rather, as Sandra articulated it, if she could re-establish the practical, lived relationship with Angas Downs, future generations could live a good life *and* hold onto their land.

Tjuki's comments tell us about much more than a prospective tourism business on Angas Downs. In his clear and powerful statements about Angas Downs, he's also showing us his sovereignty and self-determination. His is a sovereignty that Munanjahli and South Sea Islander scholar Chelsea Watego describes as both embedded in and derived from an embodied relationship to land.[7] Tjuki Tjukanku Pumpjack was in no doubt that Angas Downs was his place, and that this title derived from a power far greater than himself, or that of white settler state institutions—the Tjukurpa. He lived a life in this place that left him secure in the knowledge this was his rightful place.

In declaring to the *Alice Springs News* his rights to this land and to self-determination, he was standing strong in not only his sovereignty but his power. As Watego writes, this is a power derived from being the First Peoples of the land, and is reflected in the cries of 'still here' and 'always was, always will be', and, I would add, in Tjuki's statement that they are 'keeping this land as Aṉangu land [so that] the children can hold it forever'.[8] In asserting that Aṉangu must continue to take care of the land and prevent it from being taken over, he's showing us that this sovereignty was never ceded.

That Tjuki and Sandra were not able to hold onto their land, and pass on those ideals and socialise the next generation in the way they had hoped, was the *torment of their powerlessness*.[9] Echoing Tjuki's statement, Sandra, too, talked about the importance of the younger generations running 'things for themselves' and not 'having the government constantly pushing "Do this, do that"'.[10] I was struck by the ways in which Angas Downs was often mobilised, by both Tjuki and Sandra, by way of contrast to a complicated and, what seemed at times, anxiety-inducing present. At a time of increasing unemployment, intensifying government intervention in Aṉangu lives, alarming rates of imprisonment and endemic violence, Angas Downs, evoked as ngura, was remembered and reimagined by them as an alternative, or a solution, to the structural inequality they lived with.

First Nations people in Australia are the most incarcerated people on the planet, they are dying in police custody at an alarming rate, and their children are alienated from their families in unprecedented numbers. As the 2017 'Uluru Statement from the Heart' makes clear, this isn't because First Nations people are innately criminal, or because they don't love their families; rather, these dimensions reveal *the structural nature of the problem*.[11] Settler colonialism in Australia has bequeathed us with a set of laws, systems and institutions designed to affirm white settler superiority and privilege, while simultaneously denying First Nations peoples shared humanity, sovereignty and power. Despite Tjuki's and Sandra's persistent statements about their sovereignty that stemmed from Angas Downs, they found themselves living within a system that circumscribed their relationship to place, on grounds of race, in order to shore up white settler claims to land and power.

While pastoralism was undoubtedly both a capitalist and colonial enterprise, the particular circumstances that arose on Angas Downs throughout the middle decades of the twentieth century affirmed Anangu sovereignty during a time of increasing government interference in First Nations' lives and land. As Anangu relationships to place were reorganised through the act of migration and the encounter with white settlers, rations and work, Anangu simultaneously set about mobilising existing social and cultural practices to make a place for themselves at Angas Downs. Capitalising on the very few economic opportunities available to them, they did so in a way that enabled the continuity of knowledge exchange—in story, song and ceremony—among kin on Country. As Tjuki's and Sandra's stories demonstrate, even as Angas Downs reorganised Anangu relationships to place, Anangu simultaneously began to transform the cattle station into 'camp', and, in turn, into Country.

Tjuki's and Sandra's statements of connection to Angas Downs are articulated in terms of a lifetime of embodied experience and knowledge accumulated in that place. They both lived a life there that left them in no doubt that was where they truly belonged. This wasn't just something they both felt deeply but carried an authority also recognised by others. It's possible to read in their oral histories, and also in their silences and times of no story, an implicit critique of a present characterised by a lack of control over their own lives. Echoing the Uluru Statement from the Heart, there's a sense in their statements that if only they were empowered to take their *rightful place* in their own Country and to have control over their own destinies, their children would flourish and walk in two worlds.[12]

The politics of place continues to be keenly felt in Australia, and the 'problem' of the remote north is now commonly described by politicians and bureaucrats as 'wicked' or 'intractable'. Many assumptions and misapprehensions circulate about the circumstances of the region in which Angas Downs is situated but, in reality, they are poorly understood. This plays out in the present in multiple policy failures: First Nations people in remote areas present a major policy 'problem' because of their continuing 'difference' from 'mainstream' Australian society; policy discussion around 'employment' and the economic viability of the remote north remains largely ignorant of structural issues embedded in the 'marginality' of much of the geography; and the white settler state continues to be the arbiter of who is and isn't entitled to land rights, based upon white Western notions of Country as static, and ownership as evidenced in uninterrupted occupation of a place.

While the issues and debates surrounding the circumstances of the remote north have been intensifying since the 1990s, they assumed particular salience following the 2007 Northern Territory Emergency Response (NTER), otherwise known as 'The Intervention'. This enacted legislation enabling the Federal Government to intervene significantly in the lives of First Nations peoples living in the Northern Territory. While the reasons for the Northern Territory Intervention have been hotly contested, two years before its rollout the then Indigenous Affairs Minister, Amanda Vanstone, tellingly described remote First Nations communities as 'cultural museums'.[13] Since then, calls for the closure of remote communities, and the transfer of First Nations people from small communities and homelands to 'normalised' or 'centralised' townships, has pulsed in and out of public debate. Echoing the rhetoric of the Welfare Branch in the 1950s and 1960s and its approach to the 'itinerants', this reveals the persistent nature of settler colonial logic, and its desire to assimilate First Nations peoples and cultures into the dominant white settler capitalist state.

Deborah Bird Rose has argued colonialism's legacy is that contemporary circumstances are the result not only of violence but a 'misguided and misleading hope for the future'. As colonisers and settlers, we are only just beginning to grapple with the reality of invasion and its consequences in the present. When the purpose and meaning behind what colonialism has bequeathed us collapses, what are the alternatives? Bird Rose writes that there are no models from the past to guide a project aimed at decolonising modern settler societies. While the extent to which modern settler societies can ever truly decolonise is contested, Bird Rose's 'ethics for decolonisation' advocates for a moral and ethical engagement with the past as a means to a more just and equitable future.[14] Drawing upon philosopher Hannah Arendt's idea of 'dark times', Bird Rose suggests that it's the web of stories we weave from our shared pasts and experiences that will light the way forward. 'Recuperative histories and ethnographies', as Bird Rose refers to them, have an important role to play in this move towards dismantling the settler colonial mindset, which involves trawling 'the past for hidden histories and the local possibilities that illuminate alternatives to our embeddedness in violence'. As she sees it, there's no 'perfect state' for this kind of history writing to return or aspire to but, rather, a moral engagement with, and openness to, plurality and difference.[15]

Angas Downs is a site where different cultures, knowledge traditions and historical practices encountered one another. And yet, it is white settler narratives of discovery, civilisation, pastoralism and progress that have dominated how we see and think about this place. In order to stake its claim, the settler colonial construction of place as a white possession actively sought to overwrite the already deeply storied landscape and obscure First Nations ways of relating to place. This settler colonial creation of place has bequeathed us a world riven by racism, violence and environmental crisis, and we all inherit the consequences. Despite great efforts to control the narrative, the settler Australian psyche remains haunted by the original stories of this vast continent and the existential threat posed by the fact of First Nations sovereignty.

Mohawk scholar Audra Simpson has demonstrated that refusal is a powerful political stance in the fight for sovereignty, equality and justice in settler colonial states. Tracing the ways in which First Nations people have refused to be folded into settler colonial narratives of assimilation and recognition, Simpson argues that this politics of refusal challenges the assumption the colonial project is complete.[16] The concept of refusal is useful in thinking through approaches to the human- and land-based injustices that have resulted from settler colonialism, and been reproduced and sustained in the Australian historical imagination. Historian Samia Khatun writes that one key to finding a way out of the 'prison-house' of colonial thought is through the refusal to interpret the world on white settler colonial terms. Khatun argues that if we reject the racist and violent binaries of colonial modernist thought, and instead approach every moment in time and space as an intersection of many ways of being and knowing, we can begin to cultivate new ways of seeing the world.[17]

In tracing the making and unmaking of Angas Downs, this book represents an effort to write a recuperative history and cultivate a way of seeing and reading the past that can transform the way in which we understand our present circumstances. As a white settler woman, I understand there are contradictions and limitations inherent in my position, but I do believe, despite this, it is a necessary project and one worth pursuing. With Tjuki and Sandra as our guides, we can see clearly the colonial ideologies that have shaped our understanding of so-called Australia, particularly the heavily mythologised 'outback'. Following their stories across the Central Australian landscape works to unmake dominant narratives of white pastoral possession, and unsettle white settler colonial claims to knowledge, land and power. In this sense, the unmaking of Angas Downs suggests how settler Australians might begin to radically reimagine their relationship with people, other species, and the stolen land that we seek to belong to. As remembered and brought into being by two people who lived through and survived extraordinary change, transforming in order to make a place for themselves, Angas Downs shows us how past places might be imagined and interpreted anew in ethical and engaged histories, with a view to a more just and equitable future.

Acknowledgements

THIS BOOK IS a co-creation; the culmination of connections, conversations and collaborations that took place over many years.

I am most indebted and feel a deep sense of gratitude to Aṉangu—this is a book about their places and it wouldn't exist without their collaboration and contributions. I am deeply grateful to Tjuki Tjukanku Pumpjack for sharing his life, knowledge and Country with me. We didn't know each other when I first turned up in Imanpa, asking about Angas Downs. Over the years that followed I kept coming back. We travelled together and talked at length about his place and in the process, he changed my perspective on the world in profound ways. Above all, he showed me what it means to *love* a place, in the deepest sense of that word. Sandra Armstrong too, shared her life and her place with me. In her unwavering sovereignty and refusal to cede her sense of custodianship when whitefellas would tell her that she didn't 'own' Angas Downs, she showed me what fierce love looks like. She never stopped fighting for her rightful place.

The connection and conversations continue with Cynthia King, Kathleen Pumpjack and Michelle Armstrong. I hope that they feel proud to finally see their grandparents' stories in print.

It was so important to me that I hear and learn the places that are central to this story in the language that gives them meaning—Pitjantjatjara. Linda Rive made that possible and this book wouldn't exist without her incredible generosity. For four years we travelled the desert with Tjuki, listening and learning, and in doing so shared something truly profound. The conversations that took place around the fire as we shared food are the beating heart of this book and words cannot convey the depth of gratitude that I feel for the gift of her collaboration. I am also grateful to the rest of the team at Ar̲a Iritija—John Dallwitz, Dora Dallwitz and Julia Burke—this book owes so much to their support. I feel privileged to have been part of a project that, in Julia's words, grew out of 'An̲angu turning history on its head'.

This book began as a doctoral thesis in the School of History at the Australian National University, which was a wonderfully supportive environment for this intellectual endeavour—I benefited from the wisdom within the Coombs building immensely. My PhD scholarship was awarded as part of an Australian Research Council Linkage Project called *Deepening Histories of Place* and I am grateful to the project team, especially Ann McGrath, for seeing something in my research and encouraging me to apply. Being a part of that project helped to shape my early thinking about what it means to write histories of place in a colonised settler nation.

I had a great supervisory panel that allowed me to lose myself in the desert for many years and then engaged with me rigorously and generously when I needed it. I am deeply grateful to Martin Thomas and Luke Taylor for their close reading and thoughtful feedback at critical moments. I am particularly indebted to my primary supervisor Maria Nugent. With Maria as my guide, the creative process of bringing this book into being felt like alchemy. I thrived on being challenged by her rigour and tasked with taking my thinking deeper and further. I treasure that magical (and at times gruelling!) experience and can only hope that I get the opportunity to go deep on a creative project like that again in my lifetime.

I am also grateful to Tim Rowse, Heather Goodall, Fred Myers for their rigorous engagement with the work and the detailed and thoughtful feedback that helped to shape the final manuscript.

My colleagues in the School of History were a great source of support and, at times, some much-needed mischief. I am especially grateful to my dear friend and Coombs neighbour, Maria Haenga-Collins. Her friendship, love and laughter kept me grounded in the things that matter most and brought so much joy.

While I wandered the Central and Western deserts for many years, this book benefited immensely from the knowledge, expertise and generosity of a number of experts and practitioners 'in the field'. When I first started researching, Patrick Hookey's grasp of Pitjantjatjara language and intimate knowledge of people and place was inspiring and modelled a way of working that I hoped to emulate. Over the years I was fortunate enough to draw on his knowledge—the kind that I could never glean from a book—and I am forever grateful for his generosity in engaging with my research and writing. Sam Osborne was a constant source of inspiration and knowledge. His unwavering commitment to ethical research practices and co-creating knowledge helped to inform my approach to community-engaged research and collaboration. So too did Beth Sometimes. I am especially grateful for the countless conversations that we shared in Mparntwe about the ethics and practice of intercultural collaboration. My time living in Mparntwe and travelling in the Central and Western deserts was characterised by an acute sense of being both in and out of place—an experience that not only changed me, but is inflected in the very texture of this book. These significant relationships kept me and the research grounded.

I thank Ronald Briggs and Kirsten Thorpe at the State Library of New South Wales, Françoise Barr at the Northern Territory Archives Services and all the librarians and archivists who have helped me over the years. I am also grateful to Frederick Rose's daughter Ruth Struwe for granting me access to her father's archive and for her support for this research over the last decade.

I am thankful for the ACT Writers Centre's wonderful Hardcopy program, especially Nigel Featherstone and the 2017 non-fiction cohort, for providing an incredibly supportive and inspiring container to begin thinking about what is involved in publishing a book. Thank you also to Frank Bongiorno for his time and generosity when I first began trying to find a publisher.

Lily Withycombe has my deep appreciation for her keen editorial eye, which was invaluable at a critical moment in completing the manuscript.

I am also really grateful to the team at Melbourne University Press for believing in this book and facilitating the circulation of these important stories of place, especially to Louise Stirling for her warm support as we crossed each hurdle of the publication process.

To Rosemary Dobson and the Bolton family for the marvellous love and light-filled home that held me throughout an intense year of writing and now holds this story, alongside all that beautiful poetry, thank you for providing me with such a nurturing container for the deepest phase of the writing process.

The love and friendship of many people sustained me throughout this decade-long journey. To Jeanette, Geoff and Dallas, your unconditional love and support is a blessing. I love you all very much.

To my love, Anthony, your deep respect for the creative process and your unwavering belief in me has carried me through. I am so deeply grateful for you and your loving presence.

It is a great gift and I am thankful to all of you.

Notes

Prologue: Walara

1 There is some spelling and pronunciation variation among the different language groups. The same word is Yarnangu in Ngaanyatjarra.

2 Author field notes, 29 August 2012.

3 'Indigenous Protected Areas – Angas Downs', Department of Environment, Water, Heritage and the Arts, PDF factsheet. According to the Federal Government, IPAs are designated areas of Aboriginal-owned land where traditional owners enter into agreements with the state to promote conservation and biodiversity, as well as develop programs that deliver cultural, social and economic benefits to people and communities. See 'Indigenous Protected Areas', Department of the Environment and Energy, accessed 12 September 2016.

4 Luritja is another dialect of the Western Desert language family, which is thought prior to European contact to have bordered the lands of Pitjantjatjara-speaking communities in the west, and Yankunytjatjara- and Antikarinya-speaking communities in the south. See 'AIATSIS map of Indigenous Australia', AIATSIS. Angas Downs is cited in the IPA information leaflet as being situated on Maṯutjara country. However, there is considerable ambiguity around the distinctions between Western Desert dialects, and Maṯutjara is widely accepted by linguists as a northern variety of Yankunytjatjara (in contrast with Mulatjara, which is a southern speech variety). And yet, both Maṯutjara and Mulatjara have also been described as Antikarinya, which is thought to have bordered Yankunytjatjara country to the east. As linguist Paul Monaghan has observed, this ambiguity is perhaps indicative of the overlap of the labels Yankunytjatjara and Antikarinya. See Paul Monaghan, 'Laying Down the Country: Norman B. Tindale and the Linguistic Construction of the North-West of South Australia' (PhD thesis, University of Adelaide, 2003), pp. 227–8. Needless to say, there would have been considerable movement between people of different speech communities in this area, and it's highly probable that people from areas defined as southern Luritja and northern Pitjantjatjara and Yankunytjatjara moved through and used the area that became known as Angas Downs.

Introduction: Encounters in place

1 Klaus Neumann, 'Fred Rose: Communist, Scientist, Lover, Spy', *Inside Story*, 3 October 2015. See also Valerie Munt, 'Australian Anthropology, Ideology and Political Repression: The Cold War Experience of Frederick G.G. Rose', *Anthropological Forum* 21, no. 2 (2011): 109–29.

2 Geoffrey G Gray, *A Cautious Silence: The Politics of Australian Anthropology / Geoffrey Gray* (Canberra: Aboriginal Studies Press, 2007), p. 16. See also Patrick Wolfe, *Settler Colonialism and Transformation of Anthropology: The Politics and Poetics of an Ethnographic Event* (London/New York: Cassell, 1999).

3 For a detailed discussion of Rose's politics and their influence on his anthropology, see Peter Monteath and Valerie Munt, *Red Professor: The Cold War Life of Fred Rose* (Mile End, SA: Wakefield Press, 2015).

4 Craig San Roque, *The Long Weekend in Alice Springs*, adapted and drawn by Joshua Santospirito (Moonah: SanKessto Publications, 2013).

5 Edward W Said, *Orientalism* (New York: Pantheon Books, c 1978), pp. 88–90.

6 Linda Tuhiwai Smith, *Decolonizing Methodologies: Research and Indigenous Peoples* (London/New York/Dunedin: Zed Books Ltd and University of Otago Press, 2006), p. 1.

7 Heather Goodall, 'Too Early Yet or Not Soon Enough: Reflections on Sharing Histories as a Process', *Australian Historical Studies* 118 (2002): 17–20. Shannyn Palmer, '(un)making Angas Downs: A Spatial History of a Central Australia Pastoral Station, 1930–1980' (PhD thesis, Australian National University, 2017); See also Shannyn Palmer, 'Making Histories "Ngapartji-Ngapartji Way": Exploring Collaboration, Exchange and Intercultural Histories in a Colonised Settler Nation', *History Compass* 11, no. 2 (2013): 117–32.

8 Beth Sometimes, 'Apmere Angkentye-Kenhe: Language as a Music Playing Us' (Masters thesis, Victorian College of the Arts, University of Melbourne, 2018): 11–13.

9 Ibid., 66. I am indebted to Beth Sometimes, who helped me to hone my thinking around the ethics and practice of intercultural collaboration, during countless conversations in the town built on Mparntwe, which is now known as Alice Springs.

10 Elizabeth Edwards, 'Material Beings: Objecthood and Ethnographic Photographs', *Visual Studies* 17, no. 1 (2002): 67–75.

11 Sam Osborne, 'Staging Standpoint Dialogue in Tristate Education: Privileging A_nangu Voices' (PhD thesis, Victoria University, Melbourne, 2016).

12 See Tony Swain, *A Place for Strangers: Towards a History of Australian Aboriginal Being* (Cambridge UK; Melbourne: Cambridge University Press, 1993); Minoru Hokari, *Gurindji Journey: A Japanese Historian in the Outback* (Sydney: UNSW Press, 2011).

13 See Deborah Bird Rose, 'Writing Place', in *Writing Histories: Imagination and Narration*, eds Ann Curthoys and Ann McGrath (Melbourne: Monash University ePress, 2009), pp. 8.1–8.13. See also Stephen Muecke, Paddy Roe and Krim Benterrak, *Reading the Country: Introduction to Nomadology* (Fremantle: Fremantle Arts Centre Press, 1984); Swain, *A Place for Strangers*; Heather Goodall, *Invasion to Embassy: Land in Aboriginal Politics in New South Wales, 1770–1972* (Sydney: Sydney University Press, 1996); Deborah Bird Rose, *Dingo Makes Us Human: Life and Land in an Aboriginal Australian Culture* (Cambridge, UK: Cambridge University Press, 1992); Deborah Bird Rose,

Nourishing Terrains: Australian Aboriginal Views of Landscape and Wilderness (Canberra: Australian Heritage Commission, 1996); Richard Baker, *Land Is Life: From Bush to Town, The Story of the Yanyuwa People* (St Leonards: Allen & Unwin, 1999). For place in a global context, see Edward Casey, *Getting Back into Place: Toward a Renewed Understanding of the Place-World* (Bloomington: Indiana University Press, 1993); Arturo Escobar, 'Culture Sits in Places: Reflections on Globalism and Subaltern Strategies of Localization', *Political Geography* 20 (2001): 139–74; Doreen Massey, *For Space* (London: Sage Publications, 2005); Doreen Massey, *Space, Place and Gender* (Minneapolis: University of Minnesota Press, 1994).

14 Bird Rose, 'Writing Place'.

15 Aileen Moreton-Robinson, *The White Possessive: Property, Power, and Indigenous Sovereignty* (Minneapolis: University of Minnesota Press, 2015); see also Marcia McKenzie and Eve Tuck, *Place in Research: Theory, Methodology, and Methods* (New York: Routledge, 2015).

16 McKenzie and Tuck, *Place in Research: Theory, Methodology, and Methods*, p. 65.

17 Ibid.

18 Escobar, 'Culture Sits in Places: Reflections on Globalism and Subaltern Strategies of Localization'.

19 Fred R Myers, *Pintupi Country, Pintupi Self: Sentiment, Place, and Politics among Western Desert Aborigines*, (Canberra: Washington and London: Australian Institute of Aboriginal Studies; Smithsonian Institution Press, 1986).

20 See Danièle M Klapproth, *Narrative as Social Practice: Anglo-Western and Australian Aboriginal Oral Traditions*, Language, Power, and Social Process 13 (Berlin; New York: Mouton de Gruyter, 2004).

21 See Jeremy Beckett, 'George Dutton's Country', in *Encounters with Indigeneity: Writing about Aboriginal and Torres Strait Islander Peoples* (Canberra: Aboriginal Studies Press, 2014), pp. 1–27; Jeremy Beckett, 'Walter Newton's History of the World—or Australia', in *Encounters with Indigeneity: Writing about Aboriginal and Torres Strait Islander Peoples* (Canberra: Aboriginal Studies Press, 2014), pp. 28–58; Minoru Hokari, 'Gurindji Mode of Historical Practice', in *The Power of Knowledge, The Resonance of Tradition*, ed. Luke Taylor et al. (Canberra: Aboriginal Studies Press, 2005), pp. 214–22; Hokari, *Gurindji Journey: A Japanese Historian in the Outback*; Anne Marie Monchamp, *Autobiographical Memory in an Aboriginal Australian Community: Culture, Place and Narrative*, Palgrave Macmillan Memory Studies (Houndmills, Basingstoke, Hampshire: Palgrave Macmillan, 2014); Fred R Myers, *Pintupi Country, Pintupi Self: Sentiment, Place, and Politics among Western Desert Aborigines*, Smithsonian Series in Ethnographic Inquiry (Canberra: Washington and London: Australian Institute of Aboriginal Studies; Smithsonian Institution Press, 1986); Sylvie Poirier, *A World of Relationships: Itineraries, Dreams, and Events in the Australian Western Desert* (Toronto: University of Toronto Press, 2005).

22 Keith H Basso, '"Speaking with Names": Language and Landscape among the Western Apache', *Cultural Anthropology* 3, no. 2 (1988): 99–130; Keith H Basso, *Wisdom Sits in Places: Landscape and Language among the Western Apache* (Albuquerque: University of New Mexico Press, 1996).

23 See Alan Rumsey, 'The Dreaming, Human Agency and Inscriptive Practice', *Oceania* 65, no. 2 (December 1994): 116.

24 Moreton-Robinson, *The White Possessive: Property, Power, and Indigenous Sovereignty*, pp. 11–12. See also Nancy Munn, 'The Transformation of Subjects into Objects in Walbiri and Pitjantjatjara Myth', in *Australian Aboriginal Anthropology* (Nedlands, WA: University of Western Australia Press, 1970), pp. 141–63; Rumsey, 'The Dreaming, Human Agency and Inscriptive Practice'.
25 See Meaghan Morris, *Identity Anecdotes: Translation and Media Culture* (London: Sage Publications, 2006), pp. 5–6. Japanese historian Minoru Hokari's study of Gurindi historical consciousness led him to argue that historians need to go beyond writing histories of cross-cultural agents themselves and seek to *cross-culturalise history itself*. More recently, historian Samia Khatun has explored the use of non-English language sources as a means of making visible historical practices and epistemologies that have been subjugated by the 'suffocating monolingualism' of Australian history writing. See Minoru Hokari, *Gurindji Journey*; Samia Khatun. *Australianama: The South Asian Odyssey in Australia* (Saint Lucia, Qld: University of Queensland Press, 2018), p. 4.
26 Morgan Brigg and Mary Graham, 'The relevance of Aboriginal political concepts (5): Country, Place, and territory', *ABC Religion & Ethics*.
27 Megan Davis, 'The truth about truth-telling: Revisiting trauma is not the road to justice for Aboriginal people', *The Monthly*, (December 2021): pp. 10–12.
28 Bessie Liddle, who owned and ran the station with her husband Arthur from the 1950s through until the early 1990s, was living in Mparntwe while I was carrying out the research for this book. I first met Bessie in March 2012. After our initial meeting, I met with her on a number of occasions at her house to talk about Angas Downs. We sat together, drinking cups of tea and looking over the Rose photographs. Despite seeming to enjoy talking about life on the station, Bessie was adamant that she didn't want to record her story as part of the project. When I met Bessie's children, Lorraine and John Liddle, they too said they didn't want to participate.
29 Alexis Wright, *Tracker* (Artarmon, NSW: Giramondo, 2017).

Chapter 1 Whitefella food

1 Tjuki Tjukanku Pumpjack, oral history recorded by author, transcribed and translated by Linda Rive, 20 September 2012, Imanpa, Northern Territory.
2 'Why Aboriginals are Leaving It: Conditions in the South-West Reserve Described', *Examiner (*Launceston, Tas: 1900–1954), 23 July 1938, accessed 20 May 2014.
3 Tjuki Tjukanku Pumpjack, oral history recorded by author, transcribed and translated by Linda Rive, 26 October 2012, Imanpa, Northern Territory.
4 Diana Young, 'Dingo Scalping and the Frontier Economy in the North-West of South Australia', in *Indigenous Participation in Australian Economies: Historical and Anthropological Perspectives*, ed. Ian Keen, vol. 1 (Canberra: ANU E Press, 2010), p. 92, accessed 24 September 2012, p. 93.
5 Rani Kerin, *Doctor Do-Good: Charles Duguid and Aboriginal Advancement, 1930s–1970s* (North Melbourne, Vic: Australian Scholarly Publishing, 2011), p. 42. See also Rani Kerin, 'Dogging for a Living: Aborigines and "Undesirables" in South Australia', in *Frontier, Race, Nation: Henry Reynolds and Australian History*, eds Bain Attwood and Tom Griffiths (North Melbourne, Vic: Australian Scholarly Publishing, 2009), pp. 136–58.
6 AP Elkin, 'The Aborigines, Our National Responsibility', *The Australian Quarterly* 6, no. 23 (1934): 56.

7 Russell McGregor, *Imagined Destinies: Aboriginal Australians and the Doomed Race Theory, 1880–1939* (Melbourne, Vic: Melbourne University Press, 1997); p. 235.
8 Kerin, 'Dogging for a Living', p. 139.
9 Tjuki Tjukanku Pumpjack, 'Walking from Ernabella to Walara', interviewed, translated and transcribed by Linda Rive, June 2011, AI-0108954-003.
10 Jim Downing, Research Material relating to *Ngurra Walytja: Country of My Spirit,* 1964–72, NTAS NTRS 629, p. 28.
11 Niningka Lewis, 'I was born near Areyonga', oral history recorded, translated and transcribed by Linda Rive, October 2009, AI-0156069-002. This oral history was recorded for the Tjanpi Desert Weavers *Kuru Alala* exhibition catalogue and has since been archived with A<u>r</u>a Iritija. It's reproduced here with the permission of Niningka Lewis, Tjanpi Desert Weavers and NPY Women's Council.
12 Don Tonkin, *A Truly Remarkable Man: The Life of H.H. Finlayson, and His Adventures in Central Australia* (South Australia: Seaview Press, 2001), p. 59. Finlayson was being guided by then Tempe Downs station manager Bryan Bowman, so it's probable it was Bowman who provided Finlayson with this information.
13 Myers, *Pintupi Country, Pintupi Self*, p. 27.
14 Richard Baker, 'Coming In?: The Yanyuwa as a Case Study in the Geography of Contact History', *Aboriginal History* 14, no. 1–2 (1990): 31–2. See also Baker, *Land Is Life*.

Chapter 2 The white experts

1 Winifred M Hilliard, *The People in Between: The Pitjantjatjara People of Ernabella* (London: Hodder & Stoughton, 1968), p. 96.
2 Kerin, *Doctor Do-Good*, p. 25.
3 Charles Duguid, *Doctor and the Aborigines* (Adelaide: Rigby, 1972), p. 115. Emphasis added.
4 Duguid to Minister, 26 June 1938, quoted in Kerin, *Doctor Do-Good*, p. 32.
5 Geoffrey Gray, '"[The Sydney School] Seem[s] to View the Aborigines as Forever Unchanging": Southeastern Australia and Australian Anthropology', *Aboriginal History* 24 (2000): 176–9. For a detailed discussion of theories of Aboriginal extinction, see: McGregor, *Imagined Destinies*; Warwick Anderson, *The Cultivation of Whiteness: Science, Health and Racial Destiny in Australia* (Melbourne: Melbourne University Press, 2002).
6 WEH Stanner, *The Dreaming & Other Essays* (Melbourne: Black Inc. Agenda, 2009), p. 134.
7 Heather Goodall, 'An Intelligent Parasite: A.P. Elkin and White Perceptions of the History of Aboriginal People in New South Wales' (Paper presented to the Australian Historical Association: Sydney, 1982), pp. 16–20. See AP Elkin, 'Reaction and Interaction: A Food Gathering People and European Settlement in Australia', *American Anthropologist* 53, no. 2 (1951): 164–86.
8 TGH Strehlow, Report on Trip to the Petermann Ranges, August 1939, NAA F1 1938/418, Aboriginal Reserve South West Corner (includes Report on a Reconnaissance in the Mount Doreen Mineral Area Central Australia by CT Madigan) 1932–1941.
9 Ibid.
10 Duguid, 1941, quoted in Kerin, '"Doctor Do-Good"?', p. 66.
11 Ibid.

12 'Living with Drought', The Bureau of Meteorology.
13 Libby Robin, 'Seasons and Nomads: Reflections on Bioregionalism in Australia', in *The Bioregional Imagination: Literature Ecology and Place*, ed. Tom Lynch et al. (Athens: University of Georgia Press, 2012), p. 281.
14 Mike Smith, *The Archaeology of Australia's Deserts* (Cambridge: Cambridge University Press, 2013), pp. 6–7.
15 WG Whitford, *Ecology of Desert Systems* (San Diego: Academic Press, 2002), p. 12.
16 Ingreth Macfarlane, 'Entangled Places: Interactive Histories in the Western Simpson Desert, Central Australia' (PhD thesis, Australian National University, 2010), p. 77.
17 Whitford, *Ecology of Desert Systems*, pp. 12–13.
18 George Seddon, *Landprints: Reflections on Place and Landscape* (Cambridge, UK: Cambridge University Press, 1997), p. 226.
19 JW Gregory, *The Dead Heart of Australia: A Journey Around Lake Eyre in the Summer of 1901–02, with Some Account of the Lake Eyre Basin and the Flowing Wells of Central Australia* (London: J. Murray, 1906).
20 Ernest Giles, *Australia Twice Traversed: The Romance of Exploration Being A Narrative Compiled from the Journals of Five Exploring Expeditions Into and Through Central South Australia and Western Australia, From 1872 to 1876* (London: Sampson Low, Marston, Searle & Rivington, 1889), vol. 1, p. xxv.
21 Ibid., vol.1, p. 83.
22 WC Gosse, 'South Australia. W.C Gosse's Explorations, 1873: Report and Diary of Mr. W.C. Gosse's Central and Western Exploring Expedition, 1873' (Adelaide: House of Assembly, 1874), p. 1.
23 Peter Read and Engineer Jack Japaljarri, 'The Price of Tobacco: The Journey of the Warlmala to Wave Hill, 1928', *Aboriginal History* 2 (1978), p. 145.
24 Stanner, *The Dreaming & Other Essays*, p. 131.
25 Cecil Cook, Chief Protector of Aboriginals Northern Territory, 9 March 1937, NAA F1 1938/481.
26 See Mike Smith, *Peopling the Cleland Hills: Aboriginal History in Western Central Australia, 1850–1980*, Aboriginal History Monograph Series no. 12 *Aboriginal History*, (2005), p. 29, pp. 51–2; Mervyn John Meggitt, *Desert People: A Study of the Walbiri Aborigines of Central Australia* (London: Angus & Robertson, 1975), p. 25; Myers, *Pintupi Country, Pintupi Self*, p. 35; Norman B Tindale, 'The Pitjandjara', in *Hunters and Gatherers Today: A Socioeconomic Study of Eleven Such Cultures in the Twentieth Century*, ed. MG Bicchieri (New York: Holt, Rinehart & Winston, 1972), pp. 217–68; Robert Layton, *Uluru: An Aboriginal History of Ayers Rock* (Canberra: Australian Institute of Aboriginal Studies, 1986), p. 59; Downing, *Ngurra Walytja*, p. 28; Phillip Toyne and Daniel Vachon, *Growing Up the Country: The Pitjantjatjara Struggle for Their Land* (Melbourne: McPhee Gribble, 1984), p. 26.
27 Layton, *Ibid.*, p. 60.
28 Strehlow, Report on Trip to the Petermanns, F1 1938/418.
29 This phenomenon is similarly reflected in Peter Read's analysis of Engineer Jack's oral history of the move of Warlmala people to Wave Hill station. See Read and Japaljarri, 'The Price of Tobacco', p. 146. See also John Carty, 'Creating Country: Abstraction, Economics and the Social Life of Style in Balgo Art' (PhD thesis,

ANU, 2011), p. 27. Similarly, the thirty sworn statements from pastoralists, missionaries and other interested parties in the 1929 Board of Inquiry into the Coniston Massacre unanimously denied any evidence of hunger or starvation. See 'Attacks on white men by natives – Killing of natives – Central Australia [Attachment titled 'Finding of Board of Enquiry with exhibits 1–13']', NAA A431 1950/2768 Part 2.

30 Tjukupati James, interviewed by John Tregenza, translated by Nancy Sheppard, 13 September 1997, Kaltukatjara (Docker River), Northern Territory, AI-0001577-001.

31 Deborah Bird Rose, 'To Dance With Time: A Victoria River Aboriginal Study', *The Australian Journal of Anthropology* 11, no. 3 (2000), p. 290.

32 Nyanu Watson, interviewed by Thisbe Purich for Tjanpi Desert Weavers, July 2008, Mantamaru (Jamieson), Western Australia, AI-0123837. This transcript is reproduced here with the permission of Nyanu Watson, Tjanpi Desert Weavers and the NPY Women's Council.

33 Tjuki Tjukanku Pumpjack, 26 October 2012.

34 Finlayson, diary entry dated 22 March 1932, quoted in Tonkin, *A Truly Remarkable Man*, p. 47.

35 Duguid, *Doctor and the Aborigines*, p. 136.

Chapter 3 Walytja

1 Giles, *Australia Twice Traversed*, vol. 1, p. iv.

2 Mervyn Hartwig, "The Progress of White Settlement in the Alice Springs District and Its Effects upon the Aboriginal Inhabitants, 1860–1894' (PhD thesis, University of Adelaide, 1965), pp. 404–6.

3 Rowse, 'Aborigines as Historical Actors: Evidence and Inference', *Historical Studies* 22, no. 87 (October 1986), p. 183.

4 Carty, 'Creating Country', p. 28.

5 Tjuki Tjukanku Pumpjack, 20 September 2012.

6 Jim Cotterill to Frederick Rose, 11 June 1963, SLNSW Frederick Rose Papers, Box 36.

7 Ibid.

8 Ibid.

9 Finlayson in Tonkin, *A Truly Remarkable Man*, p. 80.

10 Finlayson, photographs relating to the 'Petermann Range Natives At Moment Domiciled in Basedow Range' 1932, SAM AA93/1/6–27.

11 Tjuki Tjukanku Pumpjack, interviewed by author, transcribed and translated by Linda Rive, 17 July 2014, Kulata Well, Erldunda station, Northern Territory.

12 Bird Rose, *Dingo Makes Us Human*, p. 53.

13 Strehlow, letter, 30 April 1937, NAA F3 32/1 Patrol Officer Strehlow General 1936–41.

14 Rowse, 'Aborigines as Historical Actors', p. 184.

15 Tjuki Tjukanku Pumpjack, 20 September 2012.

Chapter 4 Founding moments

1 Russel Ward, *The Australian Legend* (Melbourne: Oxford University Press, 1958), p. 10.

2 Bertram Keith, 'People of the Centre: Man and Environment in the Northern Territory', *Walkabout*, September 1948.

3 Glen Ross, 'The Fantastic Face of the Continent: The Australian Geographical Walkabout Magazine', *Southern Review: Communication, Politics, Culture* 32, no. 1 (1999). See also ME McGuire, 'Whiteman's Walkabout' *Meanjin* 52, no. 3 (1993), pp. 27–41; Mitchell Rolls and Anna Johnson, '*Walkabout Magazine and Mid-Twentieth Century Australia* (London: Anthem Press, 2016); Mitchell Rolls, 'Picture Imperfect: Re-Reading Imagery of Aborigines in *Walkabout*', *Journal of Australian Studies* 33, no. 1 (2009), pp. 19–35; Lynette Russell, *Savage Imaginings: Historical and Contemporary Constructions of Australian Aboriginalities* (Melbourne: Scholarly Publishing, 2001).

4 Tjuki Tjukanku Pumpjack, 26 October 2012. Sandra Armstrong's oral history also includes a story of how Bill Liddle came to be at Angas Downs. See oral history recorded and translated by Linda Rive, 18 August 2009, Alice Springs, AI-0108943.

5 Eric Jamieson and Heather Harvey, *Red Sand in Our Shoes: The Andrew Family* (Eric Jamieson, 2001), pp. 3–4.

6 Merv Andrew, interviewed by Paul France, 16 August 1983, Alice Springs, NTAS Northern Territory Oral History Unit, TS150.

7 Ray Arbon quoted in Jamieson and Harvey, *Red Sand in Our Shoes*, p. 18.

8 Tjuki Tjukanku Pumpjack, 26 October 2012.

9 Tjuki Tjukanku Pumpjack, oral history recorded by author, translated and transcribed by Linda Rive, 13 March 2013, Wilpiya, Angas Downs, Northern Territory.

10 Tjuki Tjukanku Pumpjack, oral history recorded by author, translated and transcribed by Linda Rive, 4 October 2013, Ulanga Well, Angas Downs. Tjuki spoke in a blend of Pitjantjatjara and English on this occasion. Tjuki's English is retained as it was spoken and the translation incorporated for the Pitjantjatjara parts of the conversation.

11 WH Liddle to Deputy Administrator, 11 June 1936, NTAS NTRS 246 P/2 – PL 584, Pastoral Lease Files 1914–94.

12 Chief Clerk, Lands and Surveys Branch, 22 September 1936, in NTAS NTRS 246 P/2 – PL 584.

13 Strehlow, Report on trip to Southwestern Station area, 8 December 1938, NAA F3 32/3 Patrol Officer Strehlow Monthly Reports 1938–1942.

14 Gladys Baker in Jamieson and Harvey, *Red Sand in Our Shoes*, p. 45.

15 Snowy Pearce quoted in Constable AP Lynch to Constable Muldoon, 15 April 1937, NAA F3 32/1.

16 Liddle to Constable Muldoon, 15 April 1937, NAA F3 32/1.

17 Michael T Taussig, *Shamanism, Colonialism, and the Wild Man: A Study in Terror and Healing* (Chicago: University of Chicago Press, 1986).

18 Tjuki Tjukanku Pumpjack, 'They didn't understand properly' in Marg Bowman, ed., *Every Hill Got a Story*, p. 89.

19 Ibid.

20 Taussig, *Shamanism, Colonialism, and the Wild Man*, p. 121.

21 Mark McKenna, *Return to Uluru* (Carlton: Black Inc., 2021).

Chapter 5 Founding entanglements

1 Oral history transcript, 4 October 2013.

2 Tjuki Tjukanku Pumpjack, 4 October 2013.

3 Ibid.

4 Nicholas Gill, 'Transcending Nostalgia: Pastoralist Memory and Staking a Claim in the Land', in *Dislocating the Frontier: Essaying the Mystique of the Outback*, edited by Deborah Bird Rose and Richard Davis (Canberra: ANU E Press, 2005), p. 75.
5 Finlayson quoted in Tonkin, *A Truly Remarkable Man*, p. 63.
6 See Ann McGrath, *Born in the Cattle* (St Leonards: Allen & Unwin, 1987).
7 Finlayson quoted in Tonkin, *A Truly Remarkable Man*, p. 69.
8 Alistair Paterson, 'Early Pastoral Landscapes and Culture Contact in Central Australia', *Historical Archaeology* 39, no. 3 (1 January 2005), p. 29. See also Paterson, 'The Texture of Agency: An Example of Culture–Contact in Central Australia', *Archaeology in Oceania* 38, no. 2 (2003); PG Spooner, M Firman and Yalmambira, 'Origins of Travelling Stock Routes: Connections to Indigenous Traditional Pathways', *The Rangeland Journal* 32, no. 3 (2010); Rodney Harrison, *Shared Landscapes: Archaeologies of Attachment and the Pastoral Industry in New South Wales* (Sydney: University of New South Wales Press, 2004).
9 Goodall, *Invasion to Embassy*, p. 71. See also Harrison, *Shared Landscapes*, pp. 32–3; Mary Anne Jebb, 'Pastoral Paternalism in the Pilbara' in *Marlbatharndu Wanggagu: Once Upon A Time in the West* (Perth: FORM, 2014), p. 146; Paterson, 'The Texture of Agency', p. 56.
10 Tjuki Tjukanku Pumpjack, 26 October 2012.
11 Thalia Anthony, 'Was There Slavery in Australia? Yes. It Shouldn't Even Be Up for Debate', *The Conversation*, 11 June 2020.
12 Bruce Breaden, 'Lucky to have been educated two ways' in Bowman, *Every Hill Got a Story*, p. 63.
13 Tjuki Tjukanku Pumpjack, 4 October 2013.
14 Andrew, NTAS TS150.
15 Ibid.
16 Gillian Cowlishaw, *Rednecks, Eggheads and Blackfellas: A Study of Racial Power and Intimacy in Australia* (St Leonards: Allen & Unwin, 1999), p. 72.
17 Tim Rowse, *White Flour, White Power* (Cambridge: Cambridge University Press, 1998), p. 120.
18 Strehlow to Chief Protector of Aboriginals, 19 July 1937, NAA E740, P131, Lynda Vale 1937–39.
19 Ward, *The Australian Legend*, p. 74.
20 See Chris Healy, *Forgetting Aborigines* (Sydney: University of New South Wales Press, 2008), pp. 192–3.
21 Rowse, *White Flour, White Power*, pp. 121–2. See also Brigid Hains, *The Ice and the Inland: Mawson Flynn, and the Myth of the Frontier* (Carlton South: Melbourne University Press, 2002), pp. 121–3.
22 Tjuki Tjukanku Pumpjack, 20 September 2012.

Chapter 6 Found in translation

1 Myers, *Pintupi Country, Pintupi Self*, pp. 211–12.
2 Diane Austin-Broos, 'Places, Practices and Things: The Articulation of Arrernte Kinship with Welfare and Work', *American Ethnologist* 30, no. 1 (February 2003), p. 125.
3 Personal communications with Linda Rive, July 2015.
4 Diane Austin-Broos, '"Working for" and "Working" among Western Arrernte in Central Australia', *Oceania* 76, no. 1 (March 2006), p. 6.

5 TGH Strehlow, 'Geography and the Totemic Landscape in Central Australia: A Functional Study', in *Australian Aboriginal Anthropology*, ed. Ronald M Berndt (Nedlands: University of Western Australia Press, 1970), p. 132.
6 Bird Rose, *Dingo Makes Us Human*, p. 101.
7 Robert Kenny, *The Lamb Enters the Dreaming: Nathanael Pepper and the Ruptured World* (Carlton North: Scribe, 2010), pp. 167–8.
8 Ibid., pp. 172–3.
9 Tjuki Tjukanku Pumpjack, 26 October 2012.
10 Kenny, *The Lamb Enters the Dreaming*, p. 173.
11 Ibid., pp. 177–8.
12 Tjuki Tjukanku Pumpjack, 26 October 2012.
13 Bird Rose, *Dingo Makes Us Human*, p. 101.
14 WL Clough, 'W.H Liddle—Angus Downs Station', 6 September 1943, NTAS NTRS 246 P/2, PL584.
15 Tjuki Tjukanku Pumpjack, 20 September 2012.
16 Ibid.

Chapter 7 Ration times

1 Report on Patrol of Southern Stations, Finke Police District and South-West Reserve, 29 August 1949, NAA F1 1952/470, South West Reserve 1940–1952.
2 Drought Relief Bores–Angas Downs, 25 September 1957, NTAS NTRS 246 P/2, PL 584.
3 Tjuki Tjukanku Pumpjack, 'Bullock Business', recorded, translated and transcribed by Linda Rive, June 2011, AI-0108954.
4 Niningka Lewis, oral history recorded, translated and transcribed by Linda Rive, October 2009, AI-0156069-001. This oral history was recorded for the Tjanpi Desert Weavers *Kuru Alala* exhibition catalogue and has since been archived with A<u>r</u>a Iritija. It's reproduced here with the permission of Niningka Lewis, Tjanpi Desert Weavers and NPY Women's Council.
5 Carol Booth and Wendy Tubman, 'Water Down Under: Understanding and Managing Australia's Great Artesian Basin' (Canberra: Commonwealth of Australia, 2011), p. 12.
6 Michael Cathcart, *The Water Dreamers: The Remarkable History of Our Dry Continent* (Melbourne: Text Publishing, 2009), p. 174.
7 Booth and Tubman, 'Water Down Under: Understanding and Managing Australia's Great Artesian Basin', p. 11.
8 Tjuki Tjukanku Pumpjack, 20 September 2012.
9 Tjuki Tjukanku Pumpjack, 'Bullock Business', AI-0108954.
10 Frederick GG Rose, *The Wind of Change in Central Australia: The Aborigines at Angas Downs, 1962* (Berlin: Akademie–Verlag, 1965), p. 32. Rose had access to William Liddle's 'Daybook', which was in the possession of Jack and Jim Cotterill at the time of his fieldwork.
11 Rowse, *White Flour, White Power*.
12 Ibid., p. 8.
13 Ted Ling, *Commonwealth Government Records about the Northern Territory*, (Canberra: National Archives of Australia, 2011), p. 139.
14 TC Lovegrove to Acting District Superintendent, 6 December 1954, NAA F1 1953/488.

15 'List of "Dependents" receiving rations at Angas Downs', 1954, NAA F1 1953/488.
16 Pastor Albrecht, letter to District Welfare Officer, 20 August 1959, NAA F1 1955/552 Claims Payments and Employment of Aboriginals Angas Downs 1955–1962.
17 Rose, *The Wind of Change*, p. 61.
18 Rowse, *White Flour, White Power*, pp. 118–19. Rowse notes that in 1965–66, 12 per cent of pastoral leases accommodated 59 per cent of the Aboriginal population in the region.
19 Ibid., p. 3.
20 Alessandro Portelli, *The Death of Luigi Trastulli and Other Stories: Form and Meaning in Oral History* (Albany: State University of New York Press, 1991), p. 63.
21 Rose was particularly interested in polygyny, which referred to the practice of having multiple marriage partners, and gerontocracy, there being a significant age gap between a younger woman and her older husband. See Rose, *The Wind of Change*, p. 3.
22 Ibid., pp. 11–33.
23 Conference Paper, Berlin, 1965, SLNSW Frederick Rose Papers, Box 36.
24 Valerie Munt, 'Australian Anthropology, Ideology and Political Repression', 121. See also Monteath and Munt, 'Groote Revisited' in *Red Professor*.
25 Rose's doctorate was published in 1960. See Frederick GG Rose, *Classification of Kin, Age Structure and Marriage amongst the Groote Eylandt Aborigines: A Study in Method and a Theory of Australian Kinship* (Berlin: Akademie, 1960).
26 Rose, *The Wind of Change*, pp. 4–5.
27 Bill Harney to Frederick Rose, 22 June 1962, SLNSW Frederick Rose Papers, Box 4.
28 Ibid.

Chapter 8 The wind of change

1 Rose, *The Wind of Change*, pp. 24–5.
2 Frederick Rose, summary of lecture 'The Aborigines of Angas Downs, Central Australia 1962', July 1964, Berlin, SLNSW Frederick Rose Papers, Box 1.
3 Bryan Bowman, *A History of Central Australia 1930–1980: From Horse and Camel to Motor Car, from Motor Car to Helicopter and Jet*, 2 vols. (Alice Springs: Bryan Bowman, 1989); Max Cartwright, *From Bush Tracks to Highway: An Account of Aborigine Footprints to the Horse and Camel Tracks of the Explorers, Followed by the Motor Tracks of Later Years: In the South Western Regions of Central Australia* (Alice Springs: Max Cartwright, 1994).
4 Bowman, p. 32.
5 Alison Bashford, 'World Population and Australian Land: Demography and Sovereignty in the Twentieth Century', *Australian Historical Studies* 38, no. 130 (1 October 2007): 211–27; Hains, *The Ice and the Inland*; Russell McGregor, 'Develop the North: Aborigines, Environment and Australian Nationhood in the 1930s', *Journal of Australian Studies* 28, no. 81 (January 2004): 33–45; Russell McGregor, 'A Dog in the Manger: White Australia and Its Vast Empty Spaces', *Australian Historical Studies* 43, no. 2 (June 2012): 157–73; Libby Robin, 'The Empty North', in *How a Continent Created a Nation* (Sydney: University of New South Wales Press, 2007), pp. 123–51.

6 Northern Australia Development Committee, 'Development of Northern Australia, 1947', NAA 1972/84. See also Russell McGregor, 'Developing the North, Defending the Nation? The Northern Australian Development Committee, 1945–1949', *Australian Journal of Politics and History* 59, no. 1 (March 2013): 33–46.
7 Ted Ling, *Commonwealth Government Records about the Northern Territory* (Canberra: National Archives of Australia, 2011), p. 73.
8 Ibid.
9 Tjuki Tjukanku Pumpjack, 'Bullock Business', AI-0108954.
10 J Hunter, 'Inspection Report Angas Downs', 24 August 1959, NAA F1 1955/552, Claims Payments and Employment of Aboriginals Angas Downs 1955–62.
11 Rose, *The Wind of Change*, p. 62.
12 Ibid., p. 36.
13 See Sam Osborne, 'Staging Standpoint Dialogue in Tristate Education'.
14 Sandra Armstrong, interview recorded by author, 8 October 2013, Mitchell Library SLNSW.
15 Sandra Armstrong, interviewed by author, 7 October 2013, Mitchell Library SLNSW.
16 Sandra Armstrong, oral history recorded and translated by Linda Rive, 18 August 2009, AI-0108943.
17 Arjun Appadurai, *Modernity at Large: Cultural Dimensions of Globalisation* (Minneapolis: University of Minnesota Press, 1996). See also Hugh Raffles, '"Local Theory": Nature and the Making of an Amazonian Place', *Cultural Anthropology* 14, no. 3 (1999).
18 Tjuki Tjukanku Pumpjack, 20 September 2012.
19 Ibid.
20 Anthropologist Fred Myers has observed that ritual knowledge is the most significant sphere of exchange among men. Myers, *Pintupi Country, Pintupi Self*, p. 221.
21 Ann McGrath observed during her fieldwork in the Northern Territory that Aboriginal people had incorporated the 'learning experiences offered by the station into the necessary regimen of training which made girls women and boys men', and that links had emerged between knowledge in the cattle industry and 'manhood'. However, whereas McGrath speculated this was a move that enabled Aboriginal people to 'justify and acknowledge the validity of the move to the station, and the propriety of working for whites', Tjuki's oral histories suggest that knowledge of the cattle industry became embedded in a social process that, more than serve to 'justify' the move to the station, came to lie at the heart of a person's identity and sense of place. See McGrath, *Born in the Cattle*, p. 167.
22 Appadurai, *Modernity at Large*, p. 179.
23 Ibid.
24 Fred Myers, 'Ways of Placemaking', in *Culture, Landscape, and the Environment: The Linacre Lectures, 1997*, edited by Kate Flint and Howard Morphy (Oxford: Oxford University Press, 2000), pp. 79–80.

Chapter 9 A fortuitous location

1 Michael Cathcart, 'Uluru', in *Words for Country: Landscape and Language in Australia*, edited by Tom Griffiths and Tim Bonyhady (Sydney: UNSW Press, 2002), p. 216.

2 See 'Knox Grammar Boys Climb to Top of Ayers Rock', *Sydney Morning Herald,* 13 September 1950.
3 William Liddle, letter to Department of Works and Housing, 14 September 1947, NAA F1 1952/470.
4 W McCoy to Director of Native Affairs, 17 April 1951, NAA F1 1952/470.
5 FH Moy to Acting District Superintendent, 'Ayers Rock', NAA F1 1952/470. Emphasis added.
6 Hannah Hueneke and Richard Baker, 'Tourist Behaviour, Local Values, and Interpretation at Uluru: "The Sacred Deed at Australia's Mighty Heart"', *GeoJournal* 74 (2009): 479.
7 Ibid. See also Nicholas Gill, 'Life and Death in Australian "Heartlands": Pastoralism, Ecology and Rethinking the Outback', *Journal of Rural Studies* 21, no. 1 (January 2005), pp. 39–53; Julie Marcus, 'The Journey out to the Centre' in *Race Matters*, edited by Gillian Cowlishaw and Barry Morris (Canberra: Aboriginal Studies Press, 1997), pp. 29–52. Ann McGrath, 'Travels to a Distant Past: The Mythology of the Outback', *Australian Cultural History*, 1991: 113–24.
8 Tjuki Tjukanku Pumpjack, 20 September 2012.
9 Rose, *The Wind of Change*, p. 60.
10 Sandra Armstrong, AI-0108943. The women who Sandra worked with are Elsie Wanatjura from Mutitjulu and Melinda Mitchell from Docker River. Both women were unwell and in aged care facilities when I was carrying out fieldwork, and I wasn't able to record their experiences of tourism at Angas Downs.
11 Rose, *The Wind of Change*, p. 59.
12 Ibid.
13 Gaye Sculthorpe, 'When Whitefellas Go Walkabout', in *The Oxford Companion to Aboriginal Art and Culture*, eds Sylvia Kleinart and Margot Neale (Melbourne: Oxford University Press, 2000), p. 391. See also Maria Nugent, 'Boomerangs for Sale', *Botany Bay: Where Histories Meet* (Crows Nest: Allen & Unwin, 2005), pp. 63–90; Fiona Paisley, 'No Back Streets in the Bush: 1920s and 1930s pro-Aboriginal White Women's Activism and the Trans-Australia Railway', *Australian Feminist Studies* 12, no. 25 (April 1997): 119.
14 Nugent, *Botany Bay*, p. 72.
15 Edna Bradley, *A Rock to Remember: A Memoir* (Alice Springs: Kristina Kidd, 2009), pp. 17–18.
16 Ibid., pp. 5–6.
17 Ibid., pp. xviii–xix, p. 2.
18 Rose, *The Wind of Change*, p. 58.
19 Mickey Dewar quoted in 'Whose Never Never?', produced by Lorena Allam, *Background Briefing*, Australian Broadcasting Corporation, 12 September 1999.
20 Ruth B Phillips, 'Why Not Tourist Art? Significant Silences in Native American Museum Representations' in *After Colonialism: Imperial Histories and Postcolonial Displacements*, ed. Gyan Prakash (Princeton: Princeton University Press, 1995), p. 111.
21 Sandra Armstrong, AI-0100843.
22 Rose, *The Wind of Change*, p. 39.
23 Rose, summary of lecture, July 1964.
24 Ibid.
25 Rose, *The Wind of Change*, p. 95.

26 Diane Barwick, 'And the Lubras Are Ladies Now', in *Woman's Role in Aboriginal Society*, Second (Canberra: Australian Institute of Aboriginal Studies, 1974), pp. 54–7; Nugent, 'Boomerangs For Sale', *Botany Bay*; Maria Nugent, 'An Economy of Shells: A Brief History of La Perouse Aboriginal Women's Shell-work and its Markets, 1880–2010', in *Indigenous Participation in Australian Economies II*, ed. Ian Keen et al., vol. 2, (Canberra: ANU E Press, 2012), pp. 211–27; Sculthorpe, 'When Whitefellas Go Walkabout'.
27 Nugent, 'An Economy of Shells'.
28 Rowse, *White Flour, White Power*, p. 89.
29 See Hilliard, *The People in Between*, p. 150; Howard Morphy, *Ancestral Connections: Art and an Aboriginal System of Knowledge* (Chicago: University of Chicago Press, 1991), pp. 13–17; Howard Morphy, 'Indigenous Art as Economy', in *Culture, Economy and Governance in Aboriginal Australia*, eds Diane J. Austin-Broos and Gaynor Marilyn Macdonald (Sydney: Sydney University Press, 2005), pp. 19–21. This isn't an exhaustive list; rather, it's intended to be illustrative, given that missionary markets aren't the focus of my analysis.
30 Ruth B Phillips, *Trading Identities: The Souvenir in Native North American Art from the Northeast, 1700–1900* (Seattle: University of Washington Press, 1998); Phillips, 'Why Not Tourist Art?'. See also Nelson HH Graburn, *Ethnic and Tourist Arts: Cultural Expressions from the Fourth World* (Berkeley: University of California Press, Berkeley, 1976).
31 Phillips, 'Why Not Tourist Art?', p. 102. See also Phillips, *Trading Identities*.
32 See Barwick, 'And the Lubras Are Ladies Now'; Sylvia Kleinart, '"Jacky Jacky Was a Smart Young Fella": A Study of Art and Aboriginality in South East Australia 1900–1980' (PhD thesis, ANU, 1994); Sylvia Kleinert, 'Aboriginal Enterprises: Negotiating an Urban Aboriginality', *Aboriginal History* 34 (2010): 171; Morphy, 'Indigenous Art as Economy'; Nugent, 'Boomerangs For Sale' in *Botany Bay*; Nugent, 'An Economy of Shells'.
33 Sandra Armstrong, AI-0108943.
34 Tjuki Tjukanku Pumpjack, 20 September 2012.
35 Rose, *The Wind of Change*, pp. 34, 67, 113.
36 Tjuki Tjukanku Pumpjack, oral history recorded with author and translated by Linda Rive, 19 September 2012, Walara, Angas Downs, Northern Territory.
37 Rowse, *White Flour, White Power*, pp. 131–2.
38 Ibid, pp. 132–5.
39 Rose, *The Wind of Change*, p. 168.
40 LN Penhall to Boomerang Tours, Sampsons tours, C.A.T.A. Tours & Pioneer Tours, 16 July 1964, NTAS NTRS 629, Jim Downing, research material relating to *Ngurra Walytja: Country of My Spirit* 1964–1972.
41 Elkin, 'Reaction and Interaction', 168.
42 Rose, *The Wind of Change*, p. 98.
43 Ibid., p. 35.
44 Sandra Armstrong, AI-0108943.
45 DA Stewart, Patrol Report, 6 December 1965, NAA F133 1965/20, Angas Downs Census Files.
46 Rose, *The Wind of Change*, p. 72.
47 Ibid., p. 35.
48 Mick's daughter, Nellie Mick, lives in Imanpa and was born on Angas Downs. She's one of the first women I met when I started going to Imanpa in 2011.

We've come to know each other well over the years, and I've sat with her and relayed information about her father that's included in Rose's ethnography and fieldwork diaries. Nellie was always really pleased to hear stories about her father from the book. She's very shy and was never interested in recording any oral histories.

49 Rose, *The Wind of Change*, p. 35.
50 Ibid., p. 147.
51 Ibid., p. 149.
52 I'm paraphrasing Tjuki here. This part of the recording was never transcribed, so I've worked from the recording and the on-the-spot interpretation.
53 Basil Sansom, 'The Grammar of Exchange', in *Being Black: Aboriginal Cultures in 'Settled' Australia*, ed. Ian Keen (Canberra: Aboriginal Studies Press, 1988), pp. 159–77.
54 DJ Mulvaney, '"The Chain of Connection": The Material Evidence', in *Tribes and Boundaries in Australia*, ed. Nicolas Peterson (Canberra: Australian Institute of Aboriginal Studies, 1976), pp. 72–94; Isabel McBryde, 'Travellers in Storied Landscapes: A Case Study in Exchanges and Heritage', *Aboriginal History* 24 (2000): 152–74; Anthony Redmond and Fiona Skyring, 'Exchange and Appropriation: The Wurnan Economy and Aboriginal Land and Labour at Karunjie Station, North-Western Australia', in *Indigenous Participation in Australian Economies: Historical and Anthropological Perspectives*, ed. Ian Keen, vol. 1 (Canberra: ANU E Press, 2010), pp. 73–90.
55 Sansom, 'The Grammar of Exchange', 159.

Chapter 10 Emerging economies and making place

1 Rose, summary of lecture, July 1964.
2 Nancy Munn, 'A Report on Field Research at Areyonga 1964–65', SLNSW Frederick Rose Papers, Box 26.
3 Rowse, *White Flour, White Power*, p. 153. See also Cowlishaw, *Rednecks, Eggheads and Blackfellas*, p. 115.
4 Ibid, pp. 37–8.
5 Pastor Albrecht to Director of Welfare, October 1960, NAA F1 1955/552.
6 Rose, *The Wind of Change*, pp. 73–74.
7 Ibid., p. 74. For similar observations regarding game sharing, see Nicolas Peterson, 'Demand Sharing: Reciprocity and the Pressure for Generosity among Foragers', *American Anthropologist* 95, no. 4 (December 1993): 865–7; Nicolas Peterson and Jon C Altman, 'Rights to Game and Rights to Cash among Contemporary Australian Hunter-Gatherers', in *Hunters and Gatherers: Property, Power and Ideology*, edited by Tim Ingold et al. (Oxford: Berg, 1988), pp. 77–80.
8 Rose, *The Wind of Change*, pp. 77, 159.
9 Peterson, 'Demand Sharing'.
10 Jon C Altman, 'Gambling as a Mode of Redistributing and Accumulating Cash among Aborigines: A Case Study from Arnhem Land', in *Gambling in Australia*, edited by G Caldwell et al. (Sydney: Croom Helm, 1985), pp. 50–67; Nicolas Peterson, 'Cash, Commoditisation and Authenticity: When Do Aboriginal People Stop Being Hunter-Gatherers?', in *Cash, Commoditisation and Changing Foragers* (Osaka: National Museum of Ethnology, 1991), pp. 67–90.
11 Peterson and Altman, 'Rights to Game and Rights to Cash among Contemporary Australian Hunter-Gatherers', pp. 80–1.

12 Arjun Appadurai, 'Introduction: Commodities and the Politics of Value', in *The Social Life of Things: Commodities in Cultural Perspective*, ed. Arjun Appadurai (Cambridge: Cambridge University Press, 1986), p. 4.
13 Sandra Armstrong, AI-0108943. Rose also commented on the high demand for rasps, tomahawks and files for the production of artefacts. Rose, *The Wind of Change*, p. 46.
14 Ibid.
15 John Carty, 'Maraku Arts and Crafts', in *Ngaanyatjarra: Art of the Lands*, eds Tim Acker and John Carty (Crawley: UWA Publishing, 2012), p. 135. Carty's discussion of *punu* notes similar descriptions of the social aspects of punu production that involve families going on camping trips to collect wood, and sitting and carving together around a fire.
16 Nugent, *Botany Bay*, p. 83. See also Ilaria Vanni, 'Bridging the Gap: The Production of Tourist Objects at La Perouse', in *The Oxford Companion to Aboriginal Art and Culture* (Melbourne: Oxford University Press, 2000), p. 402.
17 Vanni, 'Bridging the Gap', p. 402.
18 Rose, *The Wind of Change*, p. 93.
19 Archival documents and objects from Ernabella Arts show branded *punu* in production in the 1950s, A̱ra Irititja, Ernabella Arts Collection. Billy Cooley, an A̱nangu man cited in John Carty's history of Maraku Arts, mentions Namatjira as an influence on the technique. Carty, 'Maraku Arts and Crafts', p. 131.
20 For a discussion of *walka* as a mode of meaningful 'marking', see Munn, 'The Transformation of Subjects into Objects', pp. 142–3.
21 Nelly Paterson quoted in Peter Brokensha, *The Pitjantjatjara and Their Crafts* (North Sydney: Aboriginal Arts Board, Australia Council, 1975), p. 47.
22 Brokensha, *The Pitjantjatjara and Their Crafts*, pp. 49, 69.
23 Rose, *The Wind of Change*, pp. 92–3.
24 Appadurai, *Modernity At Large*, p. 180.
25 Ibid.
26 Raffles, '"Local Theory"', p. 329.
27 Diane Austin-Broos, 'Places, Practices, and Things', p. 118.

Chapter 11 'We were always travelling'

1 Tim Ingold, *Being Alive: Essays on Movement, Knowledge and Description* (London: Routledge, 2011), p. 12. See also Massey, *Space, Place, Gender*; Massey, *For Space*.
2 Tim Cresswell, 'Towards a Politics of Mobility', *Environment and Planning D: Society and Space* 28, no. 1 (2010): 26.
3 Tjuki Tjukanku Pumpjack, oral history recorded by author and translated by Linda Rive, 15 March 2013, Wilpiya spring and Waltunta soak, Angas Downs, Northern Territory.
4 Ibid.
5 Lesley JF Green and David R Green, 'Space, Time, and Story Tracks: Contemporary Practices of Topographic Memory in the Palikur Territory of Arukwa, Amapá, Brazil', *Ethnohistory* 56, no. 1 (1 January 2009), 164.
6 Ibid. See also '"So Many Stories on This Day-World": History as the Retracing of Tracks' in Lesley Green and David Green, *Knowing the Day, Knowing the World: Engaging Amerindian Thought in Public Archaeology* (Tucson: University of Arizona Press, 2013), pp. 51–78.

7 Green and Green, *Knowing the Day, Knowing the World*, pp. 64–5.
8 McBryde, 'Travellers in Storied Landscapes', p. 169. See also Beckett, 'George Dutton's Country', p. 14; Harrison, *Shared Landscapes*, pp. 114–17; Spooner, Firman and Yalmambirra, 'Origins of Travelling Stock Routes', pp. 329–39. Beckett, Harrison and Spooner et al. all explore the ways in which pastoral routes followed existing pathways and patterns of movement. For an exploration of water ways as an entanglement of mythical, ecological and human historical meanings, see Sandy Toussaint, Patrick Sullivan and Sarah Yu, 'Water Ways in Aboriginal Australia: An Interconnected Analysis', *Anthropological Forum* 15, no. 1 (2005): 61–74; Heather Goodall, 'Riding the Tide: Indigenous Knowledge, History and Water in a Changing Australia', *Environment and History* 14, no. 3 (2008), pp. 355–84.
9 Tjuki Tjukanku Pumpjack, 19 September 2012.
10 Niningka Lewis, AI-0156069-002.
11 Escobar, 'Culture Sits in Places', p. 161. See also Myers, *Pintupi Country, Pintupi Self*, p. 77; Colin Harris, 'Culture and Geography: South Australia's Mound Springs as Trade and Communication Routes', *Historic Environment* 16, no. 2 (2002): 8–11; Heather Goodall and Allison Cadzow, *Rivers and Resilience: Aboriginal People on Sydney's Georges River* (Sydney: University of New South Wales Press, 2009), p. 21.
12 Sandy Blair et al., 'Making Tracks: Key Issues about the Heritage of Australian Routes and Journeys', *Historic Environment* 16, no. 2 (2002): 43. Blair et al. is a discussion of 'routes' from a heritage perspective. For a discussion of 'routes' as an analytical/theoretical frame, particularly the intersections of travel and culture, see James Clifford, *Routes: Travel and Translation in the Late Twentieth Century* (Cambridge, Massachusetts: Harvard University Press, 1997).
13 Sandra Armstrong, oral history recorded, translated and transcribed by Sam Osborne, 28 March 2012, Angas Downs, Northern Territory.
14 Sandra Armstrong, oral history recorded and translated by Sam Osborne, 5 October 2013, Stuart Lodge, Alice Springs, Northern Territory. Author present at recording.
15 Bill Harney to Frederick Rose, 22 June 1962, SLNSW Frederick Rose Papers, Box 4.
16 Rose, *The Wind of Change*, p. 37.
17 Ibid., p. 18.
18 Sandra Armstrong, 5 October 2013.
19 Sandra Armstrong, 28 March 2012.
20 Nancy Munn, 'A Report on Field Research at Areyonga 1964–65', Frederick Rose Papers, Box 26.

Chaper 12 The itinerants

1 JH Giddens, 'Report of Survey to Southwest', 25 February 1960, NAA F133 1963/466, Angas Downs Station 1960–64.
2 TC Lovegrove, 'Aboriginal Camps: Ayers Rock Area', 16 February 1965, NTAS NTRS 629.
3 HC Giese, Director of Welfare to Assistant Director (southern), 27 May 1964, NTAS NTRS 629.
4 Angus Bancroft, *Roma and Gypsy-Travellers in Europe: Modernity, Race, Space and Exclusion* (Aldershot: Ashgate, 2005), p. 16.

5 Ibid. See also Tim Cresswell, *On the Move: Mobility in the Modern Western World* (New York: Routledge, 2006), pp. 12–15.
6 Bancroft, *Roma and Gypsy-Travellers in Europe*, pp. 16–18.
7 Liisa Malkki, 'National Geographic: The Rooting of Peoples and the Territorialisation of National Identity among Scholars and Refugees', *Cultural Anthropology* 7, no. 1 (1992), p. 31.
8 Ibid., p. 33.
9 James Scott, *Seeing Like a State: How Certain Schemes to Improve the Human Condition Have Failed* (New Haven: Yale University Press, 1998), p. 1.
10 Ibid.
11 Goodall and Cadzow, *Rivers and Resilience*, p. 19.
12 Ibid., p. 67. See also Bain Attwood, 'Off the Mission Stations: Aborigines in Gippsland 1860–1890', *Aboriginal History* 10 (1986): 131–51.
13 Attwood, 'Off the Mission Stations', p. 144.
14 Bain Attwood, *The Making of the Aborigines* (Sydney: Allen & Unwin, 1989), pp. 63–5.
15 Russell McGregor, 'Wards, Words and Citizens: A.P. Elkin and Paul Hasluck on Assimilation', *Oceania* 69, no. 4 (1 June 1999): 255.
16 Attwood, *The Making of the Aborigines*, p. 67. See also Angelique Edmonds, 'Sedentary Topography: The Impact of the Christian Mission Society's "Civilising" Agenda on the Spatial Structure of Life in the Roper Region of Northern Australia' in *Transgressions: Critical Australian Indigenous Histories*, edited by Ingereth Macfarlane and Mark Hannah, Aboriginal History Monograph 16 (Canberra: ANU E Press, 2007), p. 199.
17 HC Giese to Assistant Director of Welfare Branch (Southern), 'Aboriginal Camps – Angas Downs – Ayers Rock Area', 27 May 1964, NTAS NTRS 629.
18 Giese to Assistant Director of Welfare Branch (Southern), 'Itinerant Aboriginals – S/W Area', 20 June 1965, NTAS NTRS 629.
19 Les Penhall to Director of Welfare, 18 May 1964, 'Aboriginal Camps – Angas Downs – Ayers Rock Area', NTAS NTRS 629.
20 Stewart, 'Report on Itinerant Aboriginals: South West Area', 28 October 1965, NTAS NTRS 629.
21 TC Lovegrove to Assistant Director (Southern), 'Itinerant Aboriginals – South West Area', 3 November 1965, NTAS NTRS 629.
22 Ibid.
23 See Layton, *Uluru*, p. 87.
24 Stewart to District Welfare Officer, 'Itinerant Aboriginals: South West Area', 18 July 1966, NTAS NTRS 629.
25 Ibid.
26 Penhall to Director of Welfare, 'Itinerant Aboriginals South-West Area', 4 November 1965, NTAS NTRS 629.
27 Lovegrove, 3 November 1965, NTAS NTRS 629.

Chapter 13 The walkabout leaders

1 See Layton, *Uluru*, p. 84.
2 Lovegrove to Director of Welfare Branch, 'Aboriginals – Ayers Rock Road', 19 September 1968, NTAS NTRS 629.
3 JA Cooke to Assistant Director of Welfare (Southern), 'Aboriginals – Ayers Rock Road', 17 September 1968, NTAS NTRS 629.

4 WE Harney, *To Ayers Rock and Beyond* (Adelaide: Rigby, 1969), p. 136.
5 Petronella Vaarzon-Morel, 'Camels and the Transformation of Indigenous Economic Landscapes', in *Indigenous Participation in Australian Economies II*, edited by Ian Keen et al., vol. 2 (Canberra: ANU E Press, 2012), p. 73. See also Samia Khatun, *Australianama: The South Asian Odyssey in Australia* (St Lucia: University of Queensland Press, 2018); Wright, *Tracker*, pp. 96–104.
6 Layton, *Uluru*; Tom L McKnight, *The Camel in Australia* (Melbourne: Melbourne University Press, 1969); Vaarzon-Morel, 'Camels and the Transformation of Indigenous Economic Landscapes'; Rose, *The Wind of Change*; Roger Sandall, *Camels and the Pitjantjatjara* (Canberra: Australian Institute of Aboriginal Studies, 1969).
7 Rose, *The Wind of Change*, pp. 2, 22, 25.
8 Ibid., pp. 141, 153–4.
9 Ibid., pp. 28–9.
10 Layton, *Uluru*, p. 80.
11 Tjuki Tjukanku Pumpjack, 26 October 2012.
12 Layton, *Uluru*, p. 80.
13 Harney, *To Ayers Rock and Beyond*, pp. 135–6.
14 Rose, *The Wind of Change*, p. 141.
15 Vaarzon-Morel, 'Camels and the Transformation of Indigenous Economic Landscapes', p. 84.
16 Roger Sandall, *Camels and the Pitjantjatjara (film), 1969.*
17 Stewart, 'Report on Itinerant Aboriginals South-West Area', 18 July 1966, NTAS NTRS 629.
18 HH Finlayson, *The Red Centre: Man and Beast in the Heart of Australia* (Sydney: Angus & Robertson, 1943), p. 116.
19 Hilliard, *The People in Between*, p. 97.
20 While the importance of dingo scaling has been previously under recognised, recent scholarship, in which memory is an important source, is revising earlier understandings. See Young, 'Dingo Scalping and the Frontier Economy'; Kerin, 'Dogging for a Living: Aborigines and "Undesirables" in South Australia'; Ushma Scales, 'Dingoes and Doggers', A<u>r</u>a Irititja, 2006.
21 Tjuki Tjukanku Pumpjack, 26 October 2012.
22 His A<u>n</u>angu name is taken from Layton, *Uluru*, p. 84; information about his being a Wintaylka man from Rose, *The Wind of Change*, p. 232.
23 Tjuki Tjukanku Pumpjack, 26 October 2012.
24 Rose, *The Wind of Change*, pp. 70–1.
25 Ibid., p. 86.
26 PM Mackey, 'Aboriginal Camps Ayers Rock Area', 9 October 1964, NTAS NTRS 629.
27 GF Holden to Director of Social Welfare, 14 October 1964, NTAS NTRS 629.
28 Rose, *The Wind of Change*, pp. 136, 143, 169–70.
29 DA Stewart, 'Itinerant Aboriginals South West Area', 18 July 1966, NTAS NTRS 629.
30 Historical scholarship has largely focused on the cattle industry as a mode of employment that enabled Aboriginal families to live on and maintain links to Country. See Baker, *Land Is Life*; Goodall, *Invasion to Embassy*; Jebb, *Blood, Sweat and Welfare*; McGrath, *Born in the Cattle*; Harrison, *Shared Landscapes*. Other examples include 'hop-picking' in Gippsland, as discussed by Attwood

in *The Making of the Aborigines* and 'Off the Mission Stations'. For a discussion of seasonal pea and bean picking in southern New South Wales, see also John White, 'Histories of Indigenous-Settler Relations: Reflections on Internal Colonialism and the Hybrid Economy', *Australian Aboriginal Studies* 1 (2011); 'On the Road to Nerrigundah: An Historical Anthropology of Indigenous-Settler Relations in the Eurobodalla Region of New South Wales' (PhD thesis, ANU, 2010); 'Peas, Beans and Riverbanks: Seasonal Picking and Dependence in the Tuross Valley', in *Indigenous Participation in Australian Economies: Historical and Anthropological Perspectives*, vol. 1, 2 vols. (Canberra: ANU E Press, 2010).

31 Appadurai, 'Introduction: Commodities and the Politics of Value', p. 4.

32 DL Busbridge, 'Aboriginal Employment Problems in South Australia', in *Aborigines in the Economy*, eds Colin Tatz and Ian G Sharp (Brisbane: Jacaranda Press, 1966), p. 94. See also Rowse, *White Flour, White Power*, p. 149.

33 See Jeremy Beckett, 'George Dutton's Country', p. 23.

34 G Grimwade, 'Itinerant Aboriginals - S/W Area', 29 June 1965, NTAS NTRS 629.

35 DA Stewart, 'Itinerant Aboriginals: Southwest Area', 28 October 1965, NTAS NTRS 629.

36 TC Lovegrove to Director of Welfare Branch, 19 July 1966, NTAS NTRS 629.

37 Aram A Yengoyan, 'Religion, Morality and Prophetic Traditions: Conversion of the Pitjantjatjara of Central Australia', in *Conversion to Christianity: Historical and Anthropological Perspectives on a Great Transformation*, ed. Robert W Hefner (Berkeley: University of California Press, 1993), p. 236. See also Nicolas Peterson, 'An Expanding Aboriginal Domain: Mobility and the Initiation Journey', *Oceania* 70, no. 3 (March 2000): 209; Aram A Yengoyan, 'A Comparison of Certain Marriage Features between the Pitjandjara Other Groups of the Western Desert with the Northern Groups. Also Some Comments on the Red Ochre Ceremonies', *Journal of the Anthropological Society of South Australia* 5, no. 4 (1967): 16–19.

38 Yengoyan, Ibid., p. 238.

39 Peterson, 'An Expanding Aboriginal Domain', p. 206; Tim Rowse, *Remote Possibilities: The Aboriginal Domain and the Administrative Imagination* (Darwin: North Australia Research Unit, 1992); David Trigger, 'Blackfellas and Whitefellas: The Concepts of Domain and Social Closure in the Analysis of Race Relations', *Mankind* 16, no. 2 (1986); J Von Sturmer, 'The Different Domains', in *Aborigines and Uranium: Consolidated Report on the Social Impact of Uranium Mining on the Aborigines of the Northern Territory* (Canberra: Australian Institute of Aboriginal Studies, 1984), pp. 218–37.

40 Melinda Hinkson, *Remembering the Future: Warlpiri Life through the Prism of Drawing* (Canberra: Aboriginal Studies Press, 2014), pp. 124–5.

41 Peterson, 'An Expanding Aboriginal Domain', 209–10. See also Annette Hamilton, 'Coming and Going: Aboriginal Mobility in North-West South Australia, 1970–1971', *Records of the South Australian Museum* 20 (1987): 47–57.

42 Rowse, *White Flour, White Power*, p. 149.

43 LN Penhall, 'Itinerant Aboriginals – S/W Area', 29 June 1965, NTAS NTRS 629.

44 HC Giese, 'Itinerant Aboriginals – South West Area', [no day or month on document] 1965, NTAS NTRS 629.

45 Layton, *Uluru*, p. 88.

46 JA Cooke, 'Patrol of South West Area', 29 April 1968, NTAS NTRS 629. In the same report, Cooke notes that the owner of Curtin Springs, Peter Severin, told tourists and visitors passing through that 'he feeds his Great Dane one "black fella" a day'. Cooke noted that if the 'anecdote' was to receive any publicity, he suggested that 'it be ignored'. Severin still owns Curtin Springs
47 DA Stewart, 'Aboriginals – Ayers Rock Road', 19 August 1968, NTAS NTRS 629.
48 TC Lovegrove, 'Movement of Aboriginals to Docker River', 20 August 1968, NTAS NTRS 629.
49 JA Cooke, 'Aboriginals – Ayers Rock Road', 17 September 1968, NTAS NTRS 629
50 Ibid.
51 Ann Laura Stoler, *Along the Archival Grain: Epistemic Anxieties and Colonial Common Sense* (Princeton: Princeton University Press, 2010).
52 TC Lovegrove, 'Itinerant Aboriginals South West Area', 3 November 1965, NTAS NTRS 629.
53 Jane Carey and Jane Lydon (eds), *Indigenous Networks: mobility, connections and exchange* (New York: Routledge, 2014), p. 2.
54 Tim Rowse, 'Indigenous Heterogeneity', *Australian Historical Studies* 45, no. 3 (2014), p. 305. See also Rowse, *White Flour, White Power*, pp. 139–43.
55 Malkki, 'National Geographic'. See also Samia Khatun, 'Beyond Blank Spaces: Five Tracks to Late Nineteenth-Century Beltana', *Transfers* 5, no. 3 (2015): 68–86.

Chapter 14 Return

1 Thalia Anthony, 'An Anniversary Shrouded in Myths', *Australian Policy Online*, 22 August 2006; Thalia Anthony, 'Labour Relations on Northern Cattle Stations: Feudal Exploitation and Accommodation', *The Drawing Board: An Australian Review of Public Affairs* 4, no. 3 (March 2004): 117–36; Baker, *Land Is Life*; Jebb, *Blood, Sweat and Welfare*; Rowse, *White Flour, White Power*; Fiona Skyring, 'Low Wages, Low Rents, and Pension Cheques: The Introduction of Equal Wages in the Kimberley, 1968–1969', in *Indigenous Participation in Australian Economies: Historical and Anthropological Perspectives*, vol. 2 (Canberra: ANU E Press, 2012), pp. 153–69.
2 HC Giese, 'Itinerant Aboriginals – South West Area', [no day or month on document] 1965, NTAS NTRS 629.
3 Jeremy Long, 'Returning to Country: The Docker River Project', in *Experiments in Self-Determination: Histories of the Outstation Movement in Australia*, eds Fred Myers and Nicolas Peterson (Canberra: ANU E Press, 2016), p. 52.
4 TC Lovegrove, 'Movement of Aboriginals to Docker River, 20 August 1968, NTAS NTRS 629.
5 JA Cooke, Patrol of the South West Area, 29 April 1968, NTAS NTRS 629.
6 Rowse, *White Flour, White Power*, p. 210.
7 JA Cooke, Aboriginals – Ayers Rock Road, 17 September 1968, NTAS NTRS 629.
8 JA Cooke to Assistant Director of Welfare Branch, School Buildings – Angas Downs, 15 August 1969, NAA F133 1978/435 Angas Downs Station, 1968–71.
9 Sandra Armstrong, interview with author, 20 January 2015, Alice Springs hospital, Northern Territory.

10 Sandra Armstrong, 28 March 2012.

11 See Bill Edwards, Jeremy Long, Peter Sutton and Neville White in *Experiments in Self-Determination: Histories of the Outstation Movement in Australia*, edited by Nicolas Peterson and Fred Myers (Canberra: ANU E Press, 2016). See also Downing, *Ngurra Walytja*.

12 Fred Myers and Nicolas Peterson, 'The Origins and History of Outstations as Aboriginal Life Projects' in *Experiments in Self-Determination*, pp. 2–3.

13 Ibid. See also Nicolas Peterson, 'What Can Pre-Colonial and Frontier Economies Tell Us about Engagement with the Real Economy? Indigenous Life Projects and the Conditions for Development', in *Culture, Economy and Governance in Aboriginal Australia*, eds Gaynor Marilyn Macdonald and Diane Austin-Broos (Sydney: Sydney University Press, 2005), p.7.

14 Bill Edwards, 'From Coombes to Coombs: Reflections on the Pitjantjatjara Outstation Movement' in *Experiments in Self-Determination*, p. 32.

15 Downing, *Ngurra Walytja*, p. 56.

16 Susan Tod Woenne, 'Old Country, New Territory: Some Implications of the Settlement Process' in *Aborigines and Change: Australia in the 70s*, ed. Ronald M Berndt (Canberra: Australian Institute of Aboriginal Studies, 1977), p. 57.

17 Sandy Willie in Bowman ed., *Every Hill Got a Story*, p. 232.

18 Ibid.

19 Long, 'Returning to Country', p. 56.

20 TC Lovegrove, 'Movement of Aboriginals to Docker River, 20 August 1968, NTAS NTRS 629.

21 Tod Woenne, 'Old Country, New Territory', p. 57.

22 Ibid., pp. 57–8.

23 Ibid., p. 63.

24 Tjukapati James in Bowman ed., *Every Hill Got a Story*, p. 232.

25 Sandra Armstrong, oral history recorded and translated by Sam Osborne, 22 February 2012, Yulara, Northern Territory.

26 Sandra Armstrong, 20 January 2015.

27 Tjuki Tjukanku Pumpjack, 16 July 2014.

28 Ibid.

29 Sandra Armstrong, 22 February 2012.

30 Tjuki Tjukanku Pumpjack, 16 July 2014.

31 AC Weber, Patrol to Angas Downs Station, 19 September 1969, NAA F133 1978/435.

32 Sandra Armstrong, 22 February 2012.

33 Sandra Armstrong, 28 March 2012.

34 Rowse, *White Flour, White Power*, pp. 114–17. See also, Jebb, *Blood, Sweat and Welfare*, pp. 285–90.

35 See 'The Crisis of Managed Consumption' in Rowse, *White Flour, White Power*, pp. 118–46.

36 CD Rowley, *The Remote Aborigines* (Canberra: Australian National University Press, 1971), p. 304. Tim Rowse observed that pastoralists who kept their stations solvent by encouraging large camps of subsidised 'dependents' were described as being engaged in 'nigger farming'. See Rowse, *White Flour, White Power*, p. 119. While Kimberley pastoralists didn't receive subsidies for rationing, they did administer the aged pension, and Jebb documents that in 1965 there was a formal investigation revealing the blatant misappropriation of tens of

thousands of pounds of Aboriginal pension monies by pastoralists. Jebb, *Blood, Sweat and Welfare*, p. 264.

37 In regard to section 51 (xxvi), removal of the words 'The people of any race, other than the aboriginal people in any State, for whom it is necessary to make special laws' gave the Commonwealth the power to legislate on behalf of Aboriginal people. The removal of the whole of section 127 provided for Aboriginal people to be counted in the Census. See 'The 1967 Referendum', National Archives of Australia.

38 Peterson, 'An Expanding Aboriginal Domain', 210.

39 Nicolas Peterson, 'Capitalism, Culture and Land Rights: Aborigines and the State in the Northern Territory', *Social Analysis: The International Journal of Social and Cultural Practice*, no. 18 (December 1985), p. 91. See also Nicolas Peterson, 'Aboriginal Involvement with the Australian Economy in the Central Reserve during the Winter of 1970', in *Aborigines and Change*, p. 140; Hamilton, 'Coming and Going'; Jon Altman and Melinda Hinkson, 'Mobility and Modernity in Arnhem Land: The Social Universe of Kuninjku Trucks', *Journal of Material Culture* 12, no. 2 (2007).

40 Peterson, 'Capitalism, Culture and Land Rights', p. 91.

41 McMahon quoted in Myers and Peterson, 'The Origins and History of Outstations as Aboriginal Life Projects', 9. See also Rowse, *White Flour, White Power*, p. 204.

42 Rowse, *White Flour, White Power*, p. 212.

43 WJ Gray, 'Decentralisation Trends in Arnhem Land', in *Aborigines and Change*, p. 116. See also Downing, *Ngurra Walytja*; B Meehan and R Jones, 'The Outstation Movement and Hints of a White Backlash', in *Northern Australia: Options and Implications*, ed. R Jones (Canberra: The Australian National University, 1980), pp. 131–57; Myers and Peterson, 'The Origins and History of Outstations as Aboriginal Life Projects'.

44 Downing, *Ngurra Walytja*, pp. 60–6. See also Edwards, 'From Coombes to Coombs'; Noel M Wallace, 'Pitjantjatjara Decentralisation in North-West South Australia: Spiritual and Psycho-Social Motivation', in *Aborigines and Change: Australia in the 70s*, pp. 124–35. However, Arnhem Land is generally understood as the locus of the so-called 'movement' to outstations and is where the term 'homelands movement' emanated from. By the end of 1974, 25 per cent of the Yirrkala population had moved to outstations across Arnhem Land, while 450 people, or 35 per cent of the population, had left Maningrida. The number had increased to approximately 800 people by 1977. Gray, 'Decentralisation Trends in Arnhem Land', p. 115; Meehan and Jones, 'The Outstation Movement', pp. 135–6. See also Frances Morphy and Howard Morphy, 'Thwarted Aspirations: The Political Economy of a Yolgnu Outstation, 1972 to the Present', in *Experiments in Self-Determination*, pp. 301–22. Pintupi attempts at establishing a separate community began in 1967 and culminated in 1973 with the outstation at Yayayi. See Myers, 'History, Memory and the Politics of Self-Determination at an Early Outstation', in *Experiments in Self-Determination*, pp. 81–104.

45 Downing, *Ngurra Walytja*, p. 67.

46 Sandra Armstrong, AI-0108943.

47 Wright, *Tracker*, p. 91.

48 Muntawarra Agreement, DAA, January 1979, NAA F133 1978/435.

49 Arthur Liddle to Regional Director, DAA, 11 January 1979, NAA F133 1978/435.
50 B Tilmouth, DAA Internal Minute, 16 January 1979, and B Tilmouth, DAA Inter-Office Memorandum, 27 February 1979, NAA F133 1978/435.
51 B Tilmouth, DAA Internal Minutes, 20 March 1979, and B Tilmouth DAA Internal Minutes, 4 April 1979, NAA F133 1978/435.
52 HC Coombs, 'Decentralisation Trends among Aboriginal Communities', *Search* 5, no. 4 (1974): 141.
53 See Myers and Peterson, 'The Origins and History of Outstations as Aboriginal Life Projects'; Scott Cane, 'People and Policy in the Development and Destruction of Yagga Yagga Outstation, Western Australia', in *Experiments in Self-Determination*, p. 260.
54 B Tilmouth, 4 April 1979, F133 1978/435.
55 Sandra Armstrong, 20 January 2015.
56 G Langford on behalf of Tjuki Pumpjack to Mr R Styles, Area officer DAA, 13 August 1981, NAA F133 1978/435.
57 GK Castine, Senior Assistant Director, Community Development, DAA to Tjuki Pumpjack, 27 August 1981, NAA F133 1978/435.
58 GK Castine to G Langford, 27 August 1981, NAA F133 1978/435.
59 Ian Keen, 'A Question of Interpretation: The Definition of "Traditional Aboriginal Owners" in the Aboriginal Land Rights (NT) Act', in *Aboriginal Land-Owners: Contemporary Issues in the Determination of Traditional Aboriginal Land Ownership*, ed. LR Hiatt (Sydney: University Of Sydney, 1984), pp. 25–7. See also LR Hiatt, 'Real Estates and Phantom Hordes', in *Arguments about Aborigines: Australia and the Evolution of Social Anthropology* (Cambridge: Cambridge University Press, 1996), pp. 13–35; Elizabeth Povinelli, *Labor's Lot: The Power, History, and Culture of Aboriginal Action* (Chicago: University of Chicago Press, 1993), pp. 28–30.
60 Hiatt, 'Real Estates and Phantom Hordes', p. 31. See also Francesca Merlan, 'The Regimentation of Customary Practice: From Northern Territory Land Claims to Mabo', *The Australian Journal of Anthropology* 6, no. 1 (1995), p. 76; Francesca Merlan, *Caging the Rainbow: Places, Politics, and Aborigines in a North Australian Town* (Honolulu: University of Hawai'i Press, 1998), pp. 163–75.
61 It should be noted that 1981 was also the year the Anangu Pitjantjatjara Yankunytjatjara (APY) Land Rights Act was passed in the South Australian Parliament. The *APY Land Rights Act 1981* differs significantly from the Northern Territory Act. The South Australian legislation designated an area of 102 650 square kilometres as APY lands. APY was established as a body corporate and all Anangu are considered members of the body corporate. All have unrestricted access to the APY Lands under the Act. The role of APY is to 'ascertain the wishes and opinions of traditional owners', and to 'protect the interests of traditional owners'. Thus, determinations of ownership are not made by the state in a court of law but by Anangu themselves via APY. See *Anangu Pitjantjatjara Yankunytjatjara Land Rights Act 1981*.
62 See Paul Burke, *Law's Anthropology: From Ethnography to Expert Testimony in Native Title* (Canberra: ANU Press, 2011), pp. 173–208.
63 Tracker Tilmouth in Wright, *Tracker*, pp. 82–5.
64 Merlan, 'The Regimentation of Customary Practice', pp. 79–80.
65 RA Styles, Area Officer DAA to Arthur Liddle, 14 December 1981, NAA F133 1978/435.

66 Sandra Armstrong, 20 January 2015.
67 Tod Woenne, 'Old Country, New Territory', p. 59.

Chapter 15 'There's nothing there now, but it's still our place'

1 Tjuki Tjukanku Pumpjack, 26 October 2012.
2 Kimber, 'History of Pastoral Development' in 'Angas Downs Indigenous Protected Area: Plan of Management: A Report to Lisanote Pty. Ltd. on Conservation of Biodiversity, Sustainable Production and Training Opportunities' (Canberra: Australian Wildlife Services, 2005).
3 Portelli, *The Death of Luigi Trastulli*, pp. 1, 19. Emphasis added.
4 Ibid., p. 15.
5 See also M Frisch, 'The Memory of History', in *Presenting the Past: Essays on History and the Public*, eds R Rosenzweig and S Benson (Philadelphia: Temple University Press, 1986), pp. 5–17; M Frisch, *A Shared Authority: Essays on the Craft and Meaning of Oral History and the Public* (Albany: State University of New York Press, 1991); L Passerini, *Fascism in Popular Memory: The Cultural Experience of the Turin Working Class* (Cambridge: Cambridge University Press, 1987); L Passerini, ed., *Memory and Totalitarianism: International Yearbook of Oral History and Life Stories*, vol. 1 (Oxford: Oxford University Press, 1992); Heather Goodall, '"The Whole Truth and Nothing But...": Some Intersections of Western Law, Aboriginal History and Community Memory' in *Power, Knowledge and Aborigines* edited by Bain Attwood and John Arnold (Bundoora: La Trobe University Press, 1992).
6 Portelli, *The Death of Luigi Trastulli*, p. 26.
7 Tjuki Tjukanku Pumpjack, 26 October 2012.
8 Tjuki Tjukanku Pumpjack, 20 September 2012.
9 Tjuki Tjukanku Pumpjack, 'Bullock Business', AI-0108954.
10 Rose, *The Wind of Change*, p. 56.
11 Sandra Armstrong, AI-0108943.
12 Kelly Jean Butler, *Witnessing Australian Stories: History, Testimony, and Memory in Contemporary Culture* (New Brunswick, New Jersey: Transaction Publishers, 2013), pp. 117–18.
13 Tjuki Tjukanku Pumpjack, 20 September 2012.
14 Deborah Bird Rose, 'Histories and Rituals: Land Claims in the Territory', in *In the Age of Mabo: History, Aborigines and Australia*, ed. Bain Attwood (St Leonards: Allen & Unwin, 1996), pp. 35–53. See also Merlan, 'The Regimentation of Customary Practice'; Povinelli, *Labor's Lot*; Patrick Wolfe, 'Nation and MiscegeNation: Discursive Continuity in the Post-Mabo Era', *Social Analysis* 36 (1994): 93–152; Patrick Wolfe, 'Settler Colonialism and the Elimination of the Native', *Journal of Genocide Research* 8, no. 4 (2006): 387–409.
15 Hinkson, *Remembering the Future*, p. 101.
16 Tjuki Tjukanku Pumpjack, 20 September 2012.
17 Peter Sutton, 'Kind of Rights in Country: Recognising Customary Rights as Incidents of Native Title', *National Native Title Tribunal*, Occasional Paper Series, no. 2 (2001): 19–20.
18 Burke, *Law's Anthropology*, pp. 200–5.
19 Sandra Armstrong, AI-0108943.
20 Merlan, *Caging the Rainbow*, pp. 212–13.
21 Myers, 'Ways of Placemaking', pp. 89–90.

22 Jonathan Lear, *Radical Hope: Ethics in the Face of Cultural Devastation* (Cambridge, MA: Harvard University Press, 2006), p. 10.
23 Tim Rowse, 'Paternalism's Changing Reputation', *Mankind* 18, no. 2 (1988), p. 71.
24 Tjuki Tjukanku Pumpjack, 26 October 2012.
25 Plenty Coup quoted in Lear, *Radical Hope*, p. 3.
26 Ibid., pp. 4–5.
27 For a discussion of displacement and testimonial discourse, see Jeremy Beckett, 'Autobiography and Testimonial Discourse in Myles Lalor's "Oral History"' in *Encounters with Indigeneity: Writing about Aboriginal and Torres Strait Islander Peoples* (Canberra: Aboriginal Studies Press, 2014 [first published in 2001]).
28 Portelli, *The Death of Luigi Trastulli*, p. 26.
29 Basil Sansom, 'In the Absence of Vita as Genre: The Making of the Roy Kelly Story', in *Telling Stories: Indigenous History and Memory in Australia and New Zealand*, eds Bain Attwood and Fiona Magowan (Crows Nest: Allen & Unwin, 2001), p. 118.
30 In Alexis Wright's *Tracker*, Tracker Tilmouth recalls an episode when Tjuki Pumpjack was working as a 'black tracker' at Kulgera police station. This was another period in his life that Tjuki never elaborated on. He mentioned his time working at Kulgera in passing on a few occasions, but he never told stories about this time. It seemed to me that this memory had also been 'put away'.
31 Lear, *Radical Hope*, p. 50.
32 Tjuki Tjukanku Pumpjack, 20 September 2012.
33 Appadurai, *Modernity At Large*, p. 179.
34 Merlan, *Caging the Rainbow*, p. 59.

Epilogue: Palimpsest

1 Gillian Cowlishaw, *Rednecks, Eggheads and Blackfellas*, p. 15.
2 Tjuki Pumpjack quoted in Kieran Finnane, 'Major Aboriginal Tourism Venture Near Ayers Rock', *Alice Springs News*, June 19, 2002.
3 Sandra Armstrong quoted in Ibid.
4 Sandra Armstrong, 5 October 2013.
5 Lear, *Radical Hope,* p. 140.
6 Merlan, 'The Regimentation of Customary Practice', pp. 79–80.
7 Chelsea Watego, 'Always Bet on Black (Power): The Fight Against Race in the Colony', *Meanjin,* 80:3 (Spring 2021).
8 Ibid., p. 32.
9 Italicised text quoted from the Uluru Statement from the Heart, May 2017.
10 Sandra Armstrong, 5 October 2013.
11 The Uluru Statement from the Heart.
12 Ibid.
13 'Vanstone Says Remote Indigenous Communities Becoming "Cultural Museums"', *AM* program, Radio National, ABC.
14 Deborah Bird Rose, *Reports from a Wild Country: Ethics for Decolonisation* (Sydney: UNSW Press, 2004), p. 5.
15 Ibid., p. 24.
16 Audra Simpson, *Mohawk Interruptus: Political Life across the Borders of Settler States* (Durham: Duke University Press, 2014).
17 Khatun, *Australianama,* pp. 4, 179.

Bibliography

Ara Irititja archive

AI–0108954, Tjuki Tjukanku Pumpjack, oral history recorded and translated by Linda Rive, June 2011, Alice Springs, NT.

AI–0156069–002, Niningka Lewis, oral history recorded and translated by Linda Rive, October 2009, Gold Coast City Art Gallery.

AI–0001577–001, Tjukupati James, oral history recorded by John Tregenza and translated by Nancy Sheppard, 13 September 1997, Kaltukatjara (Docker River), NT.

AI–0123837, Nyanu Watson, oral history recorded by Thisbe Purich for Tjanpi Desert Weavers, July 2008, Mantamaru (Jameson), WA.

AI–0108943, Sandra Armstrong, oral history recorded and translated by Linda Rive, 18 August 2009, Alice Springs, NT.

Ernabella Arts Collection.

Mitchell Library, State Library New South Wales

Frederick Rose Papers, MLMSS (uncatalogued)

National Archives of Australia

NAA A431 1950/2768 Part 2, Attacks on white men by natives – Killing of natives – Central Australia [Attachment titled 'Finding of Board of Enquiry with exhibits 1–13'].

NAA F126 8 Part 2, Northern Territory Medical Service, TGH Strehlow, patrol officer, Angas Downs [also Tempe Downs station] 1937–1942.

NAA F1 1943/140, Areyonga Aboriginal Reserve.

NAA F1 1938/418, Aboriginal Reserve South West Corner Territory (includes Report on a Reconnaissance in the Mount Doreen Mineral Area Central Australia by CT Madigan) 1932–1941.

NAA F1 1952/470, South West Reserve 1940 1952.

NAA F1 1952/599 Finke River Mission (Lutheran) Hermansburg [Hermannsburg] Haasts Bluff and Areyonga Policy Development 1949–53.

NAA F1 1953/488, Employment of Aboriginals Angas Downs 1952–54.

NAA F1 1955/552, Angas Downs Station Claims Payments and Employment 1955–1963.
NAA F133 1963/466, Angas Downs Station 1960–64.
NAA F133 1965/20, Angas Downs Station Census Files.
NAA F133 1978/435 Angas Downs Station 1968–1971.
NAA F3 32/1, Patrol Officer Strehlow General 1936–1941.
NAA F3 32/3, Patrol Officer Strehlow Monthly Reports 1938–1942.
NAA 1972/841, Northern Australia Development Committee, Development of Northern Australia 1947.
NAA E740, P131 Lynda Vale 1937–39.

Northern Territory archives

NTAS TS150, Merv Andrew interviewed by Paul France, 16 August 1983, Alice Springs, NT.
NTAS NTRS 246 P/2, Pastoral Lease Files 1914–94.
NTAS NTRS 629, Jim Downing, Research Material relating to *Ngurra Walytja: Country of My Spirit* 1964–72.

South Australia Museum

SAM AA93/1/6–27, H.H. Finlayson, photographs relating to the 'Petermann Range Natives at Moment Domiciled in Basedow Range' 1932.

Oral histories recorded by author

Sandra Armstrong, oral history recorded with author, 7 October 2013, Mitchell Library SLNSW.
Sandra Armstrong, oral history recorded with author, 8 October 2013, Mitchell Library SLNSW.
Sandra Armstrong, oral history recorded with author, 10 October 2013, Mitchell Library SLNSW.
Sandra Armstrong, oral history recorded with author, 20 January 2015, Alice Springs Hospital, NT.
Sandra Armstrong, oral history recorded with author, 4 February 2015, Imanpa, NT.
Tjuki Tjukanku Pumpjack, oral history recorded by author (English), 29 August 2012, Walara, Angas Downs, NT.
Tjuki Tjukanku Pumpjack, oral history recorded by author, translated and transcribed by Linda Rive, 19 September 2012, Walara, Angas Downs, NT.
Tjuki Tjukanku Pumpjack, oral history recorded by author, translated and transcribed by Linda Rive, 20 September 2012, Imanpa, NT.
Tjuki Tjukanku Pumpjack, oral history recorded by author, translated and transcribed by Linda Rive, 26 October 2012, Imanpa, NT.
Tjuki Tjukanku Pumpjack, oral history recorded by author, translated and transcribed by Linda Rive, 15 March 2013, Wilpiya, Angas Downs, NT.
Tjuki Tjukanku Pumpjack, oral history recorded by author, translated and transcribed by Linda Rive, 23 April 2013, Alice Springs, NT.
Tjuki Tjukanku Pumpjack, oral history recorded by author, translated and transcribed by Linda Rive, 24 April 2013, Alice Springs, NT.
Tjuki Tjukanku Pumpjack, oral history recorded by author, translated and transcribed by Linda Rive, 4 October 2013, Ulanga Well, Angas Downs, NT.

Tjuki Tjukanku Pumpjack, oral history recorded by author, translated and transcribed by Linda Rive, 17 July 2014, Kulata Well, Erldunda Station, NT.

Oral histories recorded by others

Sandra Armstrong, oral history recorded and translated by Sam Osborne, 22 February 2012, Yulara, NT.

Sandra Armstrong, oral history recorded and translated by Sam Osborne, 28 March 2012, Angas Downs, NT.

Sandra Armstrong, oral history recorded and translated by Sam Osborne, 5 October 2013, Stuart Lodge, Alice Springs, NT.

Newspapers and magazines

Examiner, 1938.

Walkabout, 1948.

Sydney Morning Herald, 1948.

Alice Springs News, 2002.

The Australian, 2009–15.

The Monthly, 2021.

Films

Batty, David and Francis Jupurrula Kelly. *Coniston*. PAW Media and Rebel Films, 2013.

Sandall, Roger. *Camels and the Pitjantjatjara*. Canberra: Australian Institute of Aboriginal Studies, 1969.

Reports

'Angas Downs Indigenous Protected Area: Plan of Management: A Report to Lisanote Pty. Ltd. on Conservation of Biodiversity, Sustainable Production and Training Opportunities'. Canberra: Australian Wildlife Services, 2005.

Booth, Carol and Wendy Tubman. 'Water Down Under: Understanding and Managing Australia's Great Artesian Basin'. Canberra: Commonwealth of Australia, 2011.

Latz, Peter and Michael Hewett. 'A Natural Resource Management Report of the Angas Downs Pastoral Lease'. Alice Springs, January 2003.

Munn, Nancy. 'A Report on field research at Areyonga 1964–65'. SLNSW, Frederick Rose Papers, Box 26.

Websites

AIATSIS. 'AIATSIS Map of Indigenous Australia'.

Australian Broadcasting Corporation, *AM* program, 'Vanstone says remote Indigenous communities becoming "cultural museums"'.

Bureau of Meteorology. 'Living With Drought'.

Department of Environment, Water, Heritage and the Arts, 'Indigenous Protected Areas – Angas Downs'.

Department of the Environment and Energy, 'Indigenous Protected Areas'.

National Archives of Australia, 'The 1967 Referendum'.

South Australian Government. 'A<u>n</u>angu Pitjantjatjara Yankunytjatjara Land Rights Act 1981'.

The Uluru Statement, 'The Uluru Statement from the Heart'.

Theses

Carty, John. 'Creating Country: Abstraction, Economics and the Social Life of Style in Balgo Art'. PhD Thesis, Australian National University, 2011.

Hartwig, Mervyn. 'The Progress of White Settlement in the Alice Springs District and Its Effects upon the Aboriginal Inhabitants, 1860–1894'. PhD Thesis, University of Adelaide, 1965.

Kerin, Rani. 'Doctor Do-Good?: Charles Duguid and Aboriginal Politics, 1930s–1970s'. PhD Thesis, Australian National University, 2004.

Kleinart, Sylvia. '"Jacky Jacky Was a Smart Young Fella": A Study of Art and Aboriginality in South East Australia 1900–1980'. PhD Thesis, Australian National University, 1994.

Lewis, Darrell. 'A Wild History: the making of a Victoria River Pastoral Society'. PhD Thesis, Australian National University, 2004.

Macfarlane, Ingereth. 'Entangled Places: Interactive Histories in the Western Simpson Desert, Central Australia'. PhD Thesis, Australian National University, 2010.

Monaghan, Paul. 'Laying Down the Country: Norman B. Tindale and the Linguistic Construction of the North-West of South Australia'. PhD Thesis, University of Adelaide, 2003.

Osborne, Sam. 'Staging Standpoint Dialogue in Tristate Education: Privileging A<u>n</u>angu Voices'. PhD Thesis, Victoria University, 2016.

Palmer, Shannyn. '(un)making Angas Downs: A Spatial History of a Central Australian Pastoral Station, 1930–1980'. PhD Thesis, Australian National University, 2017.

Sometimes, Beth. 'Apmere Angkentye-Kenhe: Language as a Music Playing Us'. Masters Thesis, Victorian College of the Arts, University of Melbourne, 2018.

Trudinger, David. 'Converting Salvation: Protestant Missionaries in Central Australia, 1930s-40s'. PhD Thesis, Australian National University, 2004.

White, John. 'On the Road to Nerrigundah: An Historical Anthropology of Indigenous –Settler Relations in the Eurobodalla Region of New South Wales'. PhD Thesis, Australian National University, 2010.

Unpublished sources

Bowman, Bryan. A History of Central Australia 1930–1980: From Horse and Camel to Motor Car, From Motor Car to Helicopter and Jet, vol. 1, 1989.

Cartwright, Max. From Bush Tracks to highway: An Account of Aborigine Footprints to the Horse and Camel Tracks of the Explorers, Followed by the Motor tracks of Later Years: In the South Western Regions of Central Australia, 1994.

Jamieson, Eric and Heather Harvey. Red Sand in Their Shoes: The Andrews Family, 2001.

Scales, Ushma. Dingoes and Doggers, A<u>r</u>a Iritija, 2006.

Published sources

Acker, Tim and John Carty, eds. *Ngaanyatjarra Art of the Lands*. Crawley: University of Western Australia Press, 2012.

Altman, Jon C. 'Gambling as a Mode of Redistributing and Accumulating Cash among Aborigines: A Case Study from Arnhem Land'. In *Gambling in Australia*, edited by G Caldwell, M Dickerson, B Haig and L Sylvan, pp. 50–67. Sydney: Croom Helm, 1985.

——. *Sustainable Development Options on Aboriginal Land: The Hybrid Economy in the Twenty-First Century*, Discussion Paper, Centre for Aboriginal Economic Policy Research, no. 226/2001. Canberra: Centre for Aboriginal Economic Policy Research, 2001.

——. 'Economic Development and Indigenous Australia: Contestations over Property, Institutions and Ideology'. *The Australian Journal of Agricultural and Resource Economics* 48, no. 3 (2004): 513–34.

Altman, Jon and Melinda Hinkson. 'Mobility and Modernity in Arnhem Land: The Social Universe of Kuninjku Trucks'. *Journal of Material Culture* 12, no. 2 (2007): 181–203.

——. eds. *Coercive Reconciliation: Stabilise, Normalise, Exit Aboriginal Australia*. North Carlton: Arena Publications, 2007.

——. eds. *Culture Crisis: Anthropology and Politics in Aboriginal Australia*. Sydney: UNSW Press, 2010.

Anderson, Warwick. *The Cultivation of Whiteness: Science, Health and Racial Destiny in Australia*. Melbourne: Melbourne University Press, 2002.

Anthony, Thalia. 'Labour Relations on Northern Cattle Stations: Feudal Exploitation and Accommodation'. *The Drawing Board: An Australian Review of Public Affairs* 4, no. 3 (2004): 117–136.

——. 'An Anniversary Shrouded in Myths'. *Australian Policy Online*, 22 August 2006.

——. 'Was there slavery in Australia? Yes. It shouldn't even be up for debate'. *The Conversation*, 11 June 2020.

Appadurai, Arjun. 'Introduction: Commodities and the Politics of Value'. In *The Social Life of Things: Commodities in Cultural Perspective*, edited by Arjun Appadurai, pp. 3–63. Cambridge: Cambridge University Press, 1986.

——. 'Putting Hierarchy In Its Place'. *Cultural Anthropology* 3, no. 1 (1988): 36–49.

——. *Modernity at Large: Cultural Dimensions of Globalisation*. Minneapolis: University of Minnesota Press, 1996.

Attwood, Bain. 'Of the Mission Stations: Aborigines in Gippsland 1860–1890'. *Aboriginal History* 10 (1986): 131–51.

——. 'Tarra bobby, A Brataualung Man'. *Aboriginal History* 11 (1987): 41–57.

——. *The Making of the Aborigines*. Sydney: Allen & Unwin, 1989.

——. *Telling the Truth About Aboriginal History*. Crows Nest: Allen & Unwin, 2005.

——. *Possession: Batman's Treaty and the Matter of History*. Melbourne: Miegunyah Press, 2009.

Attwood, Bain and Fiona Magowan, eds. *Telling Stories: Indigenous History and Memory in Australia and New Zealand*. Crows Nest: Allen & Unwin, 2001.

Austin-Broos, Diane. 'Places, Practices and Things: The Articulation of Arrernte Kinship with Welfare and Work'. *American Ethnologist* 30, no. 1 (February 2003): 118–35.

——. '"Working for" and "Working" among Western Arrernte in Central Australia'. *Oceania* 76, no. 1 (March 2006): 1–15.

——. *Arrernte Present, Arrernte Past: Invasion, Violence, and Imagination in Indigenous Central Australia*. Chicago: University of Chicago Press, 2009.

——. *A Different Inequality: The Politics of Debate About Remote Aboriginal Australia*. Crows Nest: Allen & Unwin, 2011.

Bachelard, Gaston. *The Poetics of Space*. Translated by Maria Jolas. Boston: Beacon Press, 1994.

Baker, Richard. 'Coming in?: The Yanyuwa as a Case Study in the Geography of Contact History'. *Aboriginal History* 14, no. 1–2 (1990): 25–60.

——. *Land is Life: From Bush to Town, The Story of the Yanyuwa People*. St Leonards: Allen & Unwin, 1999.

Baker, Richard and Hannah Hueneke. 'Tourist Behaviour, Local Values and Interpretation at Uluru: "The Sacred Deed at Australia's Mighty Heart"'. *GeoJournal* 74 (2009): 477–90.

Bancroft, Angus. *Roma and Gypsy-Travellers in Europe: Modernity, Race, Space and Exclusion*. Aldershot: Ashgate, 2005.

Barwick, Diane. 'And the Lubras Are Ladies Now'. In *Woman's Role in Aboriginal Society*, edited by Fay Gale, pp. 54–7. Canberra: Australian Institute for Aboriginal Studies, 1974.

Bashford, Alison. 'World Population and Australian Land: Demography and Sovereignty in the Twentieth Century'. *Australian Historical Studies* 38, no. 130 (October 2007): 211–27.

Basso, Keith. 'Speaking with Names: Language and Landscape among the Western Apache'. *Cultural Anthropology* 3, no. 2 (1988): 99–130.

——. *Wisdom Sits in Places: Landscape and Language among the Western Apache*. Albuquerque: University of New Mexico Press, 1996.

Beckett, Jeremy. 'Torres Strait Islanders and the Pearling Industry: A Case of Internal Colonialism'. In *Encounters with Indigeneity: Writing about Aboriginal and Torres Strait Islander Peoples*, pp. 102–27. Canberra: Aboriginal Studies Press, 2014 (first published in 1977).

——. 'George Dutton's Country'. In *Encounters with Indigeneity: Writing about Aboriginal and Torres Strait Islander Peoples*, pp. 1–27. Canberra: Aboriginal Studies Press, 2014 (first published in 1978).

——. 'Walter Newton's History of the World – or Australia'. In *Encounters with Indigeneity: Writing about Aboriginal and Torres Strait Islander Peoples*, pp. 28–58. Canberra: Aboriginal Studies Press, 2014 (first published in 1993).

——. 'Autobiography and Testimonial Discourse in Myles Lalor's "Oral History".' In *Encounters with Indigeneity: Writing about Aboriginal and Torres Strait Islander Peoples*, pp. 83–101. Canberra: Aboriginal Studies Press, 2014 (first published in 2001).

Bell, Diane. 'For Our Families: The Kurundi Walk-off and the Ngurrantji Venture'. *Aboriginal History* 2 (1978): 32–62.

Berndt, Ronald M. 'The Concept of "the Tribe" in the Western Desert of Australia'.' *Oceania* 30 (1959): 81–107.

Berndt, Ronald M and Catherine H Berndt. *End of an Era: Aboriginal Labour in the Northern Territory*. Canberra: Australian Institute of Aboriginal Studies, 1987.

Bhabha, Homi K. *The Location of Culture*. London: Routledge, 1994.

Bird Rose, Deborah. *Hidden Histories: Black Stories from Victoria River Downs, Humbert River and Wave Hill Stations*. Canberra: Aboriginal Studies Press, 1991.

——. *Dingo Makes Us Human: Life and Land in an Aboriginal Australian Culture*. Cambridge: Cambridge University Press, 1992.

——. 'Histories and Rituals: Land Claims in the Territory'. In *In the Age of Mabo: History, Aborigines and Australia*, edited by Bain Attwood, pp. 35–53. St Leonards: Allen & Unwin, 1996.

——. *Nourishing Terrains: Australian Aboriginal Views of Landscape and Wilderness*. Canberra: Australian Heritage Commission, 1996.

——. 'Australia Felix Rules OK!' In *Race Matters*, edited by Gillian Cowlishaw and Barry Morris, pp. 121–38. Canberra: Aboriginal Studies Press, 1997.

——. 'To Dance With Time: A Victoria River Aboriginal Study'. *The Australian Journal of Anthropology* 11, no. 3 (2000): 287–96.

——. 'Oral Histories and Knowledge'. In *Frontier Conflict: The Australian Experience*, edited by Bain Attwood and SG Foster, pp. 120–32. Canberra: National Museum of Australia, 2003.

——. 'Writing Place'. In *Writing Histories: Imagination and Narration*, edited by Ann Curthoys and Ann McGrath, 8.1–8.13. Melbourne: Monash University ePress, 2009.

Blair, Sandy, Nicholas Hall, Diana James, and Lee Brady. 'Making Tracks: Key Issues about the Heritage of Australian Routes and Journeys'. *Historic Environment* 16, no. 2 (2002): 43–6.

Bowman, Margaret, ed. *Every Hill Got A Story: We Grew Up in Country; Men and Women of Central Australia and the Central Land Council*. Richmond: Hardie Grant Books, 2015.

Boyce, James. 'Return to Eden: Van Diemen's Land and the Early British Settlement of Australia'. *Environment and History* 14, no. 2 (2008): 289–307.

——. *Van Dieman's Land*. Melbourne: Black Inc., 2010.

Bradley, Edna. *A Rock to Remember: A Memoir*. Alice Springs, Kristina Kidd, 2009.

Brigg, Morgan and Mary Graham. 'The Relevance of Aboriginal Political Concepts (5): Country, Place and Territory'. *ABC Religion & Ethics*.

Brokensha, Peter. *The Pitjantjatjara and Their Crafts*. Sydney: Aboriginal Arts Board, Australia Council, 1975.

Burke, Paul. *Law's Anthropology: From Ethnography to Expert Testimony in Native Title*. Canberra: ANU Press, 2011.

Butler, Kelly Jean. *Witnessing Australian Stories: History, Testimony, and Memory in Contemporary Culture*. New Brunswick, New Jersey: Transaction Publishers, 2013.

Cane, Scott. 'People and Policy in the Development and Destruction of Yagga Yagga Outstation, Western Australia'. In *Experiments in Self-Determination: Histories of the Outstation Movement in Australia*, edited by Nicolas Peterson and Fred Myers, pp. 253–78. Canberra: ANU E Press, 2016.

Carey, Jane and Jane Lydon. 'Indigenous Networks: Historical Trajectories and Contemporary Connections'. In *Indigenous Networks: Mobility, Connections and Exchange*, edited by Jane Carey and Jane Lydon, pp. 1–28. New York: Routledge, 2014.

Carment, David. *History and the Landscape in Central Australia*. Darwin: North Australia Research Unit, 1991.

Carrier, Peter. 'Places, Politics and the Archiving of Contemporary Memory'. In *Memory and Methodology*, edited by Susannah Radstone, pp. 37–58. Oxford: Berg, 2000.

Casey, Edward. *Getting Back into Place: Toward a Renewed Understanding of the Place-World*. Bloomington: Indiana University Press, 1993.

——. 'How to get from space to place in a fairly short stretch of time'. In *Senses of place*, edited by S Feld and K Basso, pp. 14–51. Berkeley: University of California Press, 1996.

Cathcart, Michael. 'Uluru'. In *Words for Country: Landscape and Language in Australia*, edited by Tom Griffiths and Tim Bonyhady, pp. 206–21. Sydney: UNSW Press, 2002.

——. *The Water Dreamers: The Remarkable History of Our Dry Continent*. Melbourne: Text Publishing, 2009.

Clarsen, Georgine. 'Tracing the Outline of Nation: Circling Australia by Car'. *Continuum* 13, no. 3 (November 1999): 359–69.

——.'Automobiles and Australian Modernisation: The Redex Around –Australia Trials of the 1950s'. *Australian Historical Studies* 41, no. 3 (September 2010): 352–68.

Clarsen, Georgine and Lorenzo Veracini. 'Settler Colonial Automobilities: A Distinct Constellation of Automobile Cultures?' *History Compass* 10, no. 2 (December 2012): 889–900.

Clifford, James. *The Predicament of Culture: Twentieth Century Ethnography, Literature and Art*. Cambridge, MA: Harvard University Press, 1988.

——. *Routes: Travel and Translation in the Late Twentieth Century*. Cambridge, MA: Harvard University Press, 1997.

Coombs, HC. 'Decentralisation Trends among Aboriginal Communities'. *Search* 5, no. 4 (1974): 135–43.

Cowlishaw, Gillian. 'Colour, Culture and the Aboriginalists'. *Man* 22, no. 2 (1987): 221–37.

——. *Rednecks, Eggheads and Blackfellas: A Study of Racial Power and Intimacy in Australia*. St Leonards: Allen & Unwin, 1999.

——. 'Friend or Foe? Anthropology's Encounter with Aborigines'. *Inside Story*, 19 August 2015.

Cresswell, Tim. 'The Production of Mobilities'. *New Formations* 43 (Spring 2001): 11–25.

——. *On the Move: Mobility in the Modern Western World*. New York: Routledge, 2006.

——. 'Towards a Politics of Mobility'. *Environment and Planning D: Society and Space* 28, no. 1 (2010): 17–31.

Cresswell, T and P Merriman eds. *Geographies of Mobility: Practices, Spaces, Subjects*. Aldershot: Ashgate, 2008.

Curthoys, Ann and Clive Moore. 'Working for the White People: A Historiographic Essay on Aboriginal and Torres Strait Islander Labour'. *Labour History* 69 (1995): 1–29.

Damousi, Joy. *Living with the Aftermath: Trauma, Nostalgia and Grief in Post-War Australia*. Melbourne: Cambridge University Press, 2001.

——. *Memory and Migration in the Shadow of War: Australia's Greek Immigrants after World War II and the Greek Civil War*. Melbourne: Cambridge University Press, 2015.

Darian-Smith, Kate and Paula Hamilton, eds. *Memory and History in Twentieth-Century Australia*. Melbourne: Oxford University Press, 1994.

Davis, Megan. 'The truth about truth-telling: Revisiting trauma is not the road to justice for Aboriginal people. *The Monthly* (December 2021): pp. 10–12.

Deleuze, Gilles and Félix Guattari. *A Thousand Plateaus: Capitalism and Schizophrenia*. Translated by Brian Massumi. Minneapolis: University of Minnesota Press, 1987.

Deloria, Philip J. 'What is the Middle Ground, Anyway?' *The William and Mary Quarterly* 63, no. 1 (2006): 15–22.

Donovan, PF. *A Land Full of Possibilities: A History of South Australia's Northern Territory*. St Lucia: University of Queensland Press, 1981.

Downing, Jim. *Ngurra Walytja, Country of My Spirit*. Darwin: North Australia Research Unit, 1988.

Duguid, Charles. *Doctor and the Aborigines*. Adelaide: Rigby, 1972.

Edmonds, Angelique. 'Sedentary Topography: The Impact of the Christian Mission Society's "Civilising" Agenda on the Spatial Structure of Life in the Roper Region of Northern Australia'. In *Transgressions: Critical Australian Indigenous Histories*, edited by Ingereth Macfarlane and Mark Hannah, Aboriginal History Monograph 16, pp. 193–209. Canberra: ANU E Press, 2007.

Edwards, Bill. 'From Coombes to Coombs: Reflections on the Pitjantjatjara Outstation Movement'. In *Experiments in Self-Determination: Histories of the Outstation Movement in Australia*, edited by Nicolas Peterson and Fred Myers, pp. 25–46. Canberra: ANU E Press, 2016.

Edwards, Elizabeth. 'Material Beings: Objecthood and Ethnographic Photographs'. *Visual Studies* 17, no. 1 (2002): 67–75.

Elkin, A.P. 'The Aborigines, Our National Responsibility'. *The Australian Quarterly* 6, no. 23 (1934): 52–60.

——. 'Reaction and Interaction: A Food Gathering People and European Settlement in Australia'. *American Anthropologist* 53, no. 2 (1951): 164–86.

Escobar, Arturo. 'Culture Sits in Places: Reflections on Globalism and Subaltern Strategies of Localisation'. *Political Geography* 20 (2001): 139–74.

Finlayson, HH. *The Red Centre: Man and Beast in the Heart of Australia*. Sydney: Angus & Robertson, 1943.

Folds, Ralph. *Crossed Purposes: The Pintupi and Australia's Indigenous Policy*. Sydney: University of New South Wales Press, 2001.

Foucault, Michel. *Power/Knowledge: Selected Interviews and Other Writings, 1972–1977*. Translated by Colin Gordon. Brighton: Harvester Press, 1980.

Frisch, M. 'The Memory of History'. In *Presenting the Past: Essays on History and the Public*, edited by R Rosenzweig and S Benson, pp. 5–17. Philadelphia: Temple University Press, 1986.

——. *A Shared Authority: Essays on the Craft and Meaning of Oral History and the Public*. Albany: State University of New York Press, 1991.

——. Frisch, M. 'Sharing Authority: Oral History and the Collaborative Process'. *The Oral History Review* 30, no. 1 (2003): 111–13.

Gelder, Ken. 'Thirty Years On: *Reading the Country* and Indigenous Homeliness'. *Australian Humanities Review* 58 (2015): 17–27.

Giles, Ernest. *Geographic Travels in Central Australia, from 1872 to 1874*. Melbourne: M'Carron, Bird & Co., 1875.

——. *Australia Twice Traversed: The Romance of Exploration Being A Narrative Compiled from the Journals of Five Exploring Expeditions Into and Through Central South Australia and Western Australia, From 1872 to 1876*. Vol. 1. London: Sampson Low, Marston, Searle & Rivington, 1889.

Gill, Nicholas. 'Life and Death in Australian "Heartlands": Pastoralism, Ecology and Rethinking the Outback'. *Journal of Rural Studies* 21, no. 1 (January 2005): 39–53.

——. 'Transcending Nostalgia: Pastoralist Memory and Staking a Claim in the Land'. In *Dislocating the Frontier: Essaying the Mystique of the Outback*, edited by Deborah Bird Rose and Richard Davis, pp. 67–84. Canberra: ANU E Press, 2005.

——. 'Aboriginal Pastoralism, Social Embeddedness, and Cultural Continuity in Central Australia'. *Society & Natural Resources* 18, no. 8 (2005): 699–714.

Gill, Nicholas and Alistair Paterson. 'A Work in Progress: Aboriginal People and Pastoral Cultural Heritage in Australia'. In *Geographies of Australian Heritages: Loving a Sunburnt Country?*, edited by R Jones and B Shaw, pp. 113–31. Aldershot: Ashgate, 2007.

Goodall, Heather. 'An Intelligent Parasite: A.P. Elkin and White Perceptions of the History of Aboriginal People in New South Wales'. Paper presented to the Australian Historical Association, Sydney, 1982.

——. '"The Whole Truth and Nothing But…": Some Intersections of Western Law, Aboriginal History and Community Memory'. In *Power, Knowledge and Aborigines* edited by Bain Attwood and John Arnold, pp. 104–19. Bundoora: La Trobe University Press, 1992.

——. *Invasion to Embassy: Land in Aboriginal Politics in New South Wales, 1770–1972*. Sydney: Sydney University Press, 1996.

——. 'Too Early Yet or Not Soon Enough: Reflections on Sharing Histories as a Process'. *Australian Historical Studies* 118 (2002): 17–20.

——. 'Riding the Tide: Indigenous Knowledge, History and Water in a Changing Australia'. *Environment and History* 14, no. 3 (2008): 355–84.

Goodall, Heather and Allison Cadzow. *Rivers and Resilience: Aboriginal People on Sydney's Georges River*. Sydney: University of New South Wales Press, 2009.

Gosse, William Christie. 'South Australia. W.C. Gosse's Explorations 1873: Report and Diary of Mr W.C. Gosse's Central and Western Exploring Expedition, 1873'. Adelaide: House of Assembly, June 1874.

Gould, Richard A, D Fowler, and Catherine S Fowler. 'Diggers and Doggers: Parallel Failures in Economic Acculturation'. *Southwestern Journal of Anthropology* 28, no. 3 (1972): 265–81.

Graburn, Nelson HH. *Ethnic and Tourist Arts: Cultural Expressions from the Fourth World*. Berkeley: University of California Press, 1976.

Gray, Geoffrey. '"[The Sydney school] Seem[s] to View the Aborigines as Forever Unchanging": Southeastern Australia and Australian Anthropology'. *Aboriginal History* 24, (2000): 175–99.

——. *A Cautious Silence: The Politics of Australian Anthropology*. Canberra: Aboriginal Studies Press, 2007.

Gray, WJ. 'Decentralisation Trends in Arnhem Land'. In *Aborigines and Change: Australia in the 70s*, edited by Ronald M Berndt, pp. 114–23. Canberra: Australian Institute of Aboriginal Studies, 1977.

Green, David R and Lesley JF Green. 'Space, Time and Story Tracks: Contemporary Practices of Topographic Memory in the Palikur Territory of Arukwa, Amapá, Brazil'. *Ethnohistory* 56, no. 1 (1 January 2009): 163–85.

——. *Knowing the Day, Knowing the World: Engaging Amerindian Thought in Public Archaeology*. Arizona: University of Arizona Press, 2013.

Gregory, JW. *The Dead Heart of Australia: A Journey around Lake Eyre in the Summer of 1901–02, with Some Account of the Lake Eyre Basin and the Flowing Wells of Central Australia*. London: J. Murray, 1906.

Grele, RJ with Studs Terkel, Jan Vansina, Dennis Tedlock, Saul Benison and Alice Kessler Harris. *Envelopes of Sound: The Art of Oral History*. Chicago: Precedent, 1985.

Griffiths, Tom. *Hunters and Collectors: The Antiquarian Imagination in Australia*. Melbourne: Cambridge University Press, 1996.

——. 'A Landmark Work of Australian History'. *Inside Story*, 6 May 2013.

Groom, Arthur. *I Saw a Strange Land*. Sydney: Angus & Robertson, 1952.

Hamilton, Annette. 'Coming and Going: Aboriginal Mobility in North-West South Australia, 1970–1971'. *Records of the South Australian Museum* 20 (1987): 47–57.

Harney, WE. *To Ayers Rock and Beyond*. Adelaide: Rigby, 1969.

Harris, Colin. 'Culture and Geography: South Australia's mound springs as trade and communication routes'. *Historic Environment* 16, no. 2 (2002): 8–11.

Harrison, Rodney. *Shared Landscapes: Archaeologies of Attachment and the Pastoral Industry in New South Wales*. Sydney: University of New South Wales Press, 2004.

Hains, Brigid. *The Ice and the Inland: Mawson Flynn, and the Myth of the Frontier*. Carlton South: Melbourne University Press, 2002.

Healy, Chris. *From the Ruins of Colonialism: History as Social Memory*. New York: Cambridge University Press, 1997.

——. *Forgetting Aborigines*. Sydney: University of New South Wales Press, 2008.

Heidegger, Martin. *Being and Time*. Translated by John Macquarrie and Edward Robinson. London: SCM Press, 1962.

Hiatt, LR. *Arguments about Aborigines: Australia and the Evolution of Social Anthropology*. Cambridge, UK: Cambridge University Press, 1996.

Hill, Barry. *The Rock: Travelling to Uluru*. St Leonards: Allen & Unwin, 1994.

Hilliard, Winifred. *The People in Between: The Pitjantjatjara People of Ernabella*. London: Hodder & Stoughton, 1968.

Hinkson, Melinda. *Remembering the Future: Warlpiri Life through the Prism of Drawing*. Canberra: Aboriginal Studies Press, 2014.

Hodgkin, Katherine and Susannah Radstone, eds. *Contested Pasts: The Politics of Memory*. London: Routledge, 2003.

——. *Memory, History, Nation: Contested Pasts*. New Brunswick, New Jersey: Transaction Publishers, 2007.

Hokari, Minoru. 'Gurindji Mode of Historical Practice'. In *The Power of Knowledge, the Resonance of Tradition*, edited by Luke Taylor, Graeme K Ward, Graham Henderson, Richard Davis and Lynley Wallis, pp. 214–22. Canberra: Aboriginal Studies Press, 2005.

——. *Gurindji Journey: A Japanese Historian in the Outback*. Sydney: University of New South Wales Press, 2011.

Hughes, Helen. *Lands of Shame: Aboriginal and Torres Strait Islander 'Homelands' in Transition*. St Leonards: Centre for Independent Studies, 2007.

Ingold, Tim. *Being Alive: Essays on Movement, Knowledge and Description*. London: Routledge, 2011.

Jebb, Mary Anne. *Blood Sweat and Welfare: A History of White Bosses and Aboriginal Pastoral Workers*. Nedlands: University of Western Australia Press, 2002.

——. 'Pastoral Paternalism in the Pilbara'. In *Marlbatharndu Wanggagu: Once Upon A Time in the West*, pp. 144–9. Perth: FORM, 2014.

Johnson, Miranda. 'Writing Indigenous Histories Now'. *Australian Historical Studies* 45, no. 3 (2014): 317–30.

Kaufmann, V. *Re-Thinking Mobility: Contemporary Sociology*. Aldershot: Ashgate, 2002.

Keen, Ian. 'A Question of Interpretation: The Definition of "Traditional Aboriginal Owners" in the Aboriginal Land Rights (NT) Act.' In *Aboriginal Land Owners: Contemporary Issues in the Determination of Traditional Aboriginal Land Ownership*, edited by LR Hiatt, pp. 24–45. Sydney: University of Sydney, 1984.

Keen, Ian and Christopher Lloyd. Introduction to *Indigenous Participation in Australian Economies*, vol. 2, edited by Ian Keen, Christopher Lloyd, Natasha Fijn, and Michael Pickering, pp. 1–15. Canberra: ANU E Press, 2012.

Kenny, Robert. *The Lamb Enters The Dreaming: Nathanael Pepper & The Ruptured World*. Carlton North: Scribe, 2010.

Kerin, Rani. *Doctor Do-Good: Charles Duguid and Aboriginal Advancement, 1930s–1970s*. North Melbourne: Australian Scholarly Publishing, 2011.

——. 'Dogging for a Living: Aborigines and "Undesirables" in South Australia'. In *Frontier, Race, Nation: Henry Reynolds and Australian History*, edited by Bain Attwood and Tom Griffiths, pp. 136–58. North Melbourne: Australian Scholarly Publishing, 2009.

Kerwin, Dale. *Aboriginal Dreaming Paths and Trading Routes: The Colonisation of the Australian Economic Landscape*. Brighton: Sussex Academic Press, 2010.

Keys, Cathy. 'Skin Fabric Iron Shade'. *Proceedings of the Society of Architectural Historians, Australia and New Zealand* 31 (2014): 133–43.

Khatun, Samia. *Australianama*. St Lucia: University of Queensland Press, 2018.

——. 'Beyond Blank Spaces: Five Tracks to Late Nineteenth–Century Beltana'. *Transfers* 5, no. 3 (2015): 68–86.

Kimber, RG. 'The End of the Bad Old Days: European Settlement in Central Australia, 1871–1894'. Darwin: State Library Northern Territory, 1991.

Klapproth, Danièle M. *Narrative as Social Practice: Anglo–Western and Australian Aboriginal Oral Traditions*. Berlin: Mouton de Gruyter, 2004.

Kleinart, Sylvia. 'Aboriginal Enterprises: Negotiating an Urban Aboriginality'. *Aboriginal History* 34 (2010): 171–96.

Layton, Robert. *Uluru: An Aboriginal History of Ayers Rock*. Canberra: Australian Institute of Aboriginal Studies, 1986.

Lear, Jonathan. *Radical Hope: Ethics in the Face of Cultural Devastation*. Cambridge, MA: Harvard University Press, 2006.

Ling, Ted. *Commonwealth Government Records about the Northern Territory*. Canberra: National Archives of Australia, 2011.

Long, Jeremy. 'Leaving the Desert: Actors and Sufferers in the Aboriginal Exodus from the Western Desert'. *Aboriginal History* 13, no. 1–2 (1989): 9–43.

——. 'Returning to Country: The Docker River Project'. In *Experiments in Self-Determination: Histories of the Outstation Movement in Australia*, edited by Nicolas Peterson and Fred Myers, pp. 47–60. Canberra: ANU E Press, 2016.

McBryde, Isobel. 'Travellers in Storied Landscapes: A Cast Study in Exchanges and Heritage'. *Aboriginal History* 24, (2000): 152–74.

McGrath, Ann. *Born in the Cattle*. St Leonards: Allen & Unwin, 1987.

——. 'Travels to a Distant Past: The Mythology of the Outback'. *Australian Cultural History* 10 (1991): 113–24.

McGregor, Russell. *Imagined Destinies: Aboriginal Australians and the Doomed Race Theory, 1880-1939*. Melbourne: Melbourne University Press, 1997.

——. 'Wards, Words and Citizens: A.P. Elkin and Paul Hasluck on Assimilation'. *Oceania* 69, no. 4 (1 June 1999): 243–59.

——. 'Develop the North: Aborigines, Environment and Australian Nationhood in the 1930s'. *Journal of Australian Studies* 28, no. 81 (January 2004): 33–45.

——. 'A Dog in the Manger: White Australia and Its Vast Empty Spaces'. *Australian Historical Studies* 43, no. 2 (June 2012): 157–73.

——. 'Developing the North, Defending the Nation? The Northern Australia Development Committee, 1945–1949'. *The Australian Journal of Politics and History* 59, no. 1 (2013): 33–46.

McGuire, ME. 'Whiteman's Walkabout'. *Meanjin* 52, no. 3 (1993): 517–25.

McKenna, Mark. *Return to Uluru*. Carlton: Black Inc., 2021.

——. *Looking for Blackfellas Point: An Australian History of Place*. Sydney: University of New South Wales Press, 2002.

McMenzie, Marcia and Eve Tuck. *Place in Research: Theory, Methodology, and Methods*. New York: Routledge, 2015.

McKnight, Tom L. *The Camel in Australia*. Melbourne: Melbourne University Press, 1969.

Madigan, CT. *Central Australia*. London: Oxford University Press, 1936.

Malkki, Liisa. 'National Geographic: The Rooting of Peoples and the Territorialisation of National Identity among Scholars and Refugees'. *Cultural Anthropology* 7, no. 1 (1992): 24–44.

Marcus, Julie. 'The Journey out to the Centre'. In *Race Matters*, edited by Gillian Cowlishaw and Barry Morris, pp. 29–52. Canberra: Aboriginal Studies Press, 1997.

Massey, Doreen. *For Space*. London: Sage Publications, 2005.

Mauss, Marcel. *The Gift*. Translated by WD Halls. London: Routledge, 1990.

May, Dawn. *Aboriginal Labour and the Cattle Industry: Queensland from White Settlement to the Present*. Melbourne: Cambridge University Press, 1994.

Meggitt, Mervyn John. *Desert People: A Study of the Walbiri Aborigines of Central Australia*. London: Angus & Robertson, 1975.

Meehan, B and R Jones. 'The Outstation Movement and Hints of a White Backlash'. In *Northern Australia: Options and Implications*, edited by R Jones, pp. 131–57. Canberra: The Australian National University, 1980.

Merlan, Francesca. '"Making People Quiet" in the Pastoral North: Reminiscences of Elsey Station'. *Aboriginal History* 2 (1978): 70–106.

——. 'The Regimentation of Customary Practice: From Northern Territory Land Claims to Mabo'. *The Australian Journal of Anthropology* 6, no. 1 (1995): 64–82.

——. 'Fighting over Country: Four Commonplaces'. In *Fighting over Country: Anthropological Perspectives*, Research Monograph 12, edited by D Smith and J Findlayson, pp. 1–13. Canberra: Centre for Aboriginal Economic Policy Research, Australian National University, 1997.

——. *Caging the Rainbow: Places, Politics, and Aborigines in a North Australian Town*. Honolulu: University of Hawai'i Press, 1998.

Merlau-Ponty, Maurice. *Phenomenology of Perception*. Translated by Colin Smith. London: Routledge, 1962.

Monchamp, Anne Marie. *Autobiographical Memory in an Aboriginal Australian Community: Culture, Place and Narrative*. Houndsmills: Palgrave Macmillan, 2014.

Monteath, Peter and Valerie Munt. *Red Professor: The Cold War Life of Fred Rose*. Mile End: Wakefield Press, 2015.

Moreton-Robinson, Aileen. *The White Possessive: Property, Power, and Indigenous Sovereignty*. Minneapolis: University of Minnesota Press, 2015.

Morphy, Howard and Frances Morphy. 'The "Myths" of Ngalakan History: Ideology and Images of the Past in Northern Australia'. *Man* 19, no. 3 (September 1984): 459–78.

——. 'Anthropological Theory and Government Policy in Australia's Northern Territory: The Hegemony of the "Mainstream".' *American Anthropologist* 115, no. 2 (June 2013): 174–87.

——. 'Thwarted Aspirations: The Political Economy of a Yolgnu Outstation, 1972 to the Present'. In *Experiments in Self-Determination: Histories of the Outstation Movement in Australia*, edited by Nicolas Peterson and Fred Myers, pp. 301–22. Canberra: ANU E Press, 2016.

Morphy, Howard. *Ancestral Connections: Art and an Aboriginal System of Knowledge*. Chicago: University of Chicago Press, 1991.

——. 'Indigenous Art as Economy'. In *Culture, Economy and Governance in Aboriginal Australia*, edited by Diane Austin-Broos and Gaynor Marilyn Macdonald, pp. 19–28. Sydney: Sydney University Press, 2005.

Morris, Meaghan. *Identity Anecdotes: Translation and Media Culture*. London: Sage Publications, 2006.

Mountford, Charles. *Brown Men and Red Sand: Wanderings in Wild Australia*. Melbourne: Robertson & Mullens, 1948.

——. *Ayers Rock, Its People, Their Beliefs and Their Art*. Sydney: Angus & Robertson, 1965.

Muecke, Stephen, Paddy Roe and Krim Benterrak. *Reading the Country: Introduction to Nomadology*. Fremantle: Fremantle Arts Centre Press, 1984.

Mulvaney, DJ. '"The Chain of Connection": The Material Evidence'. In *Tribes and Boundaries in Australia*, edited by Nicolas Peterson, pp. 72–94. Canberra: Australian Institute of Aboriginal Studies, 1976.

——. '…These Aboriginal Lines of Travel'. *Historic Environment* 16, no. 2 (2002): 4–7.

Munn, Nancy. 'The Transformation of Subjects into Objects in Walbiri and Pitjantjatjara Myth'. In *Australian Aboriginal Anthropology*, edited by Ronald Berndt, pp. 141–63. Nedlands: University of Western Australia Press, 1970.

Munt, Valerie. 'Australian Anthropology, Ideology and Political Repression: The Cold War Experience of Frederick G.G. Rose'. *Anthropological Forum* 21, no. 1 (2011): 109–29.

Musharbash, Yasmine. *Yuendumu Everyday: Contemporary Life in Remote Aboriginal Australia*. Canberra: Aboriginal Studies Press, 2008.

Myers, Fred. *Pintupi Country, Pintupi Self: Sentiment, Place and Politics among Western Desert Aborigines*. Canberra: Australian Institute of Aboriginal Studies, 1986.

——. 'Ways of Placemaking'. In *Culture, Landscape, and the Environment: The Linacre Lectures, 1997*, edited by Kate Flint and Howard Morphy, pp. 72–110. Oxford: Oxford University Press, 2000.

——. 'History, Memory and the Politics of Self-Determination at an Early Outstation'. In *Experiments in Self-Determination: Histories of the Outstation Movement in Australia*, edited by Nicolas Peterson and Fred Myers, pp. 81–104. Canberra: ANU E Press, 2016.

Myers, Fred and Nicolas Peterson. 'The Origins and History of Outstations as Aboriginal Life Projects'. In *Experiments in Self-Determination: Histories of the Outstation Movement in Australia*, edited by Nicolas Peterson and Fred Myers, pp. 1–24. Canberra: ANU E Press, 2016.

Neumann, Klaus. 'Fred Rose: Communist, Scientist, Lover, Spy'. *Inside Story*, 2 October 2015.

Nora, Pierre, ed. *Les Lieux de Mémoire*. 7 vols. Paris: Gallimard, 1984.

——. 'Between Memory and History: Les Lieux de Mémoire'. *Representations* 26 (Spring 1989): 7–24.

Nugent, Maria. *Botany Bay: Where Histories Meet*. Crows Nest: Allen & Unwin, 2005.

——. 'Mapping Memories: Oral History for Aboriginal Cultural Heritage in New South Wales, Australia'. In *Oral History and Public Memories*, edited by Paula Hamilton and Linda Shopes, pp. 47–64. Philadelphia: Temple University Press, 2008.

——. 'An Economy of Shells: A brief history of La Perouse Aboriginal women's shell-work and its markets, 1880–2010'. In *Indigenous Participation in Australian Economies*, vol. 2, edited by Ian Keen, Christopher Lloyd, Natasha Fijn and Michael Pickering, pp. 211–27. Canberra: ANU E Press, 2012.

Paisley, Fiona. 'No Back Streets in the Bush: 1920s and 1930s pro-Aboriginal White Women's Activism and the Trans-Australia Railway'. *Australian Feminist Studies* 12, no. 25 (April 1997): 119–37.

Palmer, Shannyn. 'Making Histories "Ngapartji-Ngapartji" Way: Exploring Collaboration, Exchange and Intercultural Histories in a Colonised Settler Nation'. *History Compass* 11, no. 2 (2013): 117–32.

——. 'Exodus? Rethinking histories of movement and migration in the Western Desert and Central Australia from an A<u>n</u>angu perspective'. *History Australia* 13, no. 4 (2016): 490–507.

Passerini, L. *Fascism in Popular Memory: The Cultural Experience of the Turin Working Class*. Cambridge: Cambridge University Press, 1987.

——, ed. *Memory and Totalitarianism: International Yearbook of Oral History and Life Stories*, vol. 1. Oxford: Oxford University Press, 1992.

Paterson, Alistair. 'The Texture of Agency: An Example of Culture–Contact in Central Australia'. *Archaeology in Oceania* 38, no. 2 (2003): 52–65.

——. 'Early Pastoral Landscapes and Culture Contact in Central Australia'. *Historical Archaeology* 39, no. 3 (1 January 2005): 28–48.

——. *Lost Legions: Culture Contact in Central Australia*. Lanham, MD: Altamira Press, 2008.

Peterson, Nicolas and Jon C Altman. 'Rights to Game and Rights to Cash among Contemporary Australian Hunter-Gatherers'. In *Hunters and Gatherers: Property, Power and Ideology*, edited by Tim Ingold, James Woodburn and David Riches, pp. 75–94. Oxford: Berg, 1988.

Peterson, Nicolas. 'Aboriginal Involvement with the Australian Economy in the Central Reserve during the Winter of 1970'. In *Aborigines and Change:*

Australia in the 70s, edited by Ronald M Berndt, pp. 136–46. Canberra: Australian Institute of Aboriginal Studies, 1977.
——. 'Capitalism, Culture and Land Rights: Aborigines and the State in the Northern Territory'. *Social Analysis: The International Journal of Social and Cultural Practice*, no. 18 (1985): 85–101.
——. *Aboriginal Territorial Organisation*. Oceania Monograph 30. Sydney: Sydney University Press, 1986.
——. 'Cash, Commoditisation and Authenticity: When Do Aboriginal People Stop Being Hunter-Gatherers?' In *Cash, Commoditisation and Changing Foragers*, edited by Nicolas Peterson and Toshio Matsuyama, pp. 67–90. Osaka: National Museum of Ethnology, 1991.
——. 'Demand Sharing: Reciprocity and the Pressure for Generosity among Foragers'. *American Anthropologist* 96, no. 4 (December 1993): 860–74.
——. 'An Expanding Aboriginal Domain: Mobility and the Initiation Journey'. *Oceania* 70, no. 3 (2000): 205–18.
——. 'What Can Pre-Colonial and Frontier Economies Tell Us about Engagement with the Real Economy? Indigenous Life Projects and the Conditions for Development'. In *Culture, Economy and Governance in Aboriginal Australia*, edited by Diane Austin-Broos and Gaynor Marilyn Macdonald, pp. 7–18. Sydney: Sydney University Press, 2005.
Phillips, Ruth B. 'Why Not Tourist Art? Significant Silences in Native American Museum Representations' In *After Colonialism: Imperial Histories and Postcolonial Displacements*, edited by Gyan Prakash, pp. 98–128. Princeton: Princeton University Press, 1995.
——. *Trading Identities: The Souvenir in Native North American Art from the Northeast, 1700–1900*. Seattle: University of Washington Press, 1998.
Phillips, Ruth B and Christopher B Steiner. 'Art, Authenticity and the Baggage of Cultural Encounter'. In *Unpacking Culture: Art and Commodity in Colonial and postcolonial Worlds*, edited by Ruth B Phillips and Christopher B Steiner, pp. 3–19. Berkeley: University of California Press, 1999.
Poirier, Sylvie. *A World of Relationships: Itineraries, Dreams, and Events in the Australian Western Desert*. Toronto: University of Toronto Press, 2005.
Portelli, Alessandro. *The Death of Luigi Trastulli and Other Stories: Form and Meaning in Oral History*. Albany: State University of New York Press, 1991.
Povinelli, Elizabeth. *Labor's Lot: The Power, History, and Culture of Aboriginal Action*. Chicago: University of Chicago Press, 1993.
Pratt, Mary Louise. 'Arts of the Contact Zone'. *Profession*, 1991: 33–40.
Radstone, Susannah. 'Working with Memory: An Introduction'. In *Memory and Methodology*, edited by Susannah Radstone, pp. 1–24. Oxford: Berg, 2000.
——. 'Reconceiving Binaries: The Limits of Memory'. *History Workshop Journal*, no. 59 (Spring 2005): 134–50.
——. 'What Place Is This? Transcultural Memory and the Locations of Memory Studies'. *Parallax* 17, no. 4 (2011): 109–23.
Radstone, Susannah and Bill Schwarz, eds. *Memory: Histories, Theories, Debates*. New York: Fordham University Press, 2010.
Raffles, Hugh. '"Local Theory": Nature and the Making of an Amazonian Place'. *Cultural Anthropology* 14, no. 3 (1999): 323–60.
——. 'Intimate Knowledge'. *International Social Science Journal* 54, no. 173 (2002): 325–35.

Read, Peter and Engineer Jack Japaljarri. 'The Price of Tobacco: The Journey of the Warlmala to Wave Hill, 1928'. *Aboriginal History* 2 (1978): 141–8.

Read, Peter, Frances Peters-Little and Anna Haebich, editors. *Indigenous Biography and Autobiography*. Canberra: ANU E Press, 2008.

Redmond, Anthony and Fiona Skyring. 'Exchange and Appropriation: The Wurnan Economy and Aboriginal Land and Labour at Karunjie Station, North-Western Australia'. In *Indigenous Participation in Australian Economies: Historical and Anthropological Perspectives*, vol. 1, edited by Ian Keen, pp. 73–90. Canberra: ANU E Press, 2010.

Reece, Bob. 'Inventing Aborigines'. *Aboriginal History* 11 (1987): 14–23.

Rigney, Ann. 'Plenitude, Scarcity and the Circulation of Cultural Memory'. *Journal of European Studies* 35, no. 1 (2005): 11–28.

Robin, Libby. *How a Continent Created a Nation*. Sydney: University of New South Wales Press, 2007.

——. 'Seasons and Nomads: Reflections on Bioregionalism in Australia'. In *The Bioregional Imagination: Literature, Ecology and Place*, edited by Tom Lynch, Karla Ambruster and Cheryll Glotfelty, pp. 278–94. Athens: University of Georgia Press, 2012.

Rodman, Margaret. 'Empowering Place: Multilocality and Multivocality'. *American Anthropologist* 94 (1992): 640–56.

Rolls, Mitchell and Anna Johnson. *Travelling Home, 'Walkabout Magazine' and Mid-Twentieth Century Australia*. London: Anthem Press, 2016.

Rolls, Mitchell. 'Picture Imperfect: Re-reading Imagery of Aborigines in Walkabout'. *Journal of Australian Studies* 33, no. 1 (March 2009): 19–35.

Rose, Frederick GG. *Classification of Kin, Age Structure and Marriage amongst the Groote Eylandt Aborigines: A Study in Method and a Theory of Australian Kinship*. Berlin: Akademie–Verlag, 1960.

——. *The Wind of Change in Central Australia: The Aborigines at Angas Downs, 1962*. Berlin: Akademie–Verlag, 1965.

Ross, Glen. 'The Fantastic Face of the Continent: The Australian Geographical Walkabout Magazine'. *Southern Review: Communication, Politics, Culture* 32, no. 1 (1999): 27–41.

Rowley, CD. *The Remote Aborigines*. Canberra: Australian National University Press, 1971.

Rowse, Tim. 'Aborigines as Historical Actors: Evidence and Inference'. *Historical Studies* 22, no. 87 (October 1986): 176–98.

——. 'Paternalism's Changing Reputation'. *Mankind* 18, no. 2 (1988): 57–73.

——. *Remote Possibilities: The Aboriginal Domain and the Administrative Imagination*. Darwin: North Australia Research Unit, 1992.

——. *White Flour, White Power*. Cambridge: Cambridge University Press, 1998.

——. 'Indigenous Autobiography in Australia and the United States'. *Australian Humanities Review* 33 (2004).

——. 'Indigenous Heterogeneity'. *Australian Historical Studies* 45, no. 3 (2014): 297–310.

Rumsey, Alan. 'The Dreaming, Human Agency and Inscriptive Practice'. *Oceania* 65, no. 2 (December 1994): 116–30.

——. 'Tracks, Traces, and Links to Land in Aboriginal Australia, New Guinea and Beyond'. In *Emplaced Myth: Space, Narrative, and Knowledge in Aboriginal*

Australia and Papa New Guinea, edited by Alan Rumsey and James Weiner, pp. 19–42. Honolulu: University of Hawai'i Press, 1999.

Russell, Lynette. *Savage Imaginings: Historical and Contemporary Constructions of Australian Aboriginalities*. Melbourne: Scholarly Publishing, 2001.

Said, Edward. *Orientalism*. New York: Pantheon Books, 1978.

San Roque, Craig. *The Long Weekend in Alice Springs*, adapted and drawn by Joshua Santospirito. Moonah: Sankessto Publications, 2013.

Sansom, Basil. 'The Grammar of Exchange'. In *Being Black: Aboriginal Cultures in 'Settled' Australia*, edited by Ian Keen, pp. 159–77. Canberra: Aboriginal Studies Press, 1988.

——. 'In the Absence of Vita as Genre: The Making of the Roy Kelly Story'. In *Telling Stories: Indigenous History and Memory in Australia and New Zealand*, edited by Bain Attwood and Fiona Magowan, pp. 99–122. Crows Nest: Allen & Unwin, 2001.

Scott, James. *Seeing Like a State: How Certain Schemes to Improve the Human Condition Have Failed*. New Haven: Yale University Press, 1998.

Sculthorpe, Gaye. 'When Whitefellas Go Walkabout'. In *The Oxford Companion to Aboriginal Art and Culture*, edited by Sylvia Kleinart and Margot Neale, pp. 391–7. Melbourne: Oxford University Press, 2000.

Seddon, George. *Landprints: Reflections on Place and Landscape*. Cambridge, UK: Cambridge University Press, 1997.

Sharp, Ian and Colin Tatz eds. *Aborigines in the Economy: Employment, Wages and Training*. Brisbane: Jacaranda, Monash University, 1966.

Shaw, Bruce and Sandy McDonald. 'They Did It Themselves: Reminiscences of Seventy Years'. *Aboriginal History* 2 (1978): 122–39.

Shaw, Bruce. *My Country of the Pelican Dreaming: The Life of an Australian Aborigine of the Gadjerong, Grant Ngabidj, 1904–1977*. Canberra: Australian Institute for Aboriginal Studies, 1981.

——. *Banggaiyerri: The Story of Jack Sullivan*. Canberra: Australian Institute for Aboriginal Studies, 1983.

——. *Countrymen: The Life Histories of Four Aboriginal Men*. Canberra: Australian Institute for Aboriginal Studies, 1986.

Shellam, Tiffany. '"Our Natives" and "Wild Blacks": Enumeration as a Statistical Dimension of Sovereignty in Colonial Western Australia'. *Journal of Colonialism and Colonial History* 13, no. 3 (2012).

Sheller, Mimi and John Urry. 'The New Mobilities Paradigm'. *Environment and Planning A* 38, no. 2 (2006): 207–26.

Simpson, Audra. *Mohawk Interruptus: Political Life across the Borders of Settler States*. Durham: Duke University Press (2014).

Skyring, Fiona. 'Low Wages, Low Rents, and Pension Cheques: The Introduction of Equal Wages in the Kimberley, 1968–1969'. In *Indigenous Participation in Australian Economies: Historical and Anthropological Perspectives*, vol. 2, edited by Natasha Fijn, Ian Keen, Christopher Lloyd and Michael Pickering, pp. 153–69. Canberra: ANU E Press, 2012.

Smith, Diane. 'When the Starship Pintupi Meets the Klingons of Policy'. *The Australian Journal of Anthropology* 14, no. 2 (2003): 259.

Smith, MA. *Peopling the Cleland Hills: Aboriginal History in Western Central Australia, 1850–1980*, Aboriginal History Monograph Series no. 12. Canberra: *Aboriginal History*, 2005.

——. *The Archaeology of Australia's Deserts*. Cambridge: Cambridge University Press, 2013.

Spencer, Baldwin and Frank Gillen. *The Arunta: A Study of a Stone Age People*, 2 vols. London: Macmillan & Co., 1927.

Spooner, PG, M Firman and Yalmambira. 'Origins of Travelling Stock Routes: Connections to Indigenous Traditional Pathways'. *The Rangeland Journal* 32, no. 3 (2010): 329–39.

Stanner, WEH. *The Dreaming & Other Essays*. Melbourne: Black Inc., 2009.

Stevens, Frank. *Aborigines in the Northern Territory Cattle Industry*. Canberra: Australian National University Press, 1974.

Stoler, Anna Laura. *Along the Archival Grain: Epistemic Anxieties and Colonial Common Sense*. Princeton: Princeton University Press, 2010.

Strang, Veronica. *Uncommon Ground: Cultural Landscapes and Environmental Values*. Oxford: Berg, 1997.

Strehlow, TGH. 'Geography and the Totemic Landscape in Central Australia: A Functional Study'. In *Australian Aboriginal Anthropology*, edited by Ronald M Berndt, pp. 92–127. Nedlands: University of Western Australia Press, 1970.

——. *Songs of Central Australia*. Sydney: Angus & Robertson, 1971.

Sutton, Peter. 'Kinds of Rights in Country: Recognising Customary Rights as Incidents of Native Title'. *National Native Title Tribunal*, Occasional Paper Series, no. 2 (2001).

——. *The Politics of Suffering: Indigenous Australia and the End of the Liberal Consensus*. Carlton: Melbourne University Press, 2009.

Swain, Tony. *A Place for Strangers: Towards a History of Australian Aboriginal Being*. Cambridge, UK: Cambridge University Press, 1993.

Tamasari, Franca. 'Names and Naming: Speaking Forms into Place'. In *The Land is a Map: Placenames of Indigenous Origin in Australia*, edited by Louise Hercus and Flavia Hodges, pp. 87–102. Canberra: Pandanus Books, 2002.

Taussig, Michael T. *Shamanism, Colonialism and the Wild Man: A Study in Terror and Healing*. Chicago: University of Chicago Press, 1986.

Tietkens, WH. *Journal of Mr W.H. Tietkens' Central Australian Exploring Expedition*. Adelaide: S.A. Government Printer, 1890.

Tindale, Norman. 'The Pitjandjara'. In *Hunters and Gatherers Today: A Socioeconomic Study of Eleven Such Cultures in the Twentieth Century*, edited by MG Bicchieri, pp. 217–68. New York: Holt, Rinehart & Winston, 1972.

Thomas, Nicholas. *Entangled Objects: Exchange, Material Culture and Colonialism in the Pacific*. Cambridge, MA: Harvard University Press, 1991.

Thompson, Alistair. 'Anzac Memories Revisited: Trauma, Memory and Oral History'. *The Oral History Review* 42, no. 1 (2015): 1–29.

Thrush, Coll. 'Vancouver the Cannibal: Cuisine, Encounter, and the Dilemma of Difference on the Northwest Coast, 1774–1808'. *Ethnohistory* 58, no. 1 (December 2011): 1–35.

Tod Woenne, Susan. 'Old Country, New Territory: Some Implications of the Settlement Process'. In *Aborigines and Change: Australia in the 70s*, edited by Ronald M Berndt, pp. 54–64. Canberra: Australian Institute of Aboriginal Studies, 1977.

Tonkin, Don. *A Truly Remarkable Man: The Life of H.H. Finlayson and his Adventures in Central Australia*. South Australia: Seaview Press, 2001.

Tonkinson, Robert. *The Mardu Aborigines: Living the Dream in Australia's Desert*, 2nd edition. Fort Worth: Holt, Rinehart & Winston, 1991.

Toussaint, Sandy, Patrick Sullivan, and Sarah Yu. 'Water Ways in Aboriginal Australia: An Interconnected Analysis'. *Anthropological Forum* 15, no. 1 (2005): 61–74.

Toyne, Phillip and Daniel Vachon. *Growing Up the Country: The Pitjantjatjara Struggle for Their Land*. Melbourne: McPhee Gribble, 1984.

Trigger, David. 'Blackfellas and Whitefellas: The Concepts of Domain and Social Closure in the Analysis of Race Relations'. *Mankind* 16, no. 2 (1986): 99–117.

——. 'Equality and Hierarchy in Aboriginal Political Life at Doomadgee, North-West Queensland'. *Anthropological Forum* 5, no. 4 (1988): 525–44.

Trudinger, David. 'The Language(s) of Love: JRB Love and Contesting Tongues at Ernabella Mission Station, 1940-46'. *Aboriginal History* 31 (2007): 27–44.

Tuhiwai Smith, Linda. *Decolonizing Methodologies: Research and Indigenous Peoples*. London/New York/Dunedin: Zed Books Ltd. and University of Otago Press, 2006.

Urry, John. *Sociology Beyond Societies: Mobilities for the Twenty-First Century*. London: Routledge, 2000.

——. *Mobilities*. Cambridge: Polity Press, 2007.

Vanni, Ilaria. 'Bridging the Gap: The Production of Tourist Objects at La Perouse'. In *The Oxford Companion to Aboriginal Art and Culture*, edited by Sylvia Kleinart and Margot Neale, pp. 400–2. Melbourne: Oxford University Press, 2000.

Vaarzon–Morel, Petronella. 'Camels and the Transformation of Indigenous Economic Landscapes'. In *Indigenous Participation in Australian Economies*, vol. 2, edited by Ian Keen, Christopher Lloyd, Natasha Fijn and Michael Pickering, pp. 73–95. Canberra: ANU E Press, 2012.

Veracini, Lorenzo. 'Defending Settler Colonial Studies'. *Australian Historical Studies* 45, no. 3 (2014): 311–16.

Wallace, Noel M. 'Pitjantjatjara Decentralisation in North-West South Australia: Spiritual and Psycho-Social Motivation'. In *Aborigines and Change: Australia in the 70s*, edited by Ronald M Berndt, pp. 124–35. Canberra: Australian Institute of Aboriginal Studies, 1977.

Walsh, Michael. 'The Land Still Speaks? Language and Landscape in Aboriginal Australia'. In *Tracking Knowledge*, edited by Deborah Bird Rose and Anne Clarke, pp. 105–19. Darwin: North Australia Research Unit, Australian National University, 1997.

Ward, Russell. *The Australian Legend*. Melbourne: Oxford University Press, 1958.

Watego, Chelsea. 'Always Bet on Black (Power)'. *Meanjin* 80, no. 3 (2021): 22–33.

White, John. 'Peas, Beans and Riverbanks: Seasonal Picking and Dependence in the Tuross Valley'. In *Indigenous Participation in Australian Economies: Historical and Anthropological Perspectives*, vol. 1, edited by Ian Keen, pp. 109–26. Canberra: ANU E Press, 2010.

——. 'Histories of Indigenous–Settler Relations: Reflections on Internal Colonialism and the Hybrid Economy'. *Australian Aboriginal Studies* 1 (2011): 81–96.

White, Richard. *The Middle Ground: Indians, Empires, and Republics in the Great Lakes Region, 1650–1815*. New York: Cambridge University Press, 1991.

——. 'Creative Misunderstandings and New Understandings'. *The William and Mary Quarterly* 63, no. 1 (2006): 9–14.

Whitford, WG. *Ecology of Desert Systems*. San Diego: Academic Press, 2002.

Winnecke, C. *Journal of the Horn Scientific Exploring Expedition, 1984; Together with Maps and Plans; and Report of the Physical Geography of Central Australia, R. Tate and J.A. Watt.* Adelaide: CE Bristow, Government Printer, 1897.

Winter, Jay. 'Sites of Memory'. In *Memory: Histories, Theories, Debates*, edited by Susannah Radstone and Bill Schwarz, pp. 312–24. New York: Fordham University Press, 2010.

Wolfe, Patrick. *Settler Colonialism and the Transformation of Anthropology: The Politics and Poetics of an Ethnographic Event*. London/New York: Cassell, 1999.

——. 'Nation and MiscegeNation: Discursive Continuity in the Post-Mabo Era'. *Social Analysis* 36 (1994): 93–152.

——. 'Settler Colonialism and the Elimination of the Native'. *Journal of Genocide Research* 8, no. 4 (2006): 387–409.

Yengoyan, Aram A. 'A Comparison of Certain Marriage Features between the Pitjandjara and Other Groups of the Western Desert with the Northern Groups. Also Some Comments on the Red Ochre Ceremonies'. *Journal of the Anthropological Society of South Australia* 5, no. 4 (1967): 16–19.

——. 'Religion, Morality and Prophetic Traditions: Conversion of the Pitjantjatjara of Central Australia' In *Conversion to Christianity: Historical and Anthropological Perspectives on a Great Transformation*, edited by Robert W Hefner, pp. 233–58. Berkley: University of California Press, 1993.

Young, Diana. 'Dingo Scalping and the Frontier Economy in the North–West of South Australia'. In *Indigenous Participation in Australian Economies*, vol. 1, edited by Ian Keen, pp. 91–108. Canberra: ANU E Press, 2010.

Index